The Logic of Economy Discovery

The Logic of Economic Discovery

Neoclassical Economics and the Marginal Revolution

Robert M. Fisher

Assistant Professor of Economics
College of the Holy Cross

NEW YORK UNIVERSITY PRESS
Washington Square, New York

First published in the U.S.A. in 1986
by NEW YORK UNIVERSITY PRESS,
Washington Square, New York, N.Y. 10003

Library of Congress Cataloging-in-Publication Data

Fisher, Robert M., 1954–
   The logic of economic discovery.

   Bibliography: p.
   Includes index.
   1. Neoclassical school of economics.   2. Economics—
History.   I. Title.
HB98.2.F57   1986   330.15′5   86-2445
ISBN 0-8147-2581-3

To
Gail Fisher
and
Geoff Harcourt
for the compassion and tolerance which they teach

Contents

Preface

As a graduate student in economics I became disconcerted with the plethora of available theories. How was one to choose between these alternative, inconsistent frameworks? Another student, Rod Maddock, suggested that I read a book by Karl Popper, *The Poverty of Historicism.*[1] This book addressed many of the questions I had been pondering. I found Popper's writing to be cognent and convincing in regard to scientific thought. I became an avid reader of Popper, although *his* application of his ideas to social change and to economics struck me as simplistic and inconsistent with much of his framework.

At about this same time, while browsing in a bookstore, I happened upon Imre Lakatos' *Proofs and Refutations: The Logic of Mathematical Discovery.*[2] I was intrigued by the title. How could "proofs" be refuted? What could a "logic discovery" be? (I had not heard of Lakatos, nor did I know he had been a student of Popper.) Lakatos' ideas on the process of scientific discovery set my imagination whirling with possible applications to economics. It was at this stage that I decided to write on the methodology of economics.

My course was set by the stimulus of this powerful literature from the philosophy of the natural sciences and by my dissatisfaction with both the current state of economic theory and the problem of theory choice as it had been addressed by economists. I felt a need to employ these ideas from the philosophy of the natural sciences to explore metatheoretical[3] questions about economics before I could commit myself to the limitations of a particular framework. This book is one of the results of this exploration.

It is fruitful to think of this tome as two small *closely interrelated* sections; one is in the philosophy of economics, the other involves the application of that philosophy to the history of economics. In the first section I have presented a synthesis of early and late Lakatos which is richer than the "Lakatos" previously entertained by economists because the interaction between criticism and creative guessing is emphasized. A new history of economics which traces an internal dialectic of conjectures and "refutations" is implied. In the second section I apply the Lakatosian framework to the rise of marginalism. The significance is that the programmatic structure of the marginalist revolution is brought to the fore as an important explanatory variable, a variable which has not been given sufficient weight by historians of economic thought. The two sections are highly complementary as it is the history of economic thought which provides the "empirical" base with which we must critique and discuss conjectures in the methodology and philosophy of economics as a science.

I imagine that the serious student of economic thought will find the whole of this book to be of some interest. Others however may have a desire to explore the main ideas while engaging in less work. This may be done by reading with care the first five chapters, the first pages of Chapter 6, and Chapter 8 (Jevons). (I think the Jevons chapter is particularly helpful.) And then reading the remainder of the book more lightly.

To give thanks is difficult because so many have contributed to this work. For their support and guidance I thank my teachers, friends, colleagues, students, and especially my family; the present space is inadequate to thank them properly but they know who they are and I hope they know my gratitude.

Since much of this work is based on my Ph.D. Dissertation, it is important to thank the members of my committee at Duke University, which consisted of Craufurd Goodwin, Martin Bronfenbrenner, Neil deMarchi, and E. Roy Weintraub. Craufurd Goodwin, the Chairman, provided quick and yet careful commentary on each draft. His probing questions have led to a refinement of the logical structure of my argumentation. He provided reinforcement precisely when it was needed. Martin Bronfenbrenner's confrontational style of instruction has provided an impetus for much of my thought. He is an excellent teacher. If it were not for E. Roy

Weintraub I would not be an economist; when I was ready to quit graduate school he convinced me to continue. His enthusiasm for the insights provided by a Lakatosian framework and his deep interest in the structure of economic thought have provided inspiration for much of my work. Neil deMarchi was the first member of the Duke department to take a special interest in my work. He read my eccentric papers, tolerated my naive conjectures, and stimulated me to explore areas into which I might otherwise not have ventured. He was my early guide into the literature on the philosophy of science. I have fond memories of long discussions with him on methodological issues at both the opening and the closing of my dissertation work.

I also thank those members of the economics departments at Duke University, Campbell University (N. C.), the University of Adelaide (Australia), Salem College (N. C.), the College of the Holy Cross (Mass.) and the Australian National University who have taken an interest in my work and who provided constructive criticism. I am grateful to the College of the Holy Cross for a grant to complete this book.

I have been fighting methodological battles for years with Arjo Klamer and Rod Maddock. I especially thank them; they have both greatly influenced my course of thought.

My thanks also to Mrs. Pearl M. Jolicoeur for her care in typing this manuscript and for her editorial assistance.

What is of value in this work is due more to the above people than to myself. Nonetheless, the responsibility for any error lies with me as it is through the filter of my expression that the influence of these others manifests itself.

R. M. F.
Worcester, Massachusetts

NOTES

1. Karl Popper, *The Poverty of Historicism* (Boston: Beacon Press, 1957).
2. Imre Lakatos, *Proofs and Refutations* (Cambridge: Cambridge University Press, 1976).
3. A "metatheory" is a theory of theories.

1 Prolegomena to the New History of Economics

Neither the naked hand nor the understanding left to itself can effect much. It is by instruments and helps that the work is done, which are as much wanted for the understanding as for the hand. And as the instruments of the hand either give motion or guide it, so the instruments of the mind supply either suggestions for the understanding or cautions.[1]

Francis Bacon

This book is about criticism and the growth of economic knowledge. The concept of economic science presented herein is quite different from the conventional view[2] which the young economist gleans from introductory chapters, convoluted footnotes, recurrent semantic debates, and informal catechism with mentors. The conventional view is that economic science involves the collection of proven, probable, or near economic truths. In other words, to become a part of the body of economic science a conjecture must be justified. As opposed to this, the view presented here denies the possibility of justification in the conventional sense, and emphasizes instead the logic of discovery, that is, the role of creative guessing and criticism in the expansion of economic thought.

The economics discipline is characterized by a persistence of rival theories. Of economics Joan Robinson states: "with the best will in the world, it is excessively difficult to find an agreed answer to any question concerned with reality."[3] This persistence of disagreement disturbs those theorists who prefer to proclaim with the supposed authority of science. Their perturbation is linked to the thought that if a discipline is scientific, then rivalries between theories will be quickly eliminated by reference to the facts. It follows from this view that the theoretical pluralism evident in economics undermines claims to a scientific nature and hints at sciosophy.

In the above line of reasoning the nature of the scientific

1

process has been misapprehended. The persistence of rival theories does not make economics any less scientific than physics, biology, and other natural sciences where the persistence of rival theories is also visible.[4] Indeed, Paul Feyerabend argues that a "proliferation of theories is beneficial for science, while uniformity impairs critical power."[5]

Nevertheless, the economist is right to be concerned about this theoretical pluralism. Aside from the purely semantic (but sociologically important) question as to whether economics should be labelled a science, the existence of rival theories presents a problem to the economist if he is concerned about current explanatory and predictive power, the growth of knowledge (that is, future explanatory and predictive power), the pursuit of truth and, importantly, policy recommendations. It is often the case that the policy conclusions of rival economic theories will differ when these theories are combined with a particular set of ethical values.[6] In these cases the policy conclusions ultimately depend on the choice of theory. The search for criteria for deciding which theory is better is called the problem of theory choice. Technically, it is more correct to use the plural and speak of the *problems* of theory choice.

Although, as Feyerabend notes, uniformity may impair critical power, he may nonetheless, have underestimated the importance of the *attempt* to achieve unanimity in enhancing the critical discourse which is essential to the growth of knowledge. It is through the attempt to choose between theories that criticism emerges. (Note, however, that we are speaking of a process. The choices are never irrevocable.) Economists, being both social engineers and social scientists, must decide with which theory or theories to work for policy purposes (as social engineers), and on which theory or theories to work for the growth of knowledge (as social scientists). Milton Friedman, in his famous essay on positivism,[7] conflates these two distinct, although related, decisions. Though current predictive content may be a dominant factor in the theory choice made by the economist as social *engineer* it is not clear that this is the best criterion for the economist as social *scientist* who is concerned with the *growth* of knowledge and, more narrowly, the *growth* of predictive content.

The Cartesian heritage instills in economists a desire to keep economic science on a firm basis by only allowing proven, or at least probable, truths into its sacred realm. Through this careful collecting process, it is thought, we may expand truth-content. The first objection to the Cartesian-inspired conventional outlook is that, no matter how much care is taken in the justification process, the economist can never be completely sure that any particular conjecture is true; there is no procedure which precludes the possibility of the inclusion of falsity-content. Hume argues, compellingly, the impotence of induction with regard to attempts at justification. Einstein's theoretical revolution yielded a powerful counterexample to the conjecture that science is the accumulation of proven truths.

The second objection to the conventional perspective is that a careful, conservative, and always risk-averse, collection of "proven" economic truths is likely to leave much more truth-content outside the bounds of economic science than the alternative methodology presented in this book. The alternative, and opposing, approach is to forward bold guesses and then attempt to *improve* those guesses through criticism. The possibility of improving is accepted, while the possibility of proving is denied.

This approach, in the Popperian tradition, makes the best use of the asymmetry between corroboration and falsification. To take advantage of the fact that corroborations cannot prove, but a single counterexample can disprove, (that is, indicate a need for improvement), the economist's approach should be to make his or her scientific guesses as bold as possible, and continually attempt to "chip away" at falsity-content. The advantage of this approach is that the economist captures a greater range of phenomena within the scope of his or her analysis. This brings about a significant increase in truth-content. (No advantage is gained through the timidity of the conventional approach since an equal lack of certainty is shared by theoretical frameworks resulting from either.)[8]

We will be examining the metatheoretical[9] framework for theory choice provided by the philosopher of science, Imre Lakatos. Lakatos follows the Popperian tradition of reacting against justificationist metatheories which view scientific knowledge as either proven or probable. Lakatos also rejects naive falsificationistic metatheories which claim that theories can be disproven. [10] He argues that, even though theories can be neither proven nor disproven, science remains basically rational. The rational element is found in the scientific process itself, that is, in the improving of theories. Scientific rationality has its roots in the fact that theories can be compared.

In the 1970s, discontent with the current state of economic theory grew considerably even among the most orthodox practitioners of the science. With this discontent there arose a greater interest in the philosophy of economics. An initial effort was made to borrow criteria of theory choice from the natural sciences. [11] This is sensible, not because the answers will necessarily be the same for economics as for these other disciplines, but rather because the developed literature of the philosophy of the natural sciences provides a pool of mature hypotheses and distinctions, some of which may be used to provide the foundations for a metatheory of economics.

Some social scientists have an instinctive aversion to employing in their work ideas originally developed in the natural sciences. This is particularly true with methodological issues. It is argued that the social sciences are different in kind from the natural sciences. Hutchison states: "The history of science, in fact, is not actually made up of a single, epistemological homogeneous activity, because, basically the nature of the *materials* which different sciences deals with is significantly different." [12] (Italics in original.) The source of such contentions is usually a misunderstanding of the character of the natural sciences.

There are important differences *of degree* between the natural sciences and the social sciences. One such difference is that the qualities of the universe of study often appear to change more rapidly in the social sciences than in the natural sciences. If this is, indeed, the case, then the Lakatosian framework is *particularly well suited* to the social sciences.

We may use an analogy here. From the Lakatosian perspective, science is viewed as the corrective process involved in the aiming of an arrow; the bull's eye of the target is truth (by truth is meant the existence of an isomorphic relation between the theory and reality which is perfect in regard to the questions asked.) As opposed to other philosophies of science, the Lakatosian perspective explicitly discusses the mechanisms by which the aim of the arrow is readjusted should it be off-target. This is what a *logic of discovery* is all about. Philosophies of science that are concerned with a *logic of justification* only attack the problem of determining whether the arrow is aimed at the centre of the bull's eye. A logic of justification cannot help us improve our aim.

A Lakatosian methodological framework, with its emphasis on the logic of *discovery*, is particularly suited to a search for an ever-changing truth. Specifically, the corrective mechanisms, with which the Lakatosian framework concerns itself, are progressive responses to anomalies. It is clear that such mechanisms, which are tied to the recognition of anomalies, can never be discussed from a naively positivistic philosophy that views science as the accumulation of proven truths. Those social scientists who hold such a naively positivistic philosophy and who also recognize the relatively quick changes in their topic of study (i.e., quick movements of the target) either conclude that the social sciences must develop a different methodology from the natural sciences or that the social sciences must greatly restrict the range of things to which they can take a scientific approach. Hutchison arrives at both of these conclusions. Neither is warranted from a Lakatosian perspective.

A theory in isolation can never be judged as scientific because there exists no adequate logic of justification. Lakatos offers a metatheory of science which is dynamic; it involves a logic of discovery rather than a logic of justification. The scientific process is not a two-sided confrontation between a theory and the empirical base (as it is often portrayed), but rather a three-sided contraposition among two rival theories and the empirical base.[13] To study the scientific aspect of a discipline one cannot simply examine the theory at a point in time. Instead, one must examine the movement between theories. This necessarily involves a movement through time. There is a link between the history of the theoretical development of a discipline and its methodology. Examples of theory choice must be taken from the history of thought.

Philosophy of economics leads to history of economics

because history of science provides the "empirical base" with which alternative competing philosophies must be confronted. Philosophy of science is tenantless if it is without reference to scientific history. Conversely, the historian must be concerned with philosophy of science because any particular history implies some (perhaps tacit) philosophy. Without a philosophy, history is nothing more than a random collection of facts. Hutchinson states:

> It could, therefore, constitute a most welcome and significant example, as far as economics is concerned, that in their different ways, in the work of both Kuhn and Lakatos, the history of science, and its analysis of philosophy have been brought together for mutual illumination. [14]

To study the problem of theory choice in economics, we search the history of economic thought for examples of, and counterexamples to, our methodological conjectures. Philosophy of science that does not provide insight into actual scientific practice is of little use. The marginalist revolution of the 1870s, which constituted a shift in economic theory, provides a case study for the problem of theory choice. It was clear by the late 1880s that marginalist economics would become dominant within the profession and supersede classical political economy. [15]

We attempt to contribute to both the philosophy and the history of economics. This book belongs to the literature of the philosophy of economics because it constitutes an "empirical" application of a Lakatosian metatheory of science. It belongs to the literature of the history of economics because it takes a new approach to the marginalist revolution and answers some old questions in new ways. The marginal utility/total utility distinction and the idea of diminishing marginal utility had been available to economists for nearly half a century before the introduction and acceptance of the marginalist economics of Jevons, Menger, and Walras. Why did the new theories introduced in the early 1870s ascend to a dominant position within the discipline when the earlier presentations of marginalist ideas had failed to do so? Was there really a marginalist revolution? If so, what were the links between the works of Jevons, Menger, and Walras? Were Jevons, Menger, and Walras rebelling against the then orthodox theory of value? Should the marginalist revolution be termed a "multiple discovery"? Why did the professionalization of economics take place in the last quarter of the nineteenth century? Was the rise of marginalism due to factors exogenous to the economics discipline?[16]

Lakatos' framework is both normative and positive. It is normative in the sense that it prescribes what scientists ought to do. Applied as a normative theory, it nevertheless involves objective analysis if one accepts Lakatos' notion of scientific progress, because in that case the prescriptions follow logically. It becomes a positive theory when combined with the hypothesis that "scientists are 'rational' and will do what they ought to do." We apply the Lakatosian methodological framework as a positive theory when we develop hypotheses concerning the rise of marginalism.

The economics of the marginalists has become the basis of much of economic theory. The question of how we came upon a theoretical framework with such startling heuristic power and the question of the source of that heuristic power have obvious importance. An exploration of the foundation of marginalist economics through the Lakatosian metatheoretical framework will contribute to our understanding of that developmental process may lead to its refinement and provide insights into current theory choice.

Two questions dominate the writing of the history of economics: (1) "Who arrived at the 'correct' answer first?" and (2) "In what manner were the ideas related to class interests?" The first of these questions is more misleading than helpful. The second question leads to tracing the development of what we shall call the "external dialectic"; such a tracing is enlightening, but it necessarily misses an important part of the story. We will argue the need for a new history of economics which traces an "internal dialectic," a dialectic which involves the substantive content of economic theory.

Although it is fruitful to be intrepid in our claims, we are *pari passu* modest in our expectations. In this vein, we are in concordance with Descartes in his *Discourse on Method*: ". . . this tract is put forth merely as a history, or, if you will, as a tale, in which, amid some examples worthy of imitation, there will be found, perhaps, as many more which it were advisable not to follow. I hope it will prove useful to some without being hurtful to any, and, that my openness will find some favour with all." [17]

NOTES

1. Francies Bacon, *Novum Organum* included in *Man and The Universe: The Philosophers of Science* Saxe Commins and Robert N. Linscott (eds.) (New York: Washington Square Press, 1969), p. 80.
2. By "conventional" here we simply mean "widely accepted" or "standard." We are not referring to methodological conventionalism, elements of which are unavoidable in any coherent philosophy of science.
3. Joan Robinson, *Contributions to Modern Economics* (Oxford: Basil Blackwell, 1979), p. 2.
4. The philosopher of science, Imre Lakatos states: "as a matter of fact, research programmes have achieved complete monopoly only rarely and then only for relatively short periods. . . . *The history of science has been and should be a history of competing research programmes.* . . . 'Theoretical pluralism' is better than 'theoretical monism' ". (Italics in original.) Imre Lakatos and Alan Musgrave, eds., *Criticism and the Growth of Knowledge* (Cambridge: Cambridge University Press, 1970), p. 155.
5. Paul Feyerabend, *Against Method* (London: Verso 1976), p. 35.
6. Economic theories cannot have policy conclusions unless they are combined with a set of values.
7. Milton Friedman, *Essays in Positive Economics* (Chicago: University of Chicago Press, 1953).
8. Popper has demonstrated, in numerous places, that all theories are equally conjectural by any reasonable probability calculus. The heart of the argument is that for any finite number of observations there are an infinite number of theories consistent with that set of observations; hence, the probability of any one being "true" is zero. Karl Popper, *Conjectures and Refutations* (London: Routledge and Kegan Paul, 1972), *passim*; *The Logic of Scientific Discovery* (London: Hutchison, 1977), *passim*; *Objective Knowledge* (Oxford: Oxford University Press, 1979), *passim*; *The Open Society and Its Enemies* (Princeton, N. J.: Princeton University Press, 1962), *passim*; *The Poverty of Historicism* (Boston: Beacon Press, 1957), *passim*; and John Eccles, *The Self and Its Brain* (New York: Springer International, 1977), *passim*.
9. In case the reader missed Note 3 in the Preface, a "metatheory" is a theory of theories.
10. Lakatos and Musgrave, eds., *Criticism and the Growth of Knowledge*, p. 103.

11. For example, see Spiros J. Latsis, ed., *Method and Appraisal in Economics* (Cambridge: Cambridge University Press, 1976).

12. T. W. Hutchison, *Knowledge and Ignorance in Economics* (Chicago: University of Chicago Press, 1977), p. 36.

13. Lakatos and Musgrave, eds., *Criticism and the Growth of Knowledge*, p. 115.

14. T. W. Hutchison, *Knowledge and Ignorance in Economics* (Chicago: University of Chicago Press, 1977), p. 34.

15. Henry Spiegel states: "Conventional economics ... did not stand still but underwent during the closing decades of the nineteenth century a profound transformation often designated as the 'marginal revolution.' When this revolution had run its course at the turn of the century, both the structure of economics and its method differed sharply from the political economy of the classics." *The Growth of Economic Thought* (Englewood Cliffs, N. J.: Prentice-Hall, 1971), p. 505.

16. For various discussions of these questions, see R. D. Collison Black, A. W. Coats and Craufurd D. W. Goodwin, eds., *The Marginal Revolution in Economics: Interpretation and Evaluation* (Durham, N. C.: Duke University Press, 1973).

17. Descartes, Spinoza, Leibnitz, *The Rationalists* (readings) trans. respectively by John Veitch, R. H. M. Elwes, and George Montgomery with Albert R. Chandler (Garden City, N. Y.: Doubleday, 1969), p. 41.

2 A Lakatosian Approach to Economics

... there is not a single interesting theory that agrees with all the known facts in its domain.[1]

Paul Feyerabend

Implicitly, most epistemological efforts in economics have portrayed the discipline either as a collection of proven or probable truths or as truth by changing consensus. These poles are unsophisticated; the tumultuous history of science argues against the first, our sense of progress is contrary to the second. Here we offer an alternative perspective which retains the creative element in science, upon which the dogmatists are mute, as well as capturing the rational element which eludes the sociological approach.

Imre Lakatos constructed a methodological framework for mathematics, physics, and other "natural" sciences from the perspective of scientific thought as a rational process. The term "rational" broadly distinguishes his work from the work of those who would view knowledge as *simply* a (Kuhnian) social consensus or as a (Humian) psychological phenomenon. The term "process" distinguishes Lakatos' work from the work of those who take a static view of knowledge as a collection of the "provable" or "probable" at a given point in time. The only other major innovative philosopher in the same camp as Lakatos is Karl Popper, Lakatos' early mentor. The differences between Popper and Lakatos are two: (1) They have diverging metatheories about how the growth of knowledge occurs. (2) They place a completely different meaning on the term "falsification." This latter difference has been the source of much misinterpretation and confusion. The present author contends that Lakatos' metatheory is superior to Popper's.

We draw heavily upon Lakatos' *Proofs and Refutations:*

10

The Logic of Mathematical Discovery, based on his Cambridge (England) Ph.D., and upon his 1970 article "Falsification and the Methodology of Scientific Research Programmes," henceforth referred to as the *Methodology*.[2] The more important of these two works is *Proofs and Refutations* as it is essential for an understanding of the later work. For the most part, the pervasive misunderstanding of Lakatos by economists is due to a lack of attention to this early text. The need for synthesis is highlighted by McCloskey's confused comments in his article "The Rhetoric of Economics." In one passage, he praises *Proofs and Refutations* as "one outstanding piece," and cites it as the example of work concordant with his own "anarchistic theory of knowledge in economics." In another passage, he disparages Lakatos' *Methodology* as an example of methodological authoritarianism.[3] In fact, there is an intimate interrelation between these two Lakatosian works which precludes separate consideration.

It is better to think of the framework presented here as Lakatosian, rather than as that of Lakatos. First, there is the ever-present problem of the fluidity of concepts used in a new application. The question arises as to whether a concept in its new application has maintained precisely the same content as in the original. This problem is heightened because Lakatos is ambiguous in much of his presentation. He sometimes makes assertions which do not follow from the supposedly supporting analysis, and he uses his theoretical terms differently in different contexts. Decisions had to be made about what was meant and the resultant interpretation was seldom the only possible one. Furthermore, it is often fruitful to stretch meaning, and this stretching is sometimes intentional. Nonetheless, it is generally important to distinguish the new meaning from the old. Second, the methodology presented is a blend (albeit natural) of "early Lakatos" (*Proofs and Refutations*) and "late Lakatos" (*Methodology*) combined with a pinch of Kuhn and some original elements. Those readers familiar with the methodological literature in economics are forewarned that, due to the prevalence of shallow interpretations, the "Lakatos" that emerges may appear quite new.

In both *Proofs and Refutations* and *Methodology* Lakatos explores the relationship between various responses to anomalies (that is, possible reactions to criticism) and scientific progress. He contends there is an intimate and rational link between criticism and the growth of knowledge. In this chapter, various possible responses to anomalies by scientists are explored, some of which are noted to be content-increasing. The criterion for choosing *among scientific models*, which Lakatos based on content-increasing responses to anomalies, is presented. A definition of scientific progress is given, based on this criterion. Research programmes are introduced as the form in which such progress is most likely to occur. The structure of research programmes is discussed. A second criterion, related to the first, is presented for choosing *among research programmes*. New wrinkles to the Lakatosian framework are introduced so that it may be more fruitful in its application to economics. These are noted to be consistent with the Lakatosian vision. The advantages of the Lakatosian framework, as well as its normative methodological lessons, are presented in the next chapter.

A. THE LAKATOSIAN LOGIC OF DISCOVERY

i. Definitions

In *Proofs and Refutations* Lakatos defines a "proof" as: "*a thought experiment — or quasi-experiment — which suggests a decomposition of the original conjecture into subconjectures or lemmas*, thus *embedding it* in a possibly quite distant body of knowledge"[4] (italics in original). To avoid an unwarranted connotation of certainty we shall employ the term *demonstration* in the sense that Lakatos uses the term *proof*. We shall use the term "theorem," instead of Lakatos' term "conjecture," to emphasize the fact that we will be analyzing models consisting of numerous theorems and demonstrations tied to a particular set of lemmas, rather than examining, as Lakatos did in the first part of *Proofs and Refutations*, just one conjecture and its attendant proof. A *model* is defined as a collection of lemmas (postulates;

assumptions) which are combined to form various demonstrations, the conclusions of which are called *theorems* or, loosely, predictions.[5] Occasionally, it will be convenient to use the terms *theory* and *model* interchangeably. A counterexample to a lemma is called a *local counterexample* and a counterexample to a theorem (one which is not a lemma) is called a *global counterexample*.[6] (Note that a single anomaly may be a counterexample to both a lemma and a theorem simultaneously. In other words a single event may provide both a global and a local counterexample.)

ii. The Logical Relation Between Models and Observation Statements

An awareness of the asymmetry in the potential for verification and for falsification inherent in the relationship of theorem to model is fundamental to an understanding of the role of criticism in science. On the one hand, nothing may be inferred about a model or about its attendant auxiliary theories from the corroboration of a theorem. On the other hand, if a theorem is falsified by an observation, then it can be inferred that either an auxiliary theory is false, the stated initial conditions are false, or one of the lemmas of the model is false. (Popper emphasized that rationality originates from this modest point.)

If the auxiliary theories and the initial conditions are accepted as true, then it may be inferred that one of the lemmas of the model is false. In other words, the existence of a global counterexample implies the existence of a local counterexample. This type of inference is called the *modus tollens* or the principle of the retransmission of falsity.[7] It follows from the truth-transferring character of deductive logic. (Note that, in this situation, when we refer to a global and local counterexample, we refer to a single anomaly whose existence is inconsistent with both a theorem and a lemma.)

The absence of a corresponding local counterexample in the face of a global counterexample can only be due to a lack of rigour.[8] In these cases the corresponding local counterexample is provided by an implicit lemma. Note that it is also possible for an anomaly to be a local counterexample without also being a global counterexample. (In other words, a refuted lemma does not imply a refuted theorem, although often such an inference is erroneously drawn.)

iii. Responses to Anomaly

a. Content-Decreasing Responses   Reactions to anomalies may be classified as either content-decreasing or content-increasing. In *Proofs and Refutations* Lakatos describes five possible content-decreasing responses to a global counterexample. The first discussed is the *method of surrender*[9] which involves a total loss of truth-content. The model (or theory), taken as a whole, is rejected as false by the principle of the retransmission of falsity. For example, a theorem of the Walrasian theoretical framework, as found in the *Elements of Pure Economics*, is that demand curves are downward sloping.[10] The "observation" of an upward sloping demand curve for a Giffen good provides a global counterexample to the Walrasian framework. The method of surrender calls for the rejection of the Walrasian theory. This method, by which a theory facing a global counterexample is rejected, is espoused as *the* method of science by the naive falsificationists. The disadvantage of this method, as we shall see, is that we do not learn by our mistakes. With the method of surrender the danger is that "the baby will be thrown out with the bathwater." The history of science attests to the fact that scientists abhor a theoretical vacuum; a theory is only rejected as a whole in the face of a better theory; a global counterexample is generally not sufficient. Classical political economy did not fail with the attacks on the Wages Fund Doctrine in the late 1860s, but rather with the advent of marginalism.

The second alternative response to a counterexample is the method of *monster-barring*.[11] this involves rejection of the counterexample. This is done by respecifying definitions in such a manner that the "monster" is barred and the theorem and model are saved. Subsequent to this manoeuvre it is claimed that the counterexample does not meet the specification for the valid application of the model. The claim is *ad hoc*. Monster-barrers refuse to challenge the model. They prefer to hide the growth of knowledge in a maze of definitions.

Lakatos labels "attempts to expand the meaning of a term" as *concept-stretching*.[12] Monster-barring is often a response to concept-stretching. For example, suppose at an early stage in the theoretical development of the *Theory of Political Economy*,[13] Jevons derives a theorem which is meant to apply to goods in general. Suppose also that the term "goods" is defined vaguely. Finally, suppose that a discommodity is forwarded as a counterexample to this theorem. The monster-barrer would respecify the definition for the term "goods" so as to exclude discommodities. This saves the theorem in its present form. The monster-barrer would claim, perhaps legitimately, that discommodities were never meant to be included under the term "goods." Through concept-stretching, Jevons actually does introduce discommodities as anomalous at an early stage in the pedagogic development of the *Theory*.[14] However, he does not respond by monster-barring. Rather, as we shall see, he chooses the superior alternative of improving the model through a challenge. He makes several theoretical adjustments which expand predictive scope to include discommodities.[15] This allows him to analyze the range of phenomena of cost.

The third alternative is *monster-adjustment*.[16] The monster-adjuster argues that the global counterexample is only apparent. In this case the *modus tollens* is directed at the operationalization of the theory or at the auxiliary theories of observation. The empirical information is systematically reinterpreted so that the counterexample is seen to be a corroboration. Jevons uses this manoeuvre in his *Theory* to manage the problem of substitutes in consumption.[17] He brings substitutes within the scope of his model by reinterpreting them as one homogeneous commodity of variable strength. The monster-adjuster hides the growth of knowledge in the conventions of empirical interpretation.

Another possible response to a global counterexample is to improve the theorem by *exception-barring* methods.[18] The improvement consists of including a list of exceptions with the theorem. The improved theorem is then forwarded as true. Jevons uses exception-barring in his *Theory* to manage the difficulties of boundary solutions and cases of indivisibilities.[19] He lists these under the title: "Failure of the

Equations of Exchange."[20] An advantage of exception-barring is that the counterexample is taken seriously without a total surrender of truth-content. A fault with exception-barring is that the demonstration of the theorem has been ignored. The demonstration of the old theorem is not a demonstration of the new improved theorem.

The method of *lemma-incorporation* improves upon exception-barring by employing the demonstration.[21] The first step is to determine the lemma which provides the local counterexample that corresponds to the global counterexample. This procedure is called a *demonstration analysis*.[22] The lemma, once discovered, is attached to the theorem as a restriction on its range. The result is an improved theorem. For example, the upward sloping demand curve for a Giffen good provides a global counterexample to the theorem of the Walrasian framework that "demand curves are downward sloping." A demonstration analysis reveals the local counterexample to be the assumption of an additive utility function. The incorporation of this lemma produces the improved theorem that "the demand curves of individuals with additive utility functions are downward sloping." An advantage of lemma incorporation is that the old demonstration also applies to the improved theorem; in other words, the proof still proves. Lemma-incorporation yields the boldest possible unfalsified theorem; the retreat in content is smaller than with unmitigated exception-barring. This is an advantage because a retreat in content that is larger than necessary adds the danger of understatement to the ever-present danger of overstatement. For example, the unmitigated exception-barrer, in a play for safety, might have contracted the theorem to "the demand curves for normal goods are downward sloping." This would be an understatement since the demand curves for most inferior goods are also downward sloping. There would have been an unnecessary decrease in truth-content. Given the asymmetry between the potential for verification and for falsification, and intrepid approach is to be preferred as it is easier to "chip away" the falsity-content from bold conjectures than it is to add truth-content. Popper quotes Novalis: "Hypotheses are nets: only he who casts will catch."[23]

b. Content-Increasing Responses[24]   All of the above reactions to anomalies call for a decrease in empirical content. Lemma-incorporation was preferred because it minimized that reduction. A content-increasing reaction that still responds to the anomaly supersedes all others. Content-increasing responses are rendered possible by the potential for new deeper demonstrations. Let us examine first the case of an anomaly that is both a local and a global counterexample. If, by a theoretical adjustment, the observation statement which has provided the global and local counterexamples can be transformed into a corroboration while former content is retained then the resultant model is considered an improvement because of its expanded empirical content. This theoretical adjustment may involve a replacement of the lemma yielding the local counterexample, or the addition of auxiliary hypotheses, or semantic changes (perhaps through concept-stretching) or some combination of the above. For example, in the case of the upward sloping demand curve of the Giffen good, in which a global counterexample to the Walrasian framework is provided, a demonstration analysis reveals that it is the assumption of the additive utility function that provides the corresponding local counterexample. Part of the theoretical adjustment is to replace the assumption of an additive utility function with an assumption of a general utility function. (This was, in fact, a contribution made by Edgeworth.) From the reformulated model new predictions are drawn such as "the demand curves for inferior goods constituting a sufficiently large percentage of income are upward sloping." That which provided an anomaly to the earlier model provides a corroboration of the reformulated model. Situations involving additive utility functions are now seen as special cases of the reformulated model. Thus there is a retention of former unrefuted content.

There is the possibility of a local counterexample that is *not* also a global counterexample. This is an indication of the poverty of the demonstration. An observation statement might have provided a corroboration of the theorem and the model, and yet it has not been included within the explanatory scope of the model. Lakatos states: "A local, but not global, counterexample is a criticism of the proof, but not of the conjecture."[25] As above, this is an opportunity for an increase in content. Lakatos states: "If you have a counter-example which is local but not global, try to improve your proof-analysis by replacing the refuted lemma by an unfalsified one."[26] In other words, if the lemma can be replaced by another which transforms the local counterexample into a local corroboration then a new range of phenomena will have been brought within the explanatory scope of the model (since the global corroboration already exists.)

iv. The Criterion for Choosing Between Models

The above discussed content-increasing responses to anomalies produce new models which are the source of scientific progress. Lakatos formalizes the notion of progress by positing the following as a criterion of rational choice between scientific models; replace a model M_1 by another model M_2 if and only if: (1) M_2 has excess empirical content some of which is corroborated, and (2) all unrefuted content of M_1 is included in the content of M_2.[27] Label this as Lakatos' First Criterion. To have excess empirical content is to yield new predictions. The inclusion of the unrefuted content of M_1 by M_2 means that everything that is explained by M_1 must also be explained by M_2. A model which yields predictions over a new range of phenomena is called *theoretically progressive*. If some of these new predictions are substantiated by the "facts" (certain statements are decreed to be facts by convention) then the model is called *empirically progressive*. If the movement from one model to another is theoreticaly progressive, and there is a retention of unrefuted content, then the problem shift is called *progressive*. Otherwise, the shift is *degenerative*.[28] (A *problem shift* is simply the movement from one model to the next.) To summarize, one model is better than another if it can match the performance of the older model and also do a little more.

A model is not judged as scientific or not scientific *per se*, but rather the shift between one model and the next is judged as rational or irrational. Shifts are considered rational if they fulfill the two Lakatosian conditions listed above. With a rational problem shift the known anomaly for M_1 becomes a corroborating instance for M_2. M_1 is then superseded by M_2 and so on. (See Figure 1.)

$$M_1 \text{———} M_2 \text{———} M_3 \ldots$$

$\uparrow$ $\uparrow$

known anomaly   the anomaly becomes
                  a corroboration of M_2

Figure 1

Lakatos uses this normative methodological framework as a source of bold hypotheses concerning the actual development of scientific thought. He suggests that scientific progress is the result of three-cornered fight among two rival models and the facts.[29] He stretches the Popperian concept of "refutation." A model is never "refuted" by the facts alone but rather it is "refuted" (or "falsified") by the arrival of a better model. It is "refuted" when a new model has been found that can cover the same ground and more. Since new models are developed only through the confrontation of established models by anomalies, the importance of criticism for the growth of knowledge is inferred. Lakatos' scientific rationality contrasts sharply here with (the early) Popper's falsificationism. It disposes of any hint of "crucial experiments." Lakatos states: "Contrary to naive falsificationism, no experiment, experimental report, observation statement or well-corroborated low-level falsifying hypothesis alone can lead to falsification."[30]

It is only with the arrival of a better, or more promising theory (or model) that an earlier one is rejected. Lakatos finds corroboration for these hypotheses in the history of the natural sciences and mathematics. Further corroboration is provided by our examination of the marginal revolution in economics.

v. Research Programmes

Most modern scientific work is characterized by progressive series of models which are connected by a set of unifying ideas and which display a striking continuity of thought. These series of models are called *research programmes*.[31] Brilliant research programmes turn one counterinstance after another into corroborations. The set of assumptions (lemmas) which unify the programme is called the *hard core*. The *modus tollens* is never directed at the lemmas in the hard core.

Newton's programme for a planetary system is the main example used by Lakatos of a successful research programme. Lakatos states:

Newton first worked out his programme for a planetary system with a fixed point-like sun and one single point-like planet .... Then he worked out the programme for more planets as if there were only heliocentric but no interplanetary forces. Then he worked out the case where the sun and planets were not mass-points but mass balls .... Having solved this "puzzle," he started working on *spinning balls* and their wobbles. Then he admitted interplanetary forces and started work on perturbations .... It was then that he started to work on *bulging* planets, rather than round planets, etc.[32]

Newton's first model (call it M_1) involved a fixed point-like planet. This model, with its many obvious anomalies, was the first of a series. Newton's next model (M_2) involved more planets and was heliocentric but it involved no interplanetary influences. Note that a falsifying instance for Newton's first model (the existence of more than one planet) became a corroboration of his second model. The theoretical progress that results from this shift is evident. The explanatory import of the first model has been retained in the sense that predictions concerning a one-planet system may be derived from the more sophisticated model. Furthermore the second model contains excess content in the sense that predictions concerning multiple planet systems may now be advanced.[33] Newton went on, as Lakatos explains, to incorporate a number of complications such as consideration of the masses of both the sun and the planets and interplanetary influences. Note that interplanetary influences, an anomaly for M_2, becomes a corroboration for M_3. Newton further developed his calculus to facilitate the construction of this series of models.

A research programme is characterized by certain methodological rules about what sort of adjustments to a model M_1 to avoid (the *negative heuristic*) and by other methodological rules about what paths to pursue in the search for a superseding M_2 (the *positive heuristic*).[34] The exact meaning and importance of these two concepts unfolds in the following discussion. Examples are provided.

The positive heuristic is a prevision of the series of

anomalies that are to be incorporated into the series of models. Lakatos states: "The positive heuristic sets out a programme which lists a chain of ever more complicated models simulating reality,."[35] The positive heuristic keeps the problem faced by the scientist simple. At each stage of the analysis it indicates to the scientist which anomaly is to be considered significant and, therefore, is to be confronted. The precision of this vision may vary. If it is strong then further progress within the programme is reduced to the solution of mathematical or logical puzzles. In discussing the concept of positive heuristic Lakatos states:

> Most, if not all, Newtonian "puzzles," leading to a series of new variants superseding each other, were foreseeable at the time of Newton's first naive model and no doubt Newton and his colleagues *did* foresee them: Newton must have been fully aware of the blatant falsity of his first variants. Nothing shows the existence of a positive heuristic of a research programme clearer than this fact: this is why one speaks of "models" in the research programmes.[36]

For Newton, the positive heuristic included the incorporation of multiple planets, mass-bass, spinning balls, wobbles, interplanetary influences, bulging planets, and so on. The series of models developed by Jevons in his *Theory of Political Economy* provides another example of the positive heuristic of a research programme.[37] Jevons develops his initial model by incorporating a series of anomalies which includes multiple alternative uses of a commodity, the allocation across different time periods, uncertainty, propinquity, exchange as an alternative use, transport cost, multiple trading bodies, multiple commodities possessed, discommodities, production possibilities, multiple alternative production possibilities, and joint products. Certainly Jevons, like Newton, must have been "aware of the blatant falsity of his first variants."

The negative heuristic is the (implicit or explicit) set of rules which directs the adherents of a research programme to protect the hard core (the assumptions unifying the series of models).[38] It precludes the application of the method of surrender to a hard core proposition. Tactical manoeuvres to protect the hard core include monster-barring, monster-adjustment, exception-barring, and lemma-incorporation.

(Recall our earlier discussion of these manoeuvres.) There are also other tactics; for example, Jevons diverts the *modus tollens* by claiming the self-evidence of his hard core propositions. (A self-evident proposition cannot provide a local counterexample.) If the *modus tollens* is never to be directed at the hard core, then there must be a *protective belt* to which it can be directed. The protective belt includes the statement of the initial conditions, the theories of observation, the operationalization of the model, the simplifying assumptions, and the (implicit or explicit) auxiliary hypotheses *not belonging* to the hard core. The method of surrender is applied to a hard core lemma only upon the replacement of the entire research programme by another. At that point, the negative heuristic of the original programme is no longer operative.

Progress is tested within a research programme by use of Lakatos' *First Criterion*. When a new model M_2 is generated, there are four possibilities: (1) M_2 fulfills both conditions of the First Criterion, (2) M_2 has excess corroborated content but does not retain former unrefuted content, (3) M_2 retains former refuted content but does not have excess corroborated content, and (4) M_2 fulfills neither of the conditions of the First Criterion. In case one, M_2 is accepted and M_1 "refuted" (in a Lakatosian sense). In case two, it is not clear which model is superior. Model M_2 may provide the beginnings of a new research programme which is, at least temporarily, incommensurable with the old research programme by use of the First Criterion. Work on both programmes might proceed. In case three and case four, the search for a superseding M_2 continues.

vi. The Criteria for Choosing Between Research Programmes

Lakatos' First Criterion is appropriate to a choice between research programmes *in those cases where it can be applied*. In other words, if the most developed model of one research programme retains all of the unrefuted content of the most developed model of a rival research programme *and* contains some excess corroborated content, then the former is to be chosen. The supersedence of the Newtonian research programme by that of Einstein is a case where the First Criterion could be applied. As we shall see, Jevons, Menger, and Walras argued that the shift from classical political economy to marginalist economics was warranted on the grounds of the First Criterion.[39]

Although the explanatory import of two research programmes may overlap, it is seldom the case that one totally encompasses the predictions of its rival. In those cases where one research programme does not encompass another, Lakatos offers a different, although related, criterion for choice between research programmes. He suggests that the potential for, and degree of, progressiveness should be of central importance in such comparisons. Label this as Lakatos' Second Criterion. Note that to reject a research programme simply means to stop working on it; to accept one means to aim scientific effort in that direction. Recall that a research programme is progressive if it is expanding its empirical base, and that an expanding empirical base is achieved by the creation of new adjusted models that have increased corroborated content and that retain the content of their predecessor within the programme. Clearly, it is more fruitful to direct scientific efforts at progressive research programmes.

Lakatos recommends tolerance towards young progressive programmes. He states:

We must not discard a budding research programme simply because it has so far failed to overtake a powerful rival. We should not abandon it if, supposing its rival were not there, it would constitute a progressive problem shift. As long as a budding research programme can be rationally reconstructed as a progressive problem shift, it should be sheltered for a while from a powerful established rival.[40]

In other words, the expected, or even potential, supersedence of one programme by another may be as important as actual supersedence. Thus, the application of these criteria should not be pedantic. Lakatos speaks of the "end of instant rationality"[41] in *Criticism and the Growth of Knowledge* because often a research programme can be regarded as progressive only in retrospect. Indeed, a conscious recognition of the research programme itself may only emerge with the aid of hindsight when the set of unifying ideas which have given a common structure to the series of models can be declared.

To summarize, the Lakatosian criterion for choosing between models *within a research programme* and for choosing *between research programmes in those cases where this criterion can be applied* is the possession of excess corroborated content and retention of former unrefuted content; the Lakatosian criterion for choosing *between research programmes in those cases where the above criterion cannot be applied* is progressiveness.

Unsophisticated Popperians may become confused by the meaning of Lakatos' "expansion of the empirical base." They might argue (although Popper would not) that as a research programme expands and becomes an ever-closer approximation to reality it becomes *less* falsifiable, and therefore actually loses scientific value. It must be remembered here that scientists concern themselves with judging series of models and not particular statements taken out of the context of a programme. If a problem shift leads to theoretical progress, then this means that it will yield predictions over a new range of phenomena. These predictions of the programme over a new range of phenomena yield on opportunity for new anomalies to arise. It follows that empirical content has increased in a Popperian/falsificationist sense. (A corroboration of this new content is called empirical progress, although theoretical progress alone may be enough to sustain a programme in the face of weak competitors.) An example of an expansion of the empirical base through such a theoretically progressive problem shift is given by Jevons' incorporation of transport cost. At the theoretical stage prior to the incorporation of transport cost, the model cannot yield predictions over that range of phenomena which includes significant transport cost. After the incorporation of transport cost, a theoretically progressive move, predictions can be forwarded over this range of phenomena. There is more scope for "falsification" to arise. If the new predictions are corroborated then we have empirical progress.

B. ADJUSTMENTS TO THE LAKATOSIAN FRAMEWORK

In the economics literature, gross misinterpretations of Lakatosian concepts are rampant. Some of the ways in which the Lakatosian terms are "stretched" might prove fruitful in the sense that structures of interest are identified. For example, it is a common mistake to consider a methodological dictum of a programme as either part of the hard core or part of the positive heuristic. Latsis mistakenly labels as part of the positive heuristic the following metalevel rule: "Where possible construct functions which are suitable for the application of the calculus."[42] The fact that the above characteristic of an economics programme does not fit into the original categories of a Lakatosian framework is not to say that is is not important. For the sake of clarity, completeness, and the avoidance of further misinterpretation, a framework is here provided for those wandering aspects of research programmes that Lakatos did not address directly but which are judged to be of some importance in economics. The new concepts include: "core theorems," "core demonstrations," "metalevel hard core," "retreat and consolidation," "do-it-yourself positive heuristic," "ramparts," "interdiction," and the distinction between "normal" and "revolutionary" science. This last distinction is taken from the work of Thomas Kuhn[43] while the others are developed in this book. It is hoped that these theoretical adjustments to the Lakatosian framework will prove to be progressive *on the methodological level*. These amendments were developed as a result of attempts to apply the Lakatosian framework to economic theory, difficulties arising therefrom, attempts to resolve these difficulties, and renewed attempts to apply an adjusted Lakatosian framework. The following concepts are the fruit of this process, which is too cumbersome to reconstruct in the present context. They themselves provide an example of the intimate relationship between constructive criticism and the growth of knowledge. They will assist us in our exploration of responses to criticism within the economics discipline.

i. Core Theorems and Core Demonstrations

Certain theorems are redemonstrated with the development of each new model of a research programme in such a way that they may themselves by thought of as a series. A *core theorem* is the underlying idea which unites such a series of theorems. This concept may become clearer with an example. In the *Elements of Pure Economics*, Walras presents a research programme. The first model of this series he calls the "two-commodity problem." In this model Walras demonstrates the following theorem:

The exchange of two commodities for each other in a perfectly competitive market is an operation by which all holders of either one, or of both, of the two commodities can obtain the greatest possible satisfaction of their wants consistent with the condition that the two commodities are bought and sold at one and the same rate of exchange throughout the market.[44]

Walras' next major problem shift he calls the "multi-commodity problem." He demonstrates the core theorem under the conditions of the more complex model and obtains the following theorem:

The exchange of several commodities for one another in a market ruled by free competition is an operation by which all holders of one, several or all of the commodities exchanged can obtain the greatest possible satisfaction of their wants consistent with the twofold condition: (1) that any two commodities be exchanged for each other in one and the same ratio for all parties and (2) that the two ratios in which these commodities are exchanged for any third commodity be proportional to the ratio in which they are exchanged for each other.[45]

Next Walras introduces the possibility of production. He demonstrates the core theorem within the problem of production and obtains the following:

Production in a market ruled by free competition is an operation by which services can be combined and converted into products of such a nature and in such quantities as will give the greatest possible satisfaction of wants within the limits of the double conditions, that each service and each product have only one price at which the quantity supplied equals the quantity demanded and that the selling price of the products be equal to the cost of the services employed in making them[46]

Walras redemonstrates and restates this core theorem for each of the rest of the major problem shifts. The theorem demonstrated with each problem shift is actually new in the sense that is contains novel content. Predictive content increases as you move from theorem t_1 to t_2 to t_3, etc. This series of theorems, associated with Walras' series of models, is unified by the underlying idea of "the production of greatest possible satisfaction under free competition." Thus, the prediction of "greatest possible satisfaction under free competition" is a member of Walras' set of core theorems.

A *core demonstration* is the basic analytical argument that links the hard core to a core theorem. The core demonstration remains the same throughout the series of theorems from which we derive the core theorem. In the above example from Walras, the core demonstration would consist of the argument that since individuals are allowed freedom in the market they will trade right up to the point at which they are benefited the greatest and no further.

ii. Metalevel Hard Core

The hard core, core theorems, and core demonstrations unify the research programme in terms of content. In addition, a research programme may be unified by a set of methodological propositions concerning its structure. Call this set of methodological propositions the *metalevel hard core*. As an example of these new distinctions we examine an application of the Lakatosian framework by Joseph Remenyi, who has described what he considers to be the hard core of the "neoclassical" research programme. He lists the following eight propositions as the hard core:

(1) Most of the time economic activity takes place between rational actors who know their wants.

(2) Economic activity is motivated by individual self-interest.

(3) More is better than less.

(4) Given perfect knowledge and good government, economic welfare is maximized by free competition.

(5) Although welfare and economic welfare are not synonymous, the latter is a good approximation for the former.

(6) Any market for which a stable pareto-efficient equilibrium price cannot be found is: (a) not a market at all and so not relevant to economics; (b) a reflection of the lack of ingenuity on the part of the economist who has made the claim; (c) the result of a mistake in analysis; or (d) an unlikely possibility restricted to goods or services that are not significant to the economy as a whole, and therefore can be ignored.

(7) Everything has its opportunity cost.

(8) Abstract models are a valid method of analyzing economic activity.[47]

According to our amended Lakatosian terminology, only propositions (1), (2), (3), and (7) are likely candidates for a place in the hard core because these are the only members of the list to which the *modus tollens* is not to be directed and which are substantive economic lemmas. Proposition (4) is a core theorem and is clearly of a different nature than (1), (2), (3), and (7) in the sense that is is derived rather than presumed. Proposition (8) is a member of the metalevel hard core as it constitutes a methodological prescription. Proposition (5) is ambiguous, as stated, but probably should be considered part of the operationalization of the programme. Proposition (6) is a part of the negative heuristic; "(a)" is a good example of an explicit recognition of monster-barring, "(b)" is recognition that a simple marking of the existence of the positive heuristic can be used as a defensive mechanism (we discuss this later in the chapter), "(c)" is a recognition of monster-adjustment, and "(d)" a recognition of exception-barring.

iii. Retreat and Consolidation

The development of a new model subsequent to a problem shift may be complex. To keep the problem as simple as possible scientists will often *retreat* from earlier introductions of complexity. Note that such a retreat precludes the possibility of a retention of former unrefuted content. Thus it will not be possible for the newly produced model to refute the old model in a Lakatosian sense. This is counteracted by *consolidation*. After the new model has been developed, the old considerations may be reintroduced. It is this consolidation which allows the programme to be progressive. There are many examples of retreat and consolidation in the economics of the marginalist trio. For example, Jevons introduces "transport costs" early in the development of his series of models.[48] Later, to simplify the analysis, he discontinues the explicit consideration of transport costs; however, the consolidation of the later models in this regard is implicity.

iv. The Do-It-Yourself Positive Heuristic

It was noted earlier that anomalies can be produced by concept-stretching. With an appropriate response to anomaly such concept-stretching can lead to progressive theoretical adjustments. Some scientists anticipate this process and prepare the way for concept-stretching by granting flexibility to the meaning of their theoretical terms. This preparation is here called a *do-it-yourself positive heuristic*. Jevons provides a good example of the do-it-yourself positive heuristic with his term "trading body."[49] He states that he has defined this term broadly so that it might be easily applied wherever a sufficient structural similarity exists. The empirical base may then be expanded with facility by the normal scientist.

v. Defensive Mechanisms Other than the Negative Heuristic

The negative heuristic, in essence, is simply the statement "do not direct the *modus tollens* at the hard core." This statement might be communicated in many subtle ways. As opposed to the negative heuristic, which manifests itself in the specific set of tactics used to protect the hard core only, there is also a collection of tactics used by the programme to protect the predictions or core theorems. We shall call these the *ramparts*. (By the term "ramparts" we do not mean to connote any fixedness; these defensive tools are quite pliant.) It should be noted that the defensive manoeuvres used to protect the hard core will sometimes be the same as those used as ramparts for the programme. The ramparts will be discussed in the next chapter.

The final negative aspect of the programme we shall call the *interdiction*. The interdiction goes beyond the negative heuristic and the ramparts to designate particular statements, hypotheses, questions, points-of-view or activities as unacceptable to the science. This will also be discussed in the next chapter.

vi.   A Kuhnian Distinction

Thomas Kuhn makes a distinction between "normal" and "revolutionary" escientists in his *Structure of Scientific Revolutions*. We shall occasionally use these terms in the context of a Lakatosian methodological approach. By the term "normal scientist" we shall mean a practitioner of the science who is simply following the positive heuristic of the programme within which he is working and who obeys the negative heuristic (that is, he does not direct the *modus tollens* at the hard core.) By a "revolutionary scientist" we shall mean a scientist who founds a research programme or one who attempts to do so, or one who is willing to direct the *modus tollens* at the hard core in his demonstration analysis and his attempts at theoretical advance.

NOTES

1. Paul Feyerabend, *Against Method* (Norfolk: Lowe and Brydone Printers Ltd., 1976), p. 31.
2. Imre Lakatos and Alan Musgrave, eds., *Criticism and the Growth of Knowledge* (Cambridge: Cambridge University Press, 1970); Imre Lakatos, *Proofs and Refutations* (Cambridge: Cambridge University Press, 1976).
3. Donald N. McCloskey, "The Rhetoric of Economics," *Journal of Economic Literature* 21 (June 1983), pp. 481–517. On p. 483 McCloskey suggests a title that, barring some unwarranted connotations, might have been better for his article: "Outline of an Anarchistic Theory of Knowledge in Economics." See p. 492 for reference to *Proofs and Refutations*. See p. 509 for reference to *Methodology*. There are many good points in McCloskey's article.
4. Lakatos, *Proofs and Refutations*, p. 9.
5. Note that lemmas are also theorems; their demonstration consists of the statement of the lemma itself.
6. Lakatos, *Proofs and Refutations*, pp. 10–11.
7. *Ibid.*, p. 47.
8. *Ibid.*, pp. 42–7.
9. *Ibid.*, pp. 13–14.

10. Leon Walras, *Elements of Pure Economics*, trans. William Jaffe (London: George Allen and Unwin, 1954), pp. 132–42.

11. Lakatos, *Proofs and Refutations*, p. 14.

12. *Ibid.*, pp. 83–7.

13. W. Stanley Jevons, *The Theory of Political Economy*, 2nd edn. (London: Macmillan, 1879), (1st edn., 1871).

14. *Ibid.*, p. 57.

15. See Chapter 8 of this book and Jevons, *The Theory of Political Economy*, pp. 127–33.

16. Lakatos, *Proofs and Refutations*, p. 30.

17. See Chapter 8 of this book and Jevons, *The Theory of Political Economy*, p. 134.

18. Lakatos, *Proofs and Refutations*, p. 24.

19. See Chapter 8 of this book and Jevons, *The Theory of Political Economy*, pp. 118–27.

20. *Ibid.*, p. 128.

21. Lakatos, *Proofs and Refutations*, p. 33.

22. *Ibid.*, pp. 42–56. It is called a *proof analysis* in Lakatos.

23. Karl Popper, *The Logic of Scientific Discovery* (London: Hutchison, 1977), p. 1.

24. The material on content-increasing problem shifts is drawn mainly from Lakatos, *Criticism and the Growth of Knowledge*, *passim*.

25. Lakatos, *Proofs and Refutations*, p. 56.

26. *Ibid.*, p. 58.

27. Lakatos, *Criticism and the Growth of Knowledge*, p. 116. Lakatos actually states: "For sophisticated falsificationists a scientific theory T is *falsified* if and only if another theory T' has been proposed with the following characteristics: (1) T' has excess empirical content over T: that is, it predicts *novel* facts, that is, facts improbable in the light of, or even forbidden, by T; (2) T' explains the previous success of T, that is, all the unrefuted content of T is included (within the limits of observational error) in the content of T'; and (3) some of the excess content of T' is corroborated."

28. *Ibid.*, p. 118. (The above terms are defined there.)

29. *Ibid.*, p. 120.

30. *Ibid.*, p. 119.

31. *Ibid.*, p. 132.

32. *Ibid.*, pp. 135–6.

33. This leads to an expansion of the empirical base in a Popperian sense since there will be more opportunities for local and global counter-examples.

34. Lakatos, *Criticism and the Growth of Knowledge*, pp. 133–4.

35. *Ibid.*, p. 135.

36. *Ibid.*, p. 136.

37. In Chapters 6 and 7 of this book we see that this is also true of Menger's and Walras' works.

38. Lakatos, *Criticism and the Growth of Knowledge*, pp. 133–4.

39. See Chapter X of this book.

40. Lakatos, *Criticism and the Growth of Knowledge*, p. 157. This explains the possibility of a coexistence of rival programmes such as is observed in economics.
41. Lakatos, *Criticism and the Growth of Knowledge*, p. 154.
42. Spiro J. Latsis, ed., *Method and Appraisal in Economics* (Cambridge: Cambridge University Press, 1976), p. 22.
43. Thomas S. Kuhn, *The Structure of Scientific Revolutions* (Chicago: University of Chicago Press, 1970).
44. Walras, *Elements of Pure Economics*, p. 143.
45. *Ibid.*, p. 173.
46. *Ibid.*, p. 255.
47. Joseph Remenyi, *Core-Demi-Core Interaction* (Duke University: Ph.D. Thesis, 1976).
48. See Chapter 8 of this book.
49. See Chapter 8 of this book.

3 Lakatosian Virtues

> Tiger got to hunt,
> Bird got to fly;
> Man got to sit and wonder, "Why, why, why?"
> Tiger got to sleep,
> Bird got to land;
> Man got to tell himself he understand.[1]
>
> Kurt Vonnegut

To do scientific work one need not have a clear understanding of exactly what it is that one is doing. On the other hand, an improved understanding of metalevel science improves scientific praxis. In this chapter we examine various modes of scientific behaviour. Our normative criterion in assessment will be whether or not a particular mode of behaviour is likely to lead to scientific progress in the Lakatosian sense. We discuss the lessons for economics which may be derived from the Lakatosian framework. We categorize and discuss various forms of scientific criticism, some of which are fruitful and others not. Comments are offered on alternative approaches to the history of economic thought, which include the transverse approach, the functionalist approach, the socio-psychological approach, and the naive falsificationist approach. The importance of the history of economics to economic theory is adduced.

A. ON VIRTUE

i. Assessment of the Role of the Positive and the Negative Heuristics in the Development of Economic Theory

In summary, the negative heuristic is coextensive with the hard core of the programme and simply consists of the message; "do not direct the *modus tollens* at any hard core statements." If there is an attack on the hard core then the negative heuristic is called forth to shun the attack. In Lakatos' writings the intimate connection between the negative heuristic and the hard core is made clear. In his celebrated article "Falsification and the Methodology of Scientific Research Programmes," Lakatos introduces the concepts of the negative heuristic and the hard core simultaneously under the title: "Negative Heuristic; the 'hard core' of the programme."[2] Here Lakatos states: "The negative heuristic of the programme forbids us to direct the *modus tollens* at this 'hard core.'"[3] If a reconstruction of the negative heuristic of the marginalist research programme of the 1870s were desired, then it would be sufficient to cite the hard core and the metalevel hard core with the attached statement that the practitioners of the science should not construct any hypothesis, conjecture, or model inconsistent with the core.

The "hardness" of the hard core is communicated through operational statements which explain how empirical phenomena are to be translated into theoretical terms. For example, Jevons gives the following operational statement associated with the hard core assumption of the maximization of utility: "Anything which an individual is found to desire and to labour for must be assumed to possess for him utility."[4] In another place Jevons makes a similar statement: "Pleasures, in short, are, for the time being, as the mind estimates them; so that we cannot make a choice, or manifest the will in any way, without indicating thereby an excess of pleasure in some direction."[5] Operational statements are the concrete manifestations of the negative heuristic.

The maximization of utility is the most important hard core assumption for the early marginalist programme; the founders protect it with an array of operational tactics. For example, it is granted that economizing individuals may make mistakes. If one is confronted with an observation statement which indicates that an individual was not maximizing utility, either the observation statement is incorrect or the maximizing individual simply made an error in his utility calculus. In the *Principles of Economics* Menger states that:

Error and imperfect knowledge may give rise to aberrations, but these are the pathological phenomena of social economy and prove as little against the laws of economics as do the symptoms of a sick body against the laws of physiology.[6]

Jevons makes a comment along similar lines:

It is true that the mind often hesitates and is perplexed in making a choice of great importance: this indicates either varying estimates of the motives, or a feeling of incapacity to grasp the quantities concerned.[7]

After reading such statements, the practitioner of the science could have no doubt that these marginalists did not consider the assumption of utility maximization as fair game for criticism.

To look at another example, we have the following operational statement of Jevons which is associated with the hard core assumption of perfect competition. In the statement Jevons gives directions on identifying the empirical entities to which the abstract assumption is to be related. He states:

The theoretical conception of a perfect market is more or less completely carried out in practice. It is the work of brokers in any extensive market to organize exchange, so that every purchase shall be made with the most thorough acquaintance with the conditions of the trade. Each broker strives to gain the best knowledge of the conditions of supply and demand, and the earliest intimation of any change.[8]

Later, Jevons, gives the following operational statement for the protection of this assumption and its corollary of a single price in each market:

Hence follows what is undoubtedly true, with proper explanations, that *in the same open market, at any one moment, there cannot be two prices for the same kind of article.* Such differences as may practically occur arise from extraneous circumstances, such as the defective credit of the purchasers, their imperfect knowledge of the market, and so on.[9] (Italics in original)

These operational statements are manifestations of the negative heuristic. They transform hard core principles into tautological statements. Thus, the hard core principles can never be directly refuted by an empirically based criticism. The practitioners of a programme are taught by the founders how to identify the domain of a hard core law. It is through this process of learning to apply "the map to the terrain" (operationalization) that the "hardness" of a hard core statement is communicated. Hard core principles are abstract; their "truth" is seldom visible to the untrained eye. (Those who have not become acquainted with Newton's law of gravity do not see gravity; they just see things falling.) The normal scientist is trained to see the hard core principle in action by the operational statements of the negative heuristic.

The marginalists also used an alternative strategy to identify the hard core. This alternative strategy is to claim a *source* of knowledge for the truth of these principles. If one has a source of knowledge then the statements which express that knowledge must be true. If there is a source of the knowledge of the hard core then there can be no point in criticizing it, as it is true of necessity. In his *Theory*, Jevons makes a claim to sources of knowledge concerning economic principles. He states:

The science of Economics, however, is in some degree peculiar, owing to the fact, pointed out by J. S. Mill and Cairnes, that its ultimate laws are known to us immediately by intuition, or, at any rate, they are furnished to us ready made by other mental or physical sciences. [10]

In more recent history a new tactic to identify the hard core has been added to the discipline's armoury. The notion that "the realism of an assumption is unimportant" is a means of diverting the *modus tollens* from hard core statements. It is interesting to note that this manoeuvre is in conflict with the claims-to-a-source-of-knowledge manoeuvre as a means of identifying the hard core. Nevertheless, both are occasionally found together. The combination is particularly prevalent in introductory texts where the communication of the hard core is of paramount importance. Arguments are introduced which display the plausibility of a hard core principle (a source of knowledge proposition) alongside other arguments which indicate the unimportance of the plausibility of the hard core principles (the "realism of assumptions" proposal). This absurdity is resolved by recognizing the real message here: "this is a hard core principle; do not touch."

In the light of the Lakatosian framework, we may ask whether a more fruitful approach may be taken to the identification and defence of the hard core. Recall Lakatos' notion of progress. Take a theory, T, which is confronted by a global counterexample. Isolate the lemma which provides the local counterexample. If the lemma can be replaced or adjusted in such a way that the anomaly can be incorporated with both an expansion and retention of content, then progress is evident.

Notice that, in the above epistemological prescription, there is no reason why a replaced lemma might not be a member of the hard core. If the above Lakatosian conditions are fulfilled then there is progress, even though it may involved directing the *modus tollens* at the hard core. This raises the question: What possible role is there for the protection of the hard core in securing scientific progress? In *Criticism and the Growth of Knowledge*, Lakatos makes the empirical statement that most scientific progress takes place in the form of research programmes.[11] Yet it would seem that the structure of the research programme is such that progress might be thwarted. We must ask how it is that most scientific progress takes place in the form of a research programme despite the fact that the negative heuristic of the research programme forbids even a possibly progressive attack on the hard core.

Paradoxically, the answer lies in this very component of the structure of the research programme. Every aspect of the research programme is oriented toward making the demonstration analysis short and efficient (in fact, almost non-existent). The positive heuristic directs the scientist toward those areas where a theoretical adjustment is likely to be progressive. The negative heuristic directs the scientist away from those parts of the theory where it would be difficult (although not impossible) to make a progressive theoretical adjustment. These differences in the expectation of a progressive theoretical adjustment associated with different parts of the theory emerge because of the variation in the roles played by the parts of the theory. Hard core assumptions are fundamental assumptions employed in the derivation of a large proportion of the theorems. *A priori*, one would expect it to be very difficult to make a progressive theoretic adjustment to a hard core assumption because the retention of former unrefuted content is extremely unlikely. On the other hand, one would expect, *a priori*, that it would be easier to make a progressive theoretical adjustment to a simplifying assumption (that is, a member of the protective belt). Progress can be made rapidly here for two reasons. First, the simplifying assumption is not likely to have been a key to the demonstration of as many theorems as a hard core assumption. Second, and most important, the simplifying assumption is already paired off with the anomaly to which it provides the local counterexample. The programme has already done the demonstration analysis for the scientist. The creative aspect of the scientist's task is found only in the making of a progressive theoretical adjustment; the location of that adjustment is given to him. This is why rapid scientific progress comes in the form of a research programme. The link between the existence of the hard core and scientific progress is that the hard core saves the scientist time and effort by its indication that a much greater effort will be required to make progress by a theoretic adjustment in that direction. This guiding role of the positive heuristic and negative heuristic also explains the relative autonomy of theoretical science. As long as the anomalies are generated within the programme the progress is usually rapid. (We refer to this process as the "internal dialectic.")

The role of the positive and negative heuristic in generating progress also explains what often appears to be a lack of relevance in the direction of research. It sometimes happens that an anomaly is presented and deemed important by those outside the programme. If this anomaly is not in the immediately foreseeable positive heuristic, then it is often ignored. Those within the programme hope that, with enough progress along the existing positive heuristic, the path to the incorporation of the introduced anomaly will become clear. The alternative course of action is to engage in a demonstration analysis and attempt to isolate the local counterexample that corresponds to the particular anomaly. Demonstration analysis can be a difficult process. It may be found that the offending lemma is a hard core assumption. To make a pro-gressive theoretical adjustment will be difficult. It is clear why most scientists prefer to follow the positive heuristic of the programme where progress is easier. This produces a relative autonomy of the theoretical science which makes it fruitful for the historian of theory to attempt to trace an internal dialectic.

The distinction between normal and revolutionary science places an emphasis on the alternatives faced by scientists when confronted with an anomaly that is given importance from outside the programme. Those scientists who continue to follow the current positive heuristic of the programme we have called normal scientists. Those who engage in their own demonstration analysis (that is, those willing to challenge hard core assumptions in the search for a local counter-example), we have called revolutionary scientists. Clearly, there is an important role for both normal and revolutionary scientists in modern scientific work. Both revolutionary scientific activity and, separately, the relative autonomy of theoretical science are easy to observe in the economics discipline. During the depression persistent unemployment presented an anomaly to current economic analysis. The importance of this anomaly came from beyond the positive heuristic of the programme. Many economists ignored the anomaly and continued their work of articulating the domin-ant programme through adherence to its positive heuristic. Others, like Keynes, addressed the anomaly directly, searched promiscuously (but not without selection) for corresponding local counterexamples, and attempted to make theoretic adjustments which would incorporate the anomaly. They were attempting to found a new research programme.

Let us determine what lessons may be derived for econ-omics from the above considerations on the hard core. The Lakatosian framework itself offers a superior alternative method of indicating the hard core compared to the defensive manoeuvres and other techniques that are currently practised by the economics discipline. First, let us review current praxis. Claiming a source of knowledge (intuition, plausi-bility, etc.) of the hard core has the advantage that it iden-tifies the hard core, inspires belief, and therefore deters the normal scientist from wasting his efforts. The disadvantage of claiming a source of knowledge is that it may hinder the development of revolutionary scientists. If there is an entrenched belief (that is, an unscientific attitude) concerning the hard core principles, then few will dare challenge these even though the discipline may be ripe for a scientific revolution (that is, in a degenerative phase). If there is a paucity of revolutionary scientists because of entrenched beliefs then a foundation for a successful new progressive programme is less likely to be laid. Furthermore, a progressive revolutionary programme may not get a fair chance to compete if it is immediately quashed because of its disrespect for established ideas. Surely this was the nature of Jevons' complaint when he stated:

If, instead of welcoming inquiry and criticism, the admirers of a great author accept his writings as authoritative, both in their excellences and in their defects, the most serious injury is done to truth. In matters of philosophy and science authority has ever been the great opponent of truth. A despotic calm is usually the triumph of error. In the republic of the sciences sedition and even anarchy are beneficial in the long run to the greatest happiness of the greatest number. [12]

These are inspiring words for the budding revolutionary.

Claiming the unimportance of the realism of assumptions has the advantage of identifying and protecting the hard core so that the normal scientist does not waste his time but continues his efforts where the expected return is the greatest. The problem with this idea is, again, that it discourages the revolutionary scientist. If it is accepted tht the realism of assumptions is not important, individual scientists will not search the hard core for local counterexamples. Friedman's idea that a theory with unrealistic assumptions should not be rejected if it predicts well is fine as far as it goes, but it does not go far enough. Scientists are interested not only in organizing what we "know" but also in the growth of knowledge. Friedman has nothing constructive to say on this topic. He states:

Progress in positive economics will require not only the testing and elaboration of existing hypotheses but also the construction of new hypotheses. On this problem there is little to say on a formal level. The construction of hypotheses is a creative act of inspiration, intuition, invention; its essence is the vision of something new in familiar material. The process must be discussed in psychological, not logical, categories; studied in autobiographies and biographies, not treatises on scientific method; and promoted by maxim and example, not syllogism or theorem.[13]

Friedman is incorrect in his assertion that statements about the growth of knowledge must be in psychological rather than logical terms. He says this because he recognizes only a logic of justification, not a logic of discovery. The growth of knowledge *can* be examined from a Lakatosian perspective. It can be said that scientific progress may come from identifying a hard core assumption as providing a local counterexample, and then making an appropriate theoretic adjustment. In other words, scientific progress may come from a challenge to the realism of assumptions. It may be precisely the lack of plausibility which leads the revolutionary scientist to identify the hard core assumption as the local counterexample. Thus, *if we are concerned not only with present predictive power but with the growth of predictive power, the realism of a hard core assumption may be very important.*

If the Lakatosian methodological framework were explicitly adopted by the economics discipline, then all of the advantages and none of the disadvantages of the above means of identifying and protecting the hard core would be attained. In the teaching of the programme, the hard core would be identified as such and its importance for the rapid progress of the programme explained as above. It would be acknowledged that the reason why the current theory is tentatively accepted is that it is the latest (and therefore has the greatest empirical content) within a progressive series. The normal scientist would not direct the *modus tolens* at the hard core, not because the realism of assumptions is unimportant and not because he is assured of the truth of the hard core via some supposed source of knowledge, but rather because he would realize that such an act would not easily lead to progress. The normal scientist takes the option that offers a much lower risk and a somewhat lower return.

On the other hand, the revolutionary scientist will recognize that progress *may* come through the identification of a hard core assumption as a local counterexample. The revolutionary scientist realizes that he is not likely to come to any quick successes via this path. He chooses a path of much higher risk and a potentially higher return. The advantage of the Lakatosian framework is that it identifies the hard core for what it is and places clear signposts to show that the directing of the *modus tollens* at the hard core is not likely to be fruitful. Thus, specific defences of the hard core assumptions become unnecessary. On the other hand, through the Lakatosian framework we can recognize the possibility of theoretical progress through an attack on the hard core and the subsequent founding of a new research programme. Thus, *the acceptance of the Lakatosian framework yields to the revolutionary scientist sufficient methodological tolerance to ensure that his attempts at an alternative programme will be given a fair trial in competition with dominant competitors.* (Ironically, acceptance of an explicit Lakatosian framework for scientific research would somewhat lessen its descriptive accuracy as the directing of the *modus tollens* as the hard core would no longer be strictly forbidden.)

In his article "A Critique of Friedman's Critics," Lawrence Boland has argued that:

> the internal construction of Friedman's instrumentalism is logically sound, in any effective criticism of his view the only issue possibly at stake is the truth of falsity of instrumentalism itself. But no one has been able to criticize or refute instrumentalism.[14]

The "refutation" of Friedman's instrumentalism for which Boland has searched is provided by the Lakatosian approach here presented. The Lakatosian approach supersedes Friedman's methodology on the metalevel. Friedman, in his renowned article on "Positive Economics,"[15] has confused the application of scientific ideas with scientific activity itself. If one were concerned only with *current* predictive capability then Friedman's methodology would be adequate. However, a *scientist* is not concerned with current predictive capability, but rather with the *growth* of predictive capability. The growth of knowledge (predictive capability, if you must) is intimately related to fruitful criticism. Fruitful criticism may emerge *if the realism of assumptions is challenged*. Friedman has confused the economist *qua* engineer with the economist *qua* scientist. The arguments in Friedman's article are compelling only because he keeps the reader on the level of present practical usefulness — the level of engineering. When one moves to the level of scientific praxis then Friedman's framework is seen, not as illogical or incoherent, but rather as inadequate and to be replaced by a more sophisticated framework that can manage the puzzles presented by the growth of knowledge. The present author conjectures that, if Friedman worked through the Lakatosian approach here presented, he would perceive its supersedence and argue — correctly — that his own contribution was a first approximation.

ii. Assessment of the Role of Defensive Stratagems

We will now assess the role of the ramparts and the interdiction using the criterion of progressiveness. The ramparts consist of the various defensive manoeuvres of a programme faced by a global counterexample. One possible response to a counterexample is a progressive theoretical adjustment; this is always to be preferred. We include in the ramparts all possible responses *other than* progressive theoretical adjustments. An excessive use of the ramparts combined with a lack of theoretical progress is an indication of a degenerating programme. Let us be more specific about the options available within the ramparts.

The defence most often employed by economists, and by scientists in general, is the *ceteris paribus* defence since it is always a logical alternative. Economic theorems are considered valid as long as other things are held equal. Since one can never be certain that all other relevant things have been held equal, there can never by any real test of a theory in a naive falsificationist's sense. In the face of a counterexample the scientist can simply exclaim "*ceteris* was not *paribus*." Jevons points this out:

unfortunately this verification is often the least satisfactory part of the process, because, as J. S. Mill has fully explained, the circumstances of a nation are infinitely complicated, and we seldom get two or more instances which are comparable. [16]

The *ceteris paribus* condition is often employed as the

receptor of the *modus tollens*. In the passage cited below, Walras uses the *ceteris paribus* defence to protect the quantity theory of money. He states:

> But the opponents of the quantity theory deny that these fluctuations were *inversely proportional*. In reply it can easily be shown: (1) that the quantity theory relates only to the quantity of money; (2) that the theory affirms a direct proportionality to quantity; and (3) that it assumes *all other things to remain constant*, a condition which is never satisfied in reality because of the length of time required for the phenomena in question to develop. [17] (Italics in original)

Another common defensive manoeuvre in the ramparts is the mere indication of the existence of the positive heuristic. A scientist can discount the importance of an anomaly by indicating that, ultimately, he expects the further articulation of the programme, through its positive heuristic, to transform the anomaly into a corroboration. We shall call this the "young science" argument. The argument is that the phenomenon in question cannot at present be explained by the science, but the science is young and it is expected that some day an explanation based on its hard core principles may be put forward. This is what Jevons means when he states that:

> there is endless occupation for an economist in developing and improving his science ... I have ... reason to hope that little or no real error remains in the doctrines stated. The faults are in the form rather than the matter. [18]

Jevons is saying that any perceived counterexamples to his theory are due to the need for further articulation of the series of models rather than to any fault in the hard core principles. He deflects criticism from the hard core to the existence of the positive heuristic, (but not to any specific aspect of the positive heuristic). In another passage, when confronted with an apparent anomaly related to the existence of speculation, Jevons, as a defensive manoeuvre, again indicates the existence of the positive heuristic. He states:

> Speculation complicates the action of the laws of supply and demand in a high degree, but does not in the least degree arrest their action or alter their nature. We shall never have a Science of Economics unless we learn

to discern the operation of law even among the most perplexing complications and apparent interruptions.[19]

Walras uses the "young science" argument in an even more daring manner. He suggests placing the blame of an anomaly on the positive heuristic even if that positive heuristic is not expected to be incorporated. We might call this the "our science will always be young" argument. Walras states:

"Precisely," we are told, "absolutely free competition is obstructed by an infinite number of disturbing factors. It is, therefore, pointless, apart from the gratification of idle curiosity, to study free competition by itself, uninfluenced by perturbations which defy mathematical computation." The futility of this objection is obvious. Even supposing that the future development of our science will never allow these disturbing factors to be incorporated into our equations of exchange — certainly a useless prognostic, if not a rash one — nevertheless, the equations we have developed do show freedom of production to be the superior general rule.[20]

One of the more sophisticated defensive manoeuvres of the ramparts is the claim of compensating errors. The claim of compensating errors is usually closely associated with the law of large numbers although it need not be. The compensating errors argument is usually employed to defend the programme from a local counterexample. The local counterexample is argued to be unimportant because of the expectation that there will be a sufficient number of local counterexamples in various directions to cancel out each other's influence and thus produce no global counterexample. Jevons uses this manoeuvre in his *Theory*. He explains:

The use of an average, or, what is the same, an aggregate result, depends upon the high probability that accidental and disturbing causes will operate, in the long run, as often in one direction as the other, so as to neutralise each other. Provided that we have a sufficient number of independent cases, we may detect the effect of any *tendency*, however slight. Accordingly, questions which appear, and perhaps are, quite indeterminate as regards individuals, may be capable of exact investigation and solution in regard to great masses and wide averages.[21] (Italics in original)

It is certainly true that "provided that we have a 'sufficient number of independent cases, we may detect the effect of any *tendency.*" It is *not* necessarily true that "accidental and disturbing causes will operate, in the long run as often in one direction as the other." We would expect this to be the case if these disturbing causes are random, but they may not be random. There may be systematic error which we do not suspect because of our incorrect theory. When the law of large numbers is applied, a non-trivial assertion is being made that the errors are indeed compensating. In the following passage, Jevons gives the marginalist programme a general defence of the laws of economics through the compensating errors argument. He states:

I must point out that, though the theory presumes to investigate the conditions of a mind, and bases upon this information the whole of Economics, practically it is an aggregate of individuals which will be treated. The general forms of the laws of Economics are the same in the case of individuals and nations; and, in reality, it is a law operating in the case of multitudes of individuals which gives rise to the aggregates represented in the transactions of a nation. Practically, however, it is quite impossible to detect the operation of general laws of this kind in the actions of one or a few individuals. The motives and conditions are so numerous and complicated that the resulting actions have the appearance of caprice, and are beyond the analytic powers of science.[22]

Jevons has combined here the "young science" argument with the "compensating errors" argument although they may be thought of as analytically distinct. The danger of the compensating errors argument is that it opens the option of claiming that any given disturbance is one that is mutually compensated for when this may not be the case. Walras gives a concise statement of the compensating errors argument. He states:

It is unnecessary, however, to go into any great detail in order to understand the effects of various disturbing influences on the mechanism of free competition. We may neglect mutually compensating variations and those variations which are secondary or inappreciable as compared with the major variations.[23]

Another possible defensive manoeuvre is the directing of the *modus tollens* to a specific part of the protective belt. This is a slightly different defence than those previously discussed. The protective belt consists of those assumptions used to temporarily simplify the current model of the programme so that is is manageable. For example, the assumption of a two-commodity world is part of the protective belt. Recall that it is called the protective belt because the blame for an anomaly may always be directed at one of these assumptions rather than at the hard core. The thing which makes this defensive manoeuvre different to the others listed above is that it recognizes openly that the present stage of development of the programme is at fault. Such a recognition is the first step to theoretical and empirical progress which is the life-blood of the programme. In his *Theory*, Jevons manages an apparent failure of supply and demand by shifting the criticism to the protective belt. He states:

> Because, in retail trade, in English or Dutch auction, or other particular modes of traffic, we cannot at once observe the operation of the laws of supply and demand, it is not in the least to be supposed that those laws are false. In fact, Mr. Thornton seems to allow that, if prospective demand and supply are taken into account, they become substantially true. But, in the actual working of any market, the influence of future events should never be neglected, neither by a merchant nor by an economist.[24]

Another defensive option in the ramparts, discussed earlier in the context of content-decreasing responses to anomalies, is monster-adjustment. Recall, this is the case where the *modus tollens* is directed at the operationalization of the theory or at one of the theories of observation. In other words, the empirical phenomenon is reinterpreted so that it appears as a corroboration of the theory. This process may be quite systematic, as we have seen with Jevons' handling of substitutes by reinterpreting them as the same good with different intensities.

Also in the ramparts, discussed earlier, are the defensive options of exception-barring and monster-barring. Recall that exception-barring occurs in the case of an anomaly being included in a list of "exceptions" attached to the theorem. We mentioned the example of Jevons' exception-barring in managing the anomalies caused by boundary solutions and discontinuities. Monster-barring involves respecifying the theoretical terms so that a counterexample is excluded from consideration.

Finally we examine lemma-incorporation, also explored earlier, as a defensive technique in the ramparts. Directing the *modus tollens* at a specific part of the protective belt, and lemma-incorporation, are the two defensive manoeuvres most likely to lead to theoretical and empirical progress. This is because both of these techniques have the virtue of directing the normal scientist to the problem area where the theoretic adjustment will have to take place if the phenomenon in question is to be transformed from an anomaly to a corroboration. Recall that lemma-incorporation involves the isolation of the lemma which has yielded the local counterexample (which corresponds to some global counterexample) and incorporating it into the theorem. One advantage of lemma-incorporation is that it limits the range of the theorem by the minimum amount necessary to avoid the anomaly. In doing so it isolates the point where theoretical adjustment must be made for the anomaly to be brought back within the predictive scope of the theory. Walras was the most careful of the marginalist trio: he makes extensive use of lemma-incorporation in contexts where the other marginalists would employ less desirable defensive techniques. (It cannot be argued that Jevons and Menger used lemma-incorporation implicitly in these instances, since lemma-incorporation is by its essence, explicit.) To give an example, Walras uses lemma-incorporation to preclude any counterexamples which emanate from disequilibrium phenomena. He states:

Viewed in this way, the market is like a lake agitated by the wind, where the water is incessantly seeking its level without ever reaching it. But whereas there are days when the surface of a lake is almost smooth, there never is a day when the effective demand for products and services equals their effective supply and when the selling price of products equals the cost of productive services used in making them. The diversion of productive services from enterprises that are losing money to profitable enterprises takes place in various ways, the most important being through credit operations, but at best these ways are slow. It can happen and frequently does happen in real world, that under some circumstances a selling price will remain for long periods of time above cost of production and continue to rise in spite of increases in output, while under other circumstances, a fall in price, following upon this rise, will suddenly bring the selling price below cost of production and force entrepreneurs to reverse their production policies. For, just as a lake is, at times, stirred to its very depths by a storm, so also the market is sometimes thrown into violent confusion by *crises*, which are sudden and general disturbances of equilibrium. The more we know of the ideal conditions of equilibrium, the better we shall be able to control or prevent these crises.[25] (Italics in original)

This is a revealing passage from the *Elements*. In it Walras has highlighted the fact that his work applies to equilibrium phenomena only. His underlining this explicitly in the formulation of his theorems justifies labelling this a lemma-incorporation. What is interesting in the above passage is that Walras admits that, unlike the lake which is at times calm, we never observe anything even approaching equilibrium in the real world. Walras is emphasizing that his theory can never be strictly applied to reality. This completely protects the theory from empirical refutation. (The traditional sense of the term "refutation" is used here rather than the Lakatosian sense of replacement by supersedence.) This example destroys naive falsificationism as a metatheory about the development of economic thought. It is clear that these economists protected their theories carefully from the possibility of such refutation.

The use of the ramparts, as described above, to defend the programme is necessitated by a naive positivistic and justificationist philosophy of science. If science is thought of as the accumulation of proven truths, and a counterexample arises, it is necessary to place the blame for the counterexample somewhere. Since the scientist senses a great loss if the theory is rejected (even though it is flawed), he or she struggles to find another means to fend off the counterexample. Such activity is not necessary if one accepts a Lakatosian philosophy of science which concerns itself with progressiveness. The starting point of the Lakatosian philosophy is that the theory *is* flawed. Only after this is admitted can the search for the flaw begin and the possibility of progress arise. With the exception of lemma-incorporation and the use of the protective belt, all of the defensive activities in the ramparts, described above, are not only a waste of effort but distinctly detrimental to the advancement of a science because they block the recognition of a flaw in the theory. For this reason, the good Lakatosian scientist frowns upon the *ceteris paribus* defence, the pointing out of the mere existence of the positive heuristic as a defensive tactic (as opposed to directing the *modus tollens* to it), compensating errors, monster-barring, monster-adjustment, and exception-barring.

The interdiction is a statement of that which should be excluded from the scientific programme in addition to that which is in direct contradiction to the hard core. Interdiction has great potential for retarding the growth of the science if it is not handled with care, for there can be little reason to restrict the range of analysis in an *a priori* fashion if the hard core might take your further. To a large extent the interdiction is simply the statement of where the hard core is not expected to perform well, but it can sometimes be more than this and can have various motivations.

In the introduction to the *Theory*, Jevons offers a sweeping interdiction. He restricts economic analysis only to the lowest wants of man. He excludes emotional motives, such as "the claims of a family or friends," political motives, such as "the safety of a nation," and motives of "uprightness and honour" from the consideration of economic analysis.[26] He offers a lexicographical ordering of motivations and suggests that economists deal only with human activities of the lowest end of the ordering. Jevons states:

My present purpose is accomplished in pointing out this hierarchy of feeling, and assigning a proper place to the pleasures and pains with which the Economist deals. It is the lowest rank of feelings which we here treat.[27]

Jevons gives economics a modest place; it would not be expected that the end of the lexicographical ordering would be reached in many human decisions. (It is clear that modern economics has not taken this interdiction too seriously; Gary Becker's work[28] being a good example of a contravention.) All three of the marginalists exclude altruistic motives and malicious motives from the economic analysis. Psychologism is also forbidden even at the cost of losing determinacy. Menger states:

If other factors, founded on the personalities of the two economizing individuals or on other external conditions affecting the transaction, enter the picture, prices can deviate from this natural middle position between the limits explained earlier without causing the exchange operation to lose economic character. But these deviations are not economic in nature, being founded on personal characteristics or on special external causes that are not of an economic character.[29]

The interdiction of the marginalist trio is extensive. All three marginalists abide by the positive/normative distinction; any mixture of moral statements with positive assertions is forbidden. All three marginalists avoid interpersonal comparisons of utility and consider such attempts invalid. All questions concerning the absolute welfare of individuals are avoided. Concerning this point there is a prevailing misconception that interpersonal comparisons of utility are forbidden by the positive/normative distinction. This is not the case. The question of whether individuals are better or worse off in one situation than another *may* be an objective question. Happiness and health may be objective states which are either occurring or not occurring to a greater or lesser degree. Suppose, as a thought experiment, that people had "hedonometers" on their foreheads which displayed their level of happiness. In this case, whether a particular event made a person better or worse off is a positive question. Instead, suppose we buried those same hedonometers inside people's heads. Clearly, the question of people's happiness levels remains a positive question. (It would not suddenly become a normative question due to this change in physical fact.) Finally, suppose, instead, that we didn't know whether or not there were hedonometers in people's heads, but it had been suggested that this might be the case. In this last case, which is the actual one, the question of "happiness levels" remains a positive one.

To ask whether an individual is better or worse off is not the same thing as asking whether it is good or bad that the person is better or worse off. Economists have conflated the two questions for the following reason. If one assumes that individuals maximize utility then their actions indicate which situations are ones of higher utility. Economists assume that the individual is correct and criticize any other approach as moralizing. The point here is that, as far as the maximization of utility is concerned, whether or not the individual is correct in his or her decision is a *positive* question; a negative reply to that question does not suddenly make it normative.

The marginalists assume the individual is correct and employ the interdiction to preclude any further exploration of the question. This is, perhaps, why so little has been accomplished in welfare theory. One can imagine the birth of an alternative research programme in welfare economics which, by shedding a naive positivism that identifies scientific truth with the directly observable, dared to attack these important issues through bold and substantive conjectures on human "happiness" and criticism thereof. There is no scientific reason why these topics should not be addressed as positive issues within the discourse of the discipline.

Attempts to define the subject of economics are usually part of the interdiction. This is certainly the case with Jevons. He defines economics:

The problem of Economics may, as it seems to me, be stated thus: — Given, a certain population, with various needs and powers of production, in possession of certain lands and other sources of material: required, the mode of employing their labor which will maximize the utility of the produce. [30]

Jevons' formulation of "the problem of Economics" precludes any study of population, economic growth and development, underconsumption theory, and many other areas now considered to be legitimate for economic analysis. Definitions of this type serve no useful purpose. It is better to define a discipline in terms of its hard core and metalevel hard core and let the normal scientists wander where they may (that is, let the positive heuristic form "naturally" through the process of criticism without artificial restriction).

There is one possible scientific justification for the interdiction. The act of restricting the area over which one is to explore with the hard core may lead to a more efficient directing of scientific efforts if there is a reasonable *a priori* expectation that the hard core will not perform well in certain areas. There are *not* likely to be any reasonable grounds for such an expectation. Thus, the interdiction is likely to have a degenerative influence on a scientific programme if it is obeyed.

iii. Assessment of the Role of Criticism

Because there cannot be scientific progress without the recognition of both global and local counterexamples, it is clear that criticism must play a fundamental role in the advance of science. In this section we will categorize six different forms of criticism and assess each in terms of progressiveness. The six categories of criticism are: (1) criticism of sources, (2) direct criticism of the hard core, (3) criticism by counterexample, (4) criticism by demonstration of the limitation of the hard core, (5) criticism by development of a competing and progressive research programme, and (6) criticism by supersedence.

"Criticism of sources" is discussed later in this chapter and is designated as unscientific activity due to its lack of connection with progressiveness. The truth of falsity of an idea, its "usefulness" in terms of present predictive content, and its likelihood to obtain greater predictive scope through further articulation, are unrelated to the source of an idea.

Direct criticism of the hard core is the most common form of criticism and generally the least fruitful, with the exception of criticism of sources. It is not likely to be fruitful because, (a) it will not (and should not) lead to the rejection of a programme, and (b) it is not likely to lead to either a normal progressive problem shift or to a revolutionary progressive problem shift.

The direct criticism of the hard core *does not* lead to a rejection of the research programme because of the power of the positive heuristic. It *should not* lead to a rejection of the research programme because such a rejection would be a degenerative step if no superior analytic framework were available. Scientists abhor a theoretical vacuum. Normal progressive problem shifts take place through the positive heuristic. Direct criticism of the hard core can therefore play no role in normal science. The negative heuristic precludes this. Neither is a direct criticism of the hard core, in itself, likely to lead to a revolutionary problem shift. The revolutionary problem shift starts with an anomaly or global counterexample. The revolutionary scientist decides to engage in a demonstration analysis under the scrutiny of which the hard core is included. If he discovers a local counterexample in which he is interested, he may attempt a theoretical reformulation and hope to develop thereby a progressive new programme which incorporates that global counterexample. Direct criticism of the hard core *which is not linked* with a search for a local counterexample in correspondence with an interesting global counterexample *will not lead* to a revolutionary problem shift. Direct criticism of the hard core, except when it emanates from genuine revolutionary demonstration analysis, is a fruitless endeavour.

Criticism by counterexample entails pointing out anomalies (global counterexamples) to the predictions of the research programme. This is the most fruitful form of criticism, as far as the progressiveness of the particular research programme involved is concerned, because it is constructive of the positive heuristic. The positive heuristic does not gush out of thin air; it is developed through (not always obvious) criticism. Since the positive heuristic is necessary for the progress of normal science, so also is this form of criticism.

"Criticism by demonstration of the limitations of the hard core" we call fundamental criticism. It may be that certain predictions are inconsistent with the hard core. This implies that they could never become predictions of the research programme. If these predictions correspond to the reality about which one is theorizing, it is clear that the research programme will always be inadequate in that regard and that, no matter how much further the programme is articulated, it will not be able to incorporate these phenomena. This brings us to a possible form of criticism of a programme. It is conceivable that it may be demonstrated that, given a particular hard core, certain anomalies can never be incorporated because the prediction(s) necessary to incorporate these anomalies is (are) inconsistent with that hard core. For example, it is impossible for a Walrasian framework, which deals only with equilibrium phenomena (in the sense of supply equalling demand in all markets and cost of production equalling price in all markets), to make any prediction concerning the phenomenon of persistent unemployment of labour because this involves an excess supply of labour. This will remain trrue no matter how sophisticated may be the further development of the programme. It is no wonder that explanations of unemployment by neoclassical economists are always *ad hoc*. Other examples of this type of criticism are Joan Robinson's criticisms of capital theory (where she demonstrates that a basic set of predictions cannot be made beyond the one-commodity model) and J. M. Keynes' criticisms of neoclassical economics concerning non-probabilistic uncertainty.[31] Such fundamental criticisms do not imply that a research programme would or should be abandoned, but they do constitute an argument for the development of alternative programmes. Thus they are fruitful in this sense.

Of all the forms of criticism discussed so far, none will lead (nor should lead) to the rejection of a programme. A programme may be rejected by criticism in the form of a competing and progressive research programme. By "competing" we mean another programme which has a hard core inconsistent with the prior programme's hard core, and which yields predictions over some of the same phenomena. If this competing research programme is progressive and the other is degenerative, then the competing programme will become dominant in the discipline.

The final form of criticism, and the most devastating that may be directed at a research programme, is the development of an alternative programme which supersedes it.

B. THE ADVANTAGES OF A LAKATOSIAN APPROACH FOR THE HISTORY OF ECONOMIC THOUGHT

Our understanding of the current state of economic theory is enhanced by the history of economic thought. A Lakatosian history of thought has a peculiar efficiency in this respect because it captures exactly those elements from the history of the science that are necessary for the understanding of current theory. Because of this the Lakatosian approach has sheer pedagogical power with respect to both economic

theory and the history of economics. Furthermore, the
Lakatosian approach embraces valuable methodological
lessons. We discuss briefly some alternative approaches to
the history of economic thought. Our presentation involves
caricatures of the various approaches so as to highlight their
most prominent features, and a discussion of the comparative advantage of the Lakatosian approach. We note
that the Lakatosian framework underlines the importance
for modern analysis of the history of economic thought
whereas the other approaches do not.

i. Comments on Alternative Approaches to the History of Economic Thought

All histories of scientific thought are closely linked to some
particular philosophy of science. The historian of thought
interprets, orders and evaluates a morass of evidence, always
with a particular set of distinctions and similarities, and a
structure, which some philosophy of science provides.
Lakatos makes this point in regard to mathematics when he
paraphrases Kant that, without the guidance of philosophy,
the history of mathematics is blind.[32] Conversely, each
philosophy of science is associated with a particular history
of science. A history of science provides an empirical field
within which each philosophy of science develops. Lakatos
correctly suggests, again paraphrasing Kant, that the
philosophy of science is empty without the history of
science.[33]

A symbiotic relationship exists between each of the various
philosophies of science and its corresponding history of
science. A philosophy of science is needed to write a history
of science, but a history of science is needed to provide the
empirical basis for a philosophy of science. Each history of
economic thought is associated with a philosophy of
economics as a science. The suggestion that difficulties are
associated with an approach to the history of economic
thought is always concomitant with the suggestion that there
are difficulties with its corresponding philosophy of
economics as a science. In our critique of various approaches
to the history of economic thought, we must address the
underlying philosophy associated with each.

a. The Transverse Approach[34] The transverse approach to an economic work of the past is to reinterpret it with the aid of modern analysis so as to determine which aspects of it are correct by that standard and which are incorrect. The transverse approach to the history of economic thought is associated with an impercipient positivistic philosophy of science that posits science as the accumulation of proven truths. In actuality, science does *not* concern itself with proven truths (in the traditional senses of these words) and it is as much a revolutionary process as a cumulative one. However this may be, for those who accept the positivistic faith that science is the accumulation of proven truths, it follows that the current state of the science provides a standard of truth. The historian of economic thought, steeped in a positivistic tradition, goes forward with "truth" in hand in the form of modern analysis and appraises and evaluates historical works. This we call the transverse approach.

The history of economics is conceptualized by the transversing historian of thought as a search for truths, which, once discovered, are retained and never replaced. In other words, the truths are gathered like pebbles and thrown into the sack of science. A harbinger of the transverse approach is the question, "Who was the first to discover the 'correct' formulation?" This is the only interesting question that a naively positivistic philosophical framework allows one to ask. From the perspective of the transverse approach, the phylogenesis of economics becomes uninteresting because each stage of historical theorization can only be described as "mistaken" or "correct." Questions concerning the *development* of the science cannot be addressed because of the poverty of this philosophy. The transverse approach tends to relegate the history of economic thought to the realm of purely academic interest; the question of priority concerning a "correct" theoretical formulation is seldom a pressing issue of the day.

Aside from the fact that the transverse approach provides a poor framework for examining the development of economic theory, it has the further disadvantage that it is likely to lead to misinterpretation. The act of transposing an old theory into modern analysis may involve both unwarranted gains and unwarranted losses in content. That which is reported as correct in the old theory may not involve quite the same content as the modern theory. That which is reported as incorrect in the old theory may simply be different to the modern theory. The transverse approach is adopted by most historians of economic thought who are steeped in the orthodox economic tradition because a naive positivistic epistemology continues to dominate the orthodox ranks of the profession. Perhaps the most famous example of the transverse approach is recent Nobel Prize-winner George Stigler's *Production and Distribution Theories*. Stigler states:

> The writer has gone beyond mere selection and attention to logical consistency; he passes also on the empirical validity of the theories under discussion. Have the "right" assumptions been chosen? ... The basis of evaluation in this work is that body of contemporary theory which is given the nebulous description, neo-classical economics.[35]

Some examples of the misleading tendencies of the transverse approach may be adduced from Mark Blaug's *Economic Theory in Retrospect*. Blaug makes the following statement concerning Jevons: "Oddly enough ... Jevons ... did not develop a theory of the firm."[36] Further on, Blaug states:

> Jevons supplied no theory of production. His only explanation of the connection between costs of production and utility is that the marginal utility of the product obtained in equilibrium must equal the marginal disutility of producing it. This hardly depicts equilibrium for the entrepreneur because it depicts "feelings" as one of the coordinates.[37]

Blaug's statement that Jevons did not develop a theory of production because he did not depict "feelings" is incorrect. Jevons, unlike Walras and unlike later neoclassical economists, does not split his analysis into two spheres by introducing a dual law of utility and profit maximization. Jevons prefers to keep his analysis unified under a simple law of utility maximization. He states: "The theory which follows is *entirely based* on a calculus of pleasure and pain"[38] (italics mine). Blaug concludes that Jevons does not have a theory of production simply because Jevons' theory of production involves "feelings" and the modern theory does not. Blaug asserts that there is an omission in Jevons' work whereas, in fact, there is only an inconsistency between Jevons' work and modern analysis. The modern analysis is neither more nor less correct than Jevons' analysis in the sense that a research programme using Jevonian theory of production and involving "feelings" could have been developed. It is Blaug's employment of modern analysis as a criterion of truth that is the source of his error. Blaug makes precisely the same error in regard to Menger's work. Blaug states, "Menger also failed to apply marginalism to production."[39] Menger's extended analysis of goods of higher order must be considered as an analysis of production. Indeed, an educated reader who was *not* steeped in modern orthodox economic theory would probably assert that most of Menger's text is about production (because most of it is about production; it is only through dogmatic adherence to modern economic analysis that an illusion to the contrary is created). Both Jevons and Menger have theories of production but they are not the same as the modern theory of production. Blaug's conclusion that they do not have theories of production is an example of the confusion that may be caused by a transverse approach.

b. The Functionalist Approach The functionalist approach to the history of economic thought involves relating the economic work to its social context with a view to displaying its role in the society. Histories of thought based on the ideas of Marx or Weber provide examples. To illustrate some of the difficulties that may be encountered by a strictly functionalist approach let us examine an unsophisticated Marxist approach. (Similar arguments cover a Weberian analysis.) The Marxist employs the history of economic thought as another source of corroborations for the general framework of dialectical materialism. However, there is an hiatus in this Marxist analysis. The Marxist metatheory can explain why the conclusions of the economic theory were put forward but *they cannot explain how and why the economic theory is as it is*. For example, the desire of the early marginalists to reach certain ideological conclusions is an inadequate explanation of the employment of the law of diminishing marginal utility. There is no clear link between the two. Marxists emphasize the external dialectic between the discipline and the society (which certainly exists and is important) but they ignore the internal dialectic of a series of ideas. To put this another way: the particular ends toward the fulfillment of which logic and scientific technique are directed can be explained in terms of class struggle, but logic and scientific technique *themselves* cannot be explained in these terms. To attempt to explain logic and scientific ideas themselves in terms of dialectical materialism involves a paradox which is inherent to all closed systems of thought. For a system of thought to be closed, it must incorporate an explanation of itself. If a system of thought explains itself in terms which relate to empirical evidence (in the broadest possible sense), then it has a reference point outside itself and is not a closed system. If the system of thought explains itself in terms which do not relate to empirical evidence (again, in a very broad sense) then it undermines its own objectivity. It follows that *a system of thought cannot validly claim to be both objective and closed*. Furthermore, a closed system which purports to explain all thought leaves no purpose in communication, and therefore, no purpose in writing a history of economic thought. (The movement in Marxist circles away from Althusser's framework[40] appears to be due to a dissatisfaction with the constraints of a closed system.) The Marxist metatheory is enlightening concerning the interface between theory and society, but not enlightening concerning the development or truth value of the theory itself.

There is a mystical epistemology which underlies much of the Marxist history of economic thought. The Marxists and other critics of orthodoxy are concerned with showing that the origin of othodox economic theory is ideological. They assume implicitly that a display of the ideological roots of the theory will undermine its objectivity. Guy Routh's *The Origin of Economic Ideas* provides a good example of this type of criticism.[41] Such criticisms of orthodoxy conflate the source of the idea with its truth content. The source of an idea is irrelevant to its truth or falsity. A madman randomly spouting words may, by chance, hit upon a true statement. To point out that the man is mad does not made the statement false. The ideological bias of a scientist cannot alter the truth or falsity of any statement he makes. Ideas must stand or fall on their own. The attempt to discredit the source of an idea is related to the old belief that all knowledge is given to us by some divinity (absolute source). This epistemological idea is still dominant in western society and manifests itself in the noxious form of "expertism." In modern times the Judeo-Christian God has been replaced by the "authority of science" as the divine source of knowledge, but the idea remains the same. The Marxists, tacitly accepting this idea, feel that if they can show that orthodox economic theory has its source in the evil divinity of class hegemony then they have discredited the ideas. In actuality, there are no sources of knowledge. Knowledge involves a *creative* human act through which bold conjectures are formulated. These conjectures are tested against our empirical vision. Thus, it is no discredit to an idea to point out its disreputable origin. Its origin is irrelevant.

c. The Socio-Psychological Approach The socio-psychological approach relates the economic work of the past to the sociology of the discipline or to the psychological condition of the scientist. Stigler's conjecture that the cause of the marginalist revolution was due to a change in tastes within the profession (discussed in Chapter 4) is an example of a sociological approach.[42] From the history of science literature, Thomas Kuhn and M. Polanyi provide the best examples of this sort of work.[43] Lakatos descibes these two historians of thought as the "contemporary protagonists of the ideal of 'truth by consensus.'"[44]

In economics, Arjo Klamer's work offers an example of this type of approach. Klamer focuses on the psychological state of the individual economist.[45] He observes that "scientific" judgments by economists often and even typically involve "passion." He concludes that the traditionally considered "rational" aspects of science play a small role in economic discourse. The illusion under which Klamer has fallen is to confound the state of mind of an individual scientist with the state of the science itself. Implicitly, Klamer has taken the Cartesian viewpoint that the sole repository of knowledge is the individual. It follows from this presumption that if passion dominates the individual scientist then it dominates science. This is antagonistic to the Lakatosian viewpoint which, in a Hegelian tradition, sees the scientific community wholly as the repository of the corpus of scientific thought. Scientific rationality is not an individual phenomenon; it emerges in that collective activity which we call science.

The Popperian distinctions among "world one," "world two," and "world three" are useful here.[46] World one is the world of real, concrete, tangible, sensible things such as cars, pizzas, trees, sunshine and prices. World two is the subjective world of individual consciousnesses. Clearly, world one and world two often get out of line. World three is the cumulated product of world two which is embodied in such cultural institutions as language, law, ethics, common sense, books, records, the scientific/critical tradition, etc. There is an important tension between world two and world three which is what constitutes criticism.

The fallacy in Klamer's analysis is that, seeing the importance of passion in the subjectivity of individual experience — that is, in world two — he overplays the importance of passion in the development of world three, where collective forces are at work. The heart of scientific rationality is the tension between world two and world three. Scientific progress takes place through the exploration, criticism, and construction in world three. Just as the truth or falsity of a statement has nothing to do with who, be he fool, saint, or sinner, makes the statement, so also the motivation of a scientist has nothing to do with the impact of a fruitful criticism or theoretic adjustment on the body of scientific thought.

Donald McCloskey, in his article in the *Journal of Economic Literature* "The Rhetoric of Economics," also emphasizes sociological aspects of the economics discipline, and argues that, "Any Method Is Arrogant and Pretentious"[47] He describes his interpretation of the methodological literature:

The claim is that the philosopher of science can tell what makes for good, useful, fruitful, progressive science. He knows this so confidently that he can limit arguments that worthy scientists make spontaneously, casting out some as unscientific, or at best placing them firmly in the "context of discovery." The philosopher undertakes to second-guess the scientific community. [48]

Given this interpretation of the philosophy of science literature, it is no wonder that McCloskey feels it should be ignored. He argues that, instead of being concerned with methodology, economists should make a study of their own "rhetoric." He states:

The invitation to rhetoric, however, is not an invitation to irrationality in argument. Quite the contrary. It is an invitation to leave the irrationality of an artificially narrowed range of arguments and to move to the rationality of arguing like human beings. It brings out into the open the arguing that economists do anyway — in the dark, for they must do it somewhere and the various official rhetorics leave them benighted. [49]

McCloskey promises great rewards if we follow his advice. Through a study of "rhetoric" economists will have "better writing," "better teaching," "better foreign relations" with other disciplines, "better science," and "better dispositions". It is a marvellous bit of linguistic magic that allows McCloskey to offer prescriptions, which he claims will lead to "better science," while maintaining that it is best to ignore methodology and methodological prescriptions. Isn't what he offers just another "pretentious" set of methodological guidelines? McCloskey (correctly) argues the primary importance of convincing argumentation within the discipline. What he has ignored is the fact that, tacitly, methodological considerations are usually a key element in a convincing argument. A further difficulty with McCloskey's work, which is evident from the quote just above, is that he also falls into the Klamer fallacy of conflating world two and world three. Finally, he is mistaken in his interpretation of the intent of the methodological literature. The thrust of the literature on the methodology of economics is *not* to "legislate" what is good or bad economics from a heightened position outside the profession, but rather to entertain conjectures and engage in critical discourse *within* the profession on how and why economics develops as it does, and why that which is considered to be good economics is considered to be so.

Socio-psychological approaches provide no metatheory concerning the development of theory. At best, they offer a collection of uberous distinctions and good descriptions. At worst, they hide an unarticulated metatheory that will never enjoy the advantages of direct criticism. The socio-psychological approach, like the functionalist approach, is of interest but misses a major part of the story.

d. The Naive Falsificationist Approach   A naive falsificationist approach traces the development of thought as a series of conjectures and refutations. Blaug makes the following claims for falsificationism:

What methodology can do is to provide criteria for the acceptance and rejection of research programs, setting standards that will help us to discriminate between wheat and chaff. The ultimate question we can and indeed must pose about any research program is the one made familiar by Popper: what events, if they materialize, would lead us to reject that program? A program that cannot meet that question has fallen short of the highest standards that scientific knowledge can attain.[50]

The problem with naive falsificationism is that it can itself be falsified by an examination of the history of science. Theories often continue to be maintained in spite of their inconsistency with empirical evidence. Furthermore, scientists often consider simple corroborations to be very important. Lakatos discusses some counterexamples to naive falsificationism in his article in *Criticism and the Growth of Knowledge*.[51] The advantage of the falsificationist approach is that, unlike the transverse approach, the functionalist approach and the socio-psychological approach, it does concern itself with explaining the internal development of the theory. Its disadvantage is that is does not provide as good an explanation of that development as does the Lakatosian framework. (The above categorization of the various approaches to the history of economic thought is, of course, not comprehensive.)

ii. The Inseparability of Economic Theory from the History of Economics

In this section we shall argue that the understanding of economic theory is inseparable from the understanding of the history of economic theory because the science of economics involves a logic of discovery. We shall argue that this is true both for an understanding of the dominance of the overall theory and for the understanding of any particular aspect of the theory. We shall also argue that a Lakatosian reconstruction is the appropriate means to trace this logic of discovery.

The logic of economic discovery and the history of economics are intertwined. If there is a rationality to the development of a science then the actual history of that science must reflect that rationality. The notion of progress implies a link between the logical and the historical. Progress is historical because it entails a formal relation between earlier and later theories.

An example from Lakatos' *Proofs and Refutations: The Logic of Mathematical Discovery* will make these points clearer. In this book, Lakatos' aim:

is to elaborate the point that informal, quasiempirical, mathematics does not grow through a monotonous increase of the number of indubitably established theorems but through the incessant improvement of guesses by speculation and criticism, by the logic of proofs and refutations.[52]

Note that the growth of mathematics, like economics, involves shifts from guesses to improved guesses *through time*. This parallel between the logic of discovery and the actual historical development of the discipline is highlighted by Lakatos' method of placing the rational reconstruction in the body of the work and the corresponding history in the footnotes. We will take our example from the midst of his reconstruction. One of the participants in Lakatos' histrionic reconstruction presents the maturing conjecture that, "The Euler characteristic of a simple polyhedron is 2."[53] (The Euler characteristic is the number of vertices of a polyhedron minus the number of edges plus the number of faces. A simple polyhedron is one "which after having a face removed, can be stretched onto a plane.")[54] Another participant presents a cube resting on a larger cube as a counterexample to the conjecture with its attendant proof. The double cube is a simple polyhedron and its Euler characteristic is *not* two. The participants in Lakatos' reconstruction engage in a proof analysis to determine a local counterexample which corresponds to the global counterexample. They recall that one of the steps in the proof involves the statement "any face which fulfills this condition is called *simply connected.*"[55] It is noted that not all of the faces of the double cube are simply connected. The participants in the dialogue then incorporate the lemma which provides the corresponding local counterexample into the conjecture. The new improved conjecture is, "For a simple polyhedron, with all its faces simply connected, $V - E + F = 2$."[56] The double cube is not a counterexample to the new conjecture and the proof has been retained.

Now, suppose an individual were confronted with the proof and the matured conjecture at the latter stage of the above example. The best way that this individual could come to a clear understanding of why "simply connected" was included in the matured conjecture could be through a presentation, at least in outline, of the above story of the lemma-incorporation. He must be shown the counterexample with which the term "simply connected" was associated if he is to comprehend its inclusion. This example from Lakatos' *Proofs and Refutations*[57] demonstrates the principle that to understand the details of the current theory, one must explore the logic of its discovery. Since the logic of discovery is always *historical* there is an inseparability of the understanding of theory from the understanding of the history of theory. (An example from mathematics is used here instead of an example from economics because the argument is more compelling if the reader is *not* already familiar with the material.)

The idea of a link between current theory and the history of theory does not rest well with most modern economists. This is because they have been steeped in a formalist philosophy. If, in the following passage; the terms "mathematics" and "mathematician" are replaced by "economics" and "economist" respectively then the statements continue to be valid. Lakatos states:

According to formalists, mathematics is identical with formalized mathematics. But what can one *discover* in a formalized theory? Two sorts of things. *First*, one can discover the solution to problems which a suitably programmed Turing machine could solve in a finite time (such as: is a certain alleged proof a proof or not?) No mathematician is interested in following out the dreary mechanical "method" prescribed by such decision procedures. *Secondly*, one can discover the solutions to problems (such as: is a certain formula in a nondecidable theory a theorem or not?), where one can be guided only by the "method" of "unregimented insight and good fortune."

Now this bleak alternative between the rationalism of a machine and the irrationalism of blind guessing does not hold for live mathematics; an investigation of *informal* mathematics will yield a rich situational logic for working mathematicians, a situational logic which is neither mechanical nor irrational, but which cannot be recognized and still less be, stimulated, by the formalist philosophy.[58] (Italics and parenthetic remarks in original)

Recall the major points of the Lakatosian framework. Theories (or models) are always in confrontation with a set of anomalies. (Note that it is this starting point that distinctly separates the Lakatosian analysis from both falsificationism and justificationism.) There are many possible responses to anomalies; they range from those which are content-decreasing to those which are content-increasing. An adjustment to the original theory results in a new (albeit similar) theory. If a theoretic adjustment made in response to an anomaly results in both corroborated excess empirical content and the retention of unrefuted content, then it is rational to accept the new adjusted theory and to reject the old theory. The reason a theory is accepted is not because it is proven (it can never by justified in this sense), but rather because it is better than the preceding theory. The notion of scientific rationality is meaningless if a theory is considered in isolation. *It is in the movement between theories that scientific rationality manifests itself. Thus, the reasons for accepting a current theory are always historical. If we are to understand the rationality of the acceptance of the current theory then we must examine the shift from the earlier theory to that theory. This shift is always both an historical and a logical process.* That is our argument for why an understanding of the history of economic thought is essential to an understanding of the acceptance of some currently dominant theory (or programme.) The argument follows from the Lakatosian framework.

In the preceding paragraph we came to the conclusion that, to estimate the rationality of the acceptance of the most recent theory, the shift to that theory must be examined. In that context we examined the theory as a whole. To understand a particular aspect of the theory one is likely to have to delve yet deeper into its history. This occurs because every aspect of the current theory will fall into one of the following three categories: (1) the original intuitive ideas of the programme (that is, the hard core and core demonstrations), (2) the simplifying assumptions (protective belt), and (3) the results of theoretical adjustments. The historical development of the theory must be examined to understand any one of these aspects of the current theory. Corresponding to category (1) above, simply to identify the hard core and core demonstrations *one must examine the whole series of theories* from which the current theory is derived. A structured return to the original model reveals the intuitive ideas in their simplest, and therefore often most compelling, form. Corresponding to category (2), a simplifying assumption can only be understood in the context of that aspect of reality from which the scientist has abstracted. This also is obtained by tracing the *historical development* of the theory. Corresponding to category (3), any aspect of the theory which is due to a theoretic adjustment can be understood only in terms of the anomaly to which that adjustment was addressed, the local and global counterexamples which it resolved, and the expansion (and retention) of content which it allowed. These are also a matter of *history*.

The above series of arguments is the most important in this book. A naively positivistic epistemology places no importance on the history of economics. The dominance of this epistemology accounts for the decline in the importance of this subdiscipline within economics. A Lakatosian approach places prime importance on the history of economics both for pedagogical purposes and for the science itself. Let us be polemical. It may be asked, how has economics managed so well without a strong history of economics subdiscipline? First, and most obvious, it is not clear that the discipline could not have done better in terms of scientific progress, given the resources that have been directed to it. Second, and more to the point, necessary work in the history of economics has continued, but in disguise. It appears in the early chapters of college and graduate textbooks which are intended to give the student a "feel" for the discipline, and in the form of survey articles. Pick up any survey article and note that it attempts to carry the reader to the present stage of an internal dialectic through a history of the development of some particular set of ideas. It is argued here that this type of history of economics is essential for understanding economic theory, and it is suggested that this work could be done in a more efficacious manner if its role were explicitly recognized. To expect an individual to understand the current state of theory without this background would be like expecting someone to understand a heated conversation upon entering a room. The advantage of a Lakatosian approach to the history of economic thought is that it provides criteria for choosing exactly those aspects of history which enhance our understanding of the current state of the discipline. This follows from the above arguments as well.

If one considers science as the accumulation of proven truths (if one is a naive positivist) then the history of science can have only an intrinsic appeal; it can have no further usefulness. On the other hand, if one rejects justificationist philosophies as illusionary and yet agrees that there is a rationality to the development of scientific thought, then the importance of history of that thought follows as a necessary consequence. Examples from economics abound. Could any one understand the state of modern axiomatic welfare economics without examining Arrow's Impossibility Theorem of 1954 and tracing the reactions to it? Could anyone understand Keynesian economics without viewing it as a departure from neoclassical economics or without tracing the developing controversies concerning, say, the consumption or investment functions? Could anyone understand the current state of general equilibrium theory without understanding the path along which that theory was developed?

A Lakatosian reconstruction is the appropriate means to trace the "logic of discovery" in economics because it is the only available framework which offers the necessary distinctions and methodological criteria relevant to actual scientific development. (It makes us ask the "right" questions.) If one accepts Lakatos' framework as a philosophy of science, then one must accept it as an historical technique.

What is needed is a new history of economic theory, a metaparadigm of historical investigation that asks a new set of questions. We should reject the formalist tradition which only allows us to ask: "What was the first 'correct' formulation?" Instead, we should ask: "What was the initial problem context? What was the initial naive conjecture, model, or theory which addressed that problem? What were the criticisms of this first guess, and what were the natures of these criticisms? How did the scientists (economists) involved respond to these criticisms? What were the theoretical adjustments in response to the anomalies which the criticisms underlined? How did this lead to the next stage of theoretic development? What were the new criticisms brought forth at this later stage? Was the programme progressive? What were the competing programmes of research? How did they compare in terms of theoretical and empirical progress?" Through this series of questions the internal dialectic can be traced right up to the present stage of development. This is not only the most efficient path for reaching a sophisticated understanding of the current state of the science (for the reader of such material, that is); it also leads to a subtle comprehension of the nature of the activity called "economic science." It highlights that the role of the economist *qua* scientist (as opposed to the economist *qua* engineer or *qua* priest) is not just to learn the current theory, but to change it.

NOTES

1. Kurt Vonnegut, Jr., *Cat's Cradle* (New York: Dell Publishing Co:, 1963), p. 124.
2. Imre Lakatos and Alan Musgrave, eds., *Criticism and the Growth of Knowledge* (Cambridge: Cambridge University Press, 1970), p. 133.
3. *Ibid.*
4. W. Stanley Jevons, *The Theory of Political Economy*, 2nd edn. (London: Macmillan, 1879), (1st edn., 1871), p. 38.
5. *Ibid.*, p. 13.
6. Karl Menger, *Principles of Economics*, trans. and ed. James Dingwall and Bert F. Hoselitz with an introduction by Frank H. Knight (Glencoe, Illinois: The Free Press, 1950), p. 116.

7. Jevons, *Theory*, p. 13.
8. *Ibid.*, p. 86.
9. *Ibid.*, p. 91.
10. *Ibid.*, p. 18.
11. Lakatos, *Criticism and the Growth of Knowledge*, pp. 91–106. *passim.*
12. Jevons, *Theory*, pp. 275–6.
13. Milton Friedman, *Essays in Positive Economics* (Chicago: University of Chicago Press, 1953), pp. 42–3.
14. Lawrence Boland, "A Critique of Friedman's Critics," *Journal of Economic Literature* 17 (1979), p. 521.
15. Friedman, *Essays in Positive Economics*, pp. 3–43.
16. Jevons, *Theory*, p. 18.
17. Auguste Walras, *Elements of Pure Economics*, p. 367.
18. Jevons, *Theory*, p. xiv.
19. *Ibid.*, p. 111.
20. Walras, *Elements of Pure Economics*, p. 256.
21. Jevons, *Theory*, p. 16.
22. *Ibid.*, pp. 14–15.
23. Walras, *Elements of Pure Economics*, p. 255.
24. Jevons, *Theory*, p. 109.
25. Walras, *Elements of Pure Economics*, pp. 380–1.
26. Jevons, *Theory*, p. 25.
27. *Ibid.*, pp. 26–7.
28. Gary S. Becker, *The Economic Approach to Human Behaviour* (Chicago: University of Chicago Press, 1976).
29. Menger, *Principles of Economics*, p. 197.
30. Jevons, *Theory*, p. 267.
31. Joan Robinson, *Contributions to Modern Economics* (Oxford: Basil Blackwell, 1979); *Economic Heresies* (London: Macmillan, 1971); *Further Contributions to Modern Economics* (Oxford: Basil Blackwell, 1980); J. M. Keynes, *The General Theory of Employment, Interest, and Money* (New York: Harcourt, Brace & World, 1936).
32. Imre Lakatos, *Proofs and Refutations* (Cambridge: Cambridge University Press, 1976), p. 2.
33. *Ibid.*
34. Some may view the transverse approach as constituting the same classification as what is sometimes called the "absolutist" approach; it does not. The notion of an "absolutist" approach is based on a false dichotomy between dogmatism and scepticism (which dichotomy is intimately associated with positivist philosophy [a sceptic is a disappointed dogmatist]).
35. George J. Stigler, *Production and Distribution Theories* (New York: Macmillan, 1941), pp. 7–8.
36. Mark Blaug, *Economic Theory in Retrospect*, 2nd edn. (London: Heinemann Educational Books, 1977), p. 308.
37. *Ibid.*, p. 313.
38. Jevons, *Theory*, p. 23.
39. Blaug, *Economic Theory*, p. 309.

40. Louis Althusser, *Essays in Self-Criticism*, trans,. Graham Lock (London: New Left Books, 1976).
41. Guy Routh, *The Origin of Economic Ideas* (New York: Vintage Books, 1975).
42. Stigler, *Production and Distribution Theories*; see Chapter IV.
43. Thomas S. Kuhn, *The Copernican Revolution* (New York: Vintage Books, 1957); *The Essential Tension: Selected Studies in Scientific Tradition and Change* (Chicago: University of Chicago Press, 1977); *The Structure of Scientific Revolutions* (Chicago: University of Chicago Press, 1970); Michael Polanyi and Harry Prosch, *Meaning* (Chicago: University of Chicago Press, 1975); *The Tacit Dimension* (New York: Doubleday,1966).
44. Lakatos, *Criticism and the Growth of Knowledge*, p. 92.
45. Arjo Klamer, *Conversations with Economists* (Little and Brown, 1983). See also his soon to be completed "The Art of Economic Persuasion." My views on Klamer are derived from a reading of his works and from discussions with him.
46. Bryan Magee, *Karl Popper* (New York: Viking Press, 1973), pp. 54–5.
47. Donald N. McCloskey, "The Rhetoric of Economics," *Journal of Economic Literature* 21 (June 1983), p. 490.
48. *Ibid.*
49. *Ibid.*, p. 509.
50. Mark Blaug, *The Methodology of Economics: or How Economists Explain* (Cambridge: Cambridge University Press, 1980), p. 264. Quoted in McCloskey, "The Rhetorics of Economics," p. 491.
51. Lakatos, *Criticism and the Growth of Knowledge*, p. 92.
52. Lakatos, *Proofs and Refutations*, p. 5.
53. *Ibid.*, p. 34.
54. *Ibid.*
55. *Ibid.*, p. 36.
56. *Ibid.*
57. *Ibid.*
58. *Ibid.*, pp. 3–4.

4 Marginalist Puzzles

Everything new has been said before by someone who did not discover it.[1]
A. Whitehead (as paraphased by M. Blaug)

In this chapter some questions concerning the marginalist revolution are introduced and various conjectures that have been suggested as answers are reviewed critically. An alternative set of conjectures, related to the marginalist ideas becoming available for the first time in the 1870s in the form of a research programme, are adumbrated. Given that the "marginalist ideas" had been available to economists from 1738 onwards (or at least from the early 1800s) why did these ideas not rise to prominence until the marginalist revolution of the 1870s? Was there really a marginalist revolution? If so, what were the links among the works of Jevons, Menger and Walras? Were Jevons, Menger and Walras rebelling against the then orthodox theory of value? Should the marginalist revolution be termed a "multiple discovery"? Why did the professionalization of economics take place in the last quarter of the nineteenth century? Was the rise of marginalism due to a dialectic internal or external to the economics discipline? There will be a brief discussion of various answers provided by the literature. Our alternative conjectures, embedded in a Lakatosian methodological framework, will only be adumbrated in this chapter; they cannot take flesh without more preparation.

The marginal utility/total utility distinction and the idea of diminishing marginal utility had been available to economists for nearly half a century before the introduction and acceptance of the marginalist economics of Jevons, Menger and Walras. Neil deMarchi states:

For the most part, successive expositions of the utility theory were ignored by economists practicing in the dominant Ricardian tradition. This is not quite true of the leading adherents of that tradition, John Stuart Mill and J. E. Cairnes, who openly opposed it in certain respects.[2]

More poetically, Craufurd Goodwin states:

before 1870 even the most promising marginal land lay fallow . . . to change the metaphor . . . marginal bread cast upon the waters was simply eaten by the classical fish without so much as a case of indigestion.[3]

Our first question is: Why did the new theories introduced in the early 1870s rise to a dominant position within the discipline when the earlier presentations of marginalist ideas had failed to do so?[4] Before offering an alternative solution to this problem we shall review nine conjectures put forward by other authors and note the inadequacies of these tentative solutions. The first four conjectures are in terms of an internal dialectic in the sense that the rise of marginalism is attributed either to strictly methodological considerations (the first two) or to a qualitative change in the topic of study (the latter two).[5] The five conjectures following this set are in terms of an external dialectic in the sense that they posit a change in the purpose, function or direction of the economics discipline due to outside influences.

Our first conjecture is provided by Frank Knight. He has suggested that it is the manifest truth of the marginalist theories that explains their ultimate success.[6] This dogmatically-based conjecture provides a poor explanation of the supersedence of classical political economy by marginalist economics. It fails to account for the above-mentioned fact that the marginal utility/total utility distinction and the principle of diminishing marginal utility had been put forward long before the 1870s and yet were never accepted as a basis for analysis until after that time. In the following passage Frank Knight provides an example of the imbroglio that is caused by the assumption that the truth of these theories is self-evident:

The greater mystery . . . is that the utility principle, connecting use-value with scarcity, had not been universally recognized and used long before, even "from the beginning," or at least after it had received fairly clear and adequate statement in published work. It had in fact been stated in all of the same three culture-languages — by Lloyd, Senior, and Jennings in England, by Dupuit in France and (most elaborately) by Gossen in Germany, not to mention the other "forerunners" . . . . The history of economic thought is replete with cases in which it seems that the "best minds" obstinately preferred to talk nonsense when the truth lay open before their eyes, in the world and even on the printed page.[7]

Further doubt is shed on Knight's conjecture of the manifest truth of marginalist economics by the fact that, although the marginalist theories have dominated much of western orthodoxy in the twentieth century, they have never received acceptance in all quarters even in the western world.

To provide our second methodologically-based conjecture one could take a falsificationist approach and argue that the rise of marginalism was due to the fall of classical political economy. Concerning the fall of the classical framework Hutchison states: "We have here a case, almost unparalleled in the history of economic theory, of the comparatively sudden abandonment of a central theoretical core which had long and authoritatively prevailed as an established orthodoxy."[8] It is clear that a scepticism concerning the validity of the classical framework was present prior to the onslaught of marginalism in the 1870s. Hutchison states:

The extent and suddenness of the collapse of confidence in the prevailing orthodoxies was most prominently exhibited with regard to the wages-fund doctrine in the late sixties and early seventies. F. D. Longe's *Refutation* in 1866 was slightly too early to make an impact. But Cliffe Leslie and Fleeming Jenking (both 1868) were followed by W. T. Thornton (1869),who extracted the capitulation from Mill, which Sidwick saw as the critical episode in the collapse of confidence in "classical," or Ricado-Mill, political economy.[9]

These attacks on classical political economy and Mill's capitulation might be interpreted as a falsification of the classical framework. A falsificationist would expect that, subsequent to such a collapse, an unrefuted competing body of thought, such as marginalism, would rise to the fore.

The question that must be asked here is whether the decline of classical political economy left room for the rise of marginalism or whether, instead, it was the rise of marginalism that forced the classical school out of a position of dominance. On the Lakatosian methodological grounds that scientists will not reject one theoretical framework until they have what appears to be a better alternative, we may question whether the doubts expressed in the late 1860s would have been sufficient to lead to the overthrow of the classical programme if no alternative had been present. It is interesting to note that, although Sidgwick writing in 1883 marks the beginning of the termination of classical economics with "Mill's notice of Mr. Thornton's book *On Labour* in the *Fortnightly Review* of March, 1869," he adds that "a second shock was given in 1871 by the publication of Professor Jevons' *Theory of Political Economy*." [10] We shall later argue that is was the existence of an alternative framework *which had not been available prior to the 1870s* that led to the rejection of classical political economy. This may seem paradoxical since obviously the marginalist ideas had been available prior to the 1870s. We shall argue that these ideas took on a new form in the 1870s (that is, the form of a research programme) which made them viable as an alternative framework. The falsificationist's approach is confuted by the better metatheory that scientists abhor a theoretical vacuum.

The next two conjectures are related in that they posit changes in the economy in the late nineteenth century that made marginalist analysis more appropriate.

The first conjecture in this pair is that the classical assumption of the homogeneity of labour-power became obsolete with the increase in the differentiation of labour skills that occurred toward the end of the nineteenth century. Walter Bagehot made this observation in 1895. He states:

And fifty years ago, when manufactures grew but slowly, and when the arts were comparatively stationary, this mode of speaking may not have been wholly incorrect — at any rate was not perfectly false. But nowadays the different skill used in different employments varies incessantly; it tends to increase with every improvement in quality; it tends to diminish with every improvement in machinery. Even between the same employments at different times it is difficult to compare it, and between two different employments it is impossible to compare it. [11]

The second conjecture of this duo is that, due to the spread of the capitalist ethic during the nineteenth century, households became more "rational" in the economic sense. It follows that a theory based on utility maximization would have become more appropriate in the last quarter of the century. This conjecture is due to Oscar Lange whom Ronald Meek paraphrases as follows: "Only when the 'spirit of capitalism' has become all-pervasive does it begin to appear plausible to assume that household activity, too, is 'rational' in the relevant sense."[12]

The two above conjectures have as a common feature that they highlight the rise of an empirical phenomenon which is in accord with marginalism and which is not in particular accord with classical economics.[13] There is a key element lacking in these two conjectures if they are taken as explanations of the rise of marginalism. To state that marginalism was more in accord with the economic reality of the late nineteenth century than was classical economies does not constitute an explanation of the rise of marginalism unless a metatheory concerning the relation between the state of the science and the state of reality is introduced. We cannot simply assume that the state of reality will be reflected in the theories of a given time.

The next five conjectures involve the external dialectic in the sense that they posit a change in the purpose, function or direction of the economics discipline due to influences outside the discipline.

The first conjecture in this set is suggested by Craufurd Goodwin. He supposes "that marginal utility theory (like modern welfare theory) is a luxury good which will be produced only at an advanced stage of economic development."[14] Goodwin gives a supporting argument as follows:

So long as the marginal utilities of all goods are very high, this argument runs, as they must be on the frontier or in underdeveloped countries, it is unreasonable to expect economists to spend their time analyzing the phenomenon of declining utility.[15]

In contradistinction to Goodwin's supporting argument for this hypothesis, the benefits of analyzing declining marginal utility will be greater in a frontier or underdeveloped economy where marginal utility is large. Losses through inefficiency have more severe and unpleasant consequences in underdeveloped economies *due to the high marginal utilities.* It follows that it is *more* important in an underdeveloped economy to allocate resources rationally (in the sense of setting the extra benefit to extra cost ratios equal in all uses) than in a developed economy.

A better supporting argument for Goodwin's conjecture would be that an underdeveloped society cannot command sufficient resources to support a marginalist economics programme of thought because of the high level of difficulty inherent in marginal analysis. This argument is indirectly supported by the fact that the rise of marginalism and the professionalization of economics were concurrent. (The implication is that the complexities of marginal analysis demand the attention [and greater resources] which can only be given by a professional.) A difficulty with this latter supporting argument and with the conjecture itself is that the levels of economic development in England, France and Austria were not comparable in the 1870s. England was by far the more developed of the three countries.

Let us move on to another conjecture. George Stigler is perplexed, like many others, by the fact that the utility idea had been available to prominent economists for at least forty years before it began to gain acceptance. Stigler suggests that, as economics became an academic discipline in the last quarter of the nineteenth century, there was a change in tastes which favoured the acceptance of marginalist economics. (There is a certain element of irony in a Chicago economist positing a change of tastes as an explanation.) The academic tastes that economists are supposed to have acquired included "a special premium upon generality" and "the paraphernalia of scholarship." Stigler states:

A dominant value of the scholarly world is a certain disengagement from the contemporary scene and a search for knowledge more fundamental and durable than that required for practical and immediate purposes . . . . The form of work takes on a value independent of its content: a scholar should be literate, and his work should be pursued with non-vulgar instruments.[16]

In support of his conjecture Stigler notes that a high proportion of prominent economists working on utility theory in this period were academics and that a high proportion of prominent economists who were not academics worked on applied topics. [17] He also submits "that there does not appear to be any serious rival explanation." [18] Of course, this last argument is sound methodologically from a Lakatosian perspective, however we hope to "falsify" it be providing a coherent alternative conjecture.

There are several difficulties with Stigler's explanation. It is not clear that, prior to the marginal revolution, prominent economists were devoid of the tastes that Stigler labels as academic and to which he ascribes the revolution. "Rigour and elegance" would seem an apt description of Ricardo's *Principles*. [19] Adam Smith's *Theory of Moral Sentiments* and J. S. Mill's concern with logic and methodology[20] indicate a "certain disengagement from the contemporary scene and a search for knowledge more fundamental and durable than that required for practical and immediate purposes." [21] Furthermore, it is not clear that the economics of the classical school did not have sufficient academic appeal. The revival of the classical framework with Sraffa's 1960 *Production of Commodities by Means of Commodities*[22] demonstrates that work based in the classical tradition may be in good academic taste. Stigler himself notes the lack of marginalist economics in Germany as an anomaly to his argument. He states:

The remarkable fact that Germany, the leading scientific nation of the world in the late Victorian period, had not a single important utility theorist is of some relevance. German economics had an established dominant academic base before almost any other European nation. [23]

Stigler's supporting evidence that a high proportion of utility theorists were academics may be explained by the plausible alternative conjecture that those economists with an inclination toward theoretical problems would also be those that would be attracted by an academic lifestyle.

The obverse of Stigler's hypothesis is that there was a shift of tastes toward obfuscation with the academization of the discipline. The third conjecture of this set of five is that marginalism was preferred because its more difficult mathematics and formal character could be employed as a "union card" or barrier to entry. Craufurd Goodwin expresses this third conjecture as follows:

To some extent, one suspects, the complexities of marginalism were welcomed by many economists as much for their professional significance as for their capacity to explain economic phenomena. It is the essence of a profession that the skills required therein are not possessed by those without. Marginalism was the first body of economic thought which provided the essential barrier of entry to the profession.[24]

The objections to this hypothesis are similar to the objections to Stigler's hypothesis. It is not clear that classical economics could not have been sufficiently mathematicized and involuted to form a restricted code.

Mark Blaug provides the fourth conjecture of this set. He has suggested that the need for "intellectual ammunition against Marx and Henry George" assured the success of the marginalist revolution. He states:

It was the rise of Marxism and Fabianism in the 1880s and 1890s that finally made subjective value theory socially and politically relevant; as the new economics began to furnish effective intellectual ammunition against Marx and Henry George, the view that value theory really did not matter became more difficult to sustain.[25]

We shall combine our comments on Blaug's conjecture with our comments on the fifth conjecture, which is offered by E. K. Hunt, who suggests a similarly ideologically based argument. Hunt proposes that in the early nineteenth century the emphasis within the classical framework on the distinction between productive and unproductive labour was useful for industrial capitalists who were concerned with the problem of accumulation. Simultaneously, the utility based theory, which emphasized the benefits derived from exchange, supplied useful ideological support to finance-capitalists and landlords. Towards the end of the nineteenth century the nature of capitalism changed. The industrial capitalists became more removed from the "industrial floor"; they became more like the finance-capitalists. At the same time, with the growth of Marxism, the labour theory of value began to take on radical connotations. Utility theory rose to dominance as the industrial capitalists joined the finance-capitalists and landlords in their acceptance of the ideological support provided by that theory. The labour theory of value had lost its attractiveness for industrial capitalists and their class.[26]

Ideological bias cannot be sufficient explanation of the supplanting of classical political economy by the marginalist theories, since the policy conclusions espoused by the major proponents of the two frameworks were basically the same. Henry Spiegel states: "In matters of economic policy, there was continuity rather than a break with the ideas of the classics."[27] Furthermore a particular theory of value does not entail the ideological position of its adherents. A comparison of Marx's work with Ricardo's shows that the labour theory of value could provide a basis for either an attack on or a defence of laissez-faire capitalism. This is also true of a theory of value based on utility. Craufurd Goodwin states:

marginalism did not have a clear set of policy precepts attached to it. A marginalist could be a free trader or a protectionist, a monometallist or a bimetallist. Except for the early controversy between European Marxists and marginalists, there was no crucial incident which committed marginalists for or against specific policies.[28]

There are ample examples of the employment of utility theory for both Conservative and leftist purposes. On the one hand, utility theory was used to support Conservative propositions by Jevons, by Pareto, who was a senator in the Mussolini regime, and by many others. On the other hand, utility theory was used to argue for the equality of income (or at least a movement in that direction) by the followers of Pigou. Wicksell made a similar argument:

If we assume that the rich man carries his consumption so far that the marginal utility, the utility of the last unit, is little or nothing to him, whilst on the other hand, the poor man must discontinue his consumption of practically all commodities at a point at which they possess for him a high marginal utility, then it is not difficult to imagine . . . that an exchange between a rich man and a poor man may lead to a much greater total utility for both together — and therefore for society as a whole — if it is effected at a suitable price fixed by society, than if everything is left to the haphazard working of free competition.[29]

E. K. Hunt cites two examples of the employment of utility

theory for leftist purposes. He states: "Thompson and Hodgskin had argued, on utilitarian grounds, that exchange would be even more beneficial in an economy where workers owned their own means of production."[30] George Bernard Shaw, an active member of the Fabian Society, attempted to develop an utility theory of socialism through a synthesis of Jevons' utility framework and Marxist analysis. Craufurd Goodwin states: "One can observe such later marginalists as Herbert Davenport and Thomas Nixon Carver proposing creation of interventionist economic institutions which would have horrified many of the marginalist pioneers."[31] Even the much mooted theorem of maximum social utility can be pivoted in a socialist direction. Hutchison states:

Theoretically, both a competitive and a collectivist economy can, with a given distribution of income, reach a position of maximum ophelimity (utility) . . . there is a slightly less unrealistic reason which makes this theoretical attainment much more difficult for the competitive economy than for the collectivist. This reason is that in a competitive economy it is difficult or practically impossible for a private firm to use price-discrimination or two-part tariffs in cases where there are fixed costs.[32]

Despite the work of certain Austrians, in the long run marginalist economics proved to be a boon to leftist economics. First, as Ronald Meek observes, marginalism has provided the foundation for and the justification of the economics of planning. Meek argues that in a modern planned economy marginalism should supersede Marxist analysis for many purposes.[33] Marx's writings were on capitalism; he had little to say on socialism and communism. Marginalism picks up where Marx left off. Schumpeter states: "Marx would have used it as a matter of course if he had been born fifty years later."[34] Second, the marginalist revolution contributed to the decline of "the concept of political economy as a collection of immutable rules for personal behaviour, more akin a catechism than to a science."[35] Up until the 1870s political economy had been asssociated with "Moral Philosophy and especially Protestant theology."[36] (Marx's work had been the exception to this.) The role that the marginalist revolution played in bursting this oppressive cultural grid — and we will argue that it was a leading one — was of assistance to radical economics.

We have noted some difficulties associated with each of the above conjectures concerning the marginalist revolution. These conjectures are not all mutually exclusive; elements of truth are to be found in many of them. In this book we shall present an alternative conjecture that we consider to be an improvement. Our conjecture does not preclude the possibility that some of the above conjectures have captured contributory elements to the revolution. It must be kept in mind that events are never monocausal. Our conjecture, which is methodologicallly based, will provide a necessary condition for the rise of marginalism. With it more sense can be made of the available evidence.

Our alternative explanation is that marginalism gained ascendence when it became available as a *research programme*. Recall that a research programme is a series of models interconnected by a set of unifying ideas and characterized by a series of anomalies which are to be incorporated. Unlike their marginalist forebears, Jevons, Menger and Walras forged the marginalist ideas into a research programme with a potential for theoretical and empirical growth *and* disseminated this prospectus to their colleagues. The fulfillment of both of these conditions was necessary for the success of marginalism, and they were not fulfilled until the 1870s. Although each of the marginalist trio intended to found an unique research programme and initially was not aware of his co-discoverers, their contribution as a group can be viewed as the foundation for a broad marginalist research programme. This is due to the similarity in both the form and content of their separate works. The similarity in content is due to an affinity among the hard cores, core theorems, and core demonstrations. The similarity of form is granted by the fact that each of these marginalists presented his work as a research programme. The *availability* of this marginalist programme to the economic community was ensured by the near simultaneity of their major publications, their personal diligence,[37] the enthusiasm of their supporters, their diversity of style (and, therefore, of appeal), and the fact that their writtings covered three different major European languages.

George Stigler is incorrect when he says that "utility theory was fully accessible to economics"[38] prior to the marginalist revolution. The *idea* with which one might construct such a theory were available, but the theory itself was not. The early marginalist ideas were, for the most part, *ad hoc* asides to handle particular puzzles. With one exception, which we shall examine below, the early marginalist ideas were never made a part of an overall theoretical framework such as constitutes a research programme. The notion of marginal utility was used by Bernoulli to solve the St. Petersburg paradox. Neither he nor the other writers concerned with this puzzle (Laplace, Fourier, Quetelet, Cournot, Buffon) employed utility theory as a general framework for explaining economic phenomena.[39] Bentham and his disciple Dumont limited their analysis to moral problems and did not develop an explanatory framework. Stigler states: "the role of utility as a moral guide . . . I believe it was the intellectual tragedy of Bentham's life that he limited his analysis of utility primarily to this role."[40] Concerning J. B. Say, Henry Spiegel states that he was a "forerunner of the subjective theory of value, but a forerunner more of thought than of the full-fledged theory."[41] Concerning the discoverers of the 1830s we may quote Blaug: "Lloyd, Longfield, Senior made little substantive use of marginal utility and thus only illustrate Whitehead's adage that everything new has been said before by someone who did not discover it."[42] Senior is typical of early marginalist writers in that he explored the notion of marginal utility and yet continued to base much of his economic analysis on a labour theory of value.[43] Dupuit only applied the marginalist ideas to a puzzle concerning the effect upon welfare of a toll. Stigler states the following in regard to Dupuit's work: "One is impressed by the narrowness of his vision; the explicit formulation of the concept of consumer surplus is elegant, but there is no intuition of the difficulties in the concept, *nor is there an attempt to construct the larger theoretical framework necessary to solve his problem*"[44] (italics mine). Jennings and Hearn formulated the principle of diminishing marginal utility but they did not apply it in their economic analysis.[45] With one exception, no economist prior to Jevons, Menger and Walras had forged the marginalist ideas into a programme of thought with which the universe of economic phenomena was to be explained. The only exception, Heinrich Gossen's work in Germany (1854),[46] was written in such an abstruse manner that it was never read widely enough to be an *available* alternative programme for the economic community. It is interesting to note that Gossen is the only "predecessor" upon which both Jevons and Walras could agree as being a true predecessor.[47] This is because he is the only one to have presented a research programme. It is unfortunate for Gossen that his programme did not become available until after the marginalist revolution.

Lakatos suggests that if one programme "explains the previous success of its rival and supersedes it by a further display of heuristic power"[48] then it will be considered superior. These are exactly the grounds on which the marginalist trio argued for the acceptance of their programme.[49] The meaning and significance of marginalism as a research programme will become clearer as the book progresses. The marginalist ideas available before 1871, the marginal utility/total utility distinction and the concept of diminishing marginal utility, could never alone have constituted a challenge to the dominant classical programme because they did not constitute a research programme and therefore had no potential for theoretical or empirical growth.

We now move to our second question: Was there a marginalist revolution? The decision as to whether or not to label the rise of marginalism as a revolution depends on the answers to some questions of degree. A. W. Coats asks: "How far did the marginal revolution constitute a break with the past? How far were any or all of the key concepts already present in the classical literature?"[50] Donald Winch offers an explication of the term "marginal revolution." He states: "Those who speak of a marginal revolution necessarily commit themselves to the view that the introduction of marginalism marks a decisive change in the direction, and possibly even the nature, of economics as an organized body of knowledge."[51]

The philosopher of science Thomas Kuhn suggests that one may consider a scientist or group of scientists to have induced a revolution if they fulfill two conditions. He states as conditions that:

Their achievement was sufficiently unprecedented to attract an enduring group of adherents away from competing modes of scientific activity. Simultaneously, it was sufficiently open-ended to leave all sorts of problems for the redefined group of practitioners to solve.[52]

Whether or not the rise of marginalism from the 1870s should be considered a revolution is an unresolved controversy. Blaug describes the "standard version" as "that which dates the revolution near 1871 and links together the names of Jevons, Menger, and Walras as having written essentially about the same thing."[53] This "standard version" has been challenged by a number of economists including Blaug, who states: "it was not a marginal utility revolution; it was not an abrupt change, but only a gradual transformation in which the old ideas were never definitely rejected; and it did not happen in the 1870s".[54] There are two streams of criticism of the "standard version." On the one hand many authors, including Eric Streissler,[55] have emphasized particular differences in the works of Jevons, Menger and Walras and have argued from this point that the work of the trio did not constitute an overall revolution. On the other hand, there are those who emphasize continuity in the growth of economic thought and who, accordingly, deny the revolutionary character of marginal utility theory. Prominent, and most interesting, in this group is Alfred Marshall, who himself was a major force in the latter stages of the revolution. Marshall was concerned that economics be granted the authority of science. The naively positivistic epistemology of the day demanded that a science appear as an accumulation of proven truths. In scientific "common sense" prior to Einstein, the notion of a revolution in science was anathema. As Harrod states:

he [Marshall] was extremely anxious to maintain the unity of the subject, both in time and place. He knew that economic controversies exposed it to the contempt of the ordinary man. He sought to find some good in various schools of thought and to preserve historical continuity, such as exists in the more developed sciences.[56]

In this book we uphold a revised standard version that in fact there was a marginalist revolution, that Jevons, Menger and Walras were basically writing about the same thing, and that the revolution began in the early 1870s. Not surprisingly, our argument will be based on the programmatic nature of the works of Jevons, Menger and Walras. We shall argue that the introduction and rise to dominance of a new research programme necessarily involves the fulfilment of both Winch's and Kuhn's criteria. In our assessment we shall consider both the similarities and differences in the works of Jevons, Menger and Walras.

If there was a revolution then what was the link between Jevons, Menger and Walras? There is a nice passage in Blaug's article from the Bellagio conference which captures most of the competing ideas concerning the links among the works of the marginalist trio. Blaug asks:

Was it a new emphasis on demand rather than supply, on consumer utility rather than on production costs? Was it something as ambitious as a subjective theory of value, which was to supplant the objective labor-cost theories of the past? Was it rather the extension of the principle of maximization from business firms to households, making the consumer and not the entrepreneur the epitome of rational action? Was it perhaps the equimarginal principle, enshrined in the proportionality of marginal utilities to prices as the condition of consumer equilibrium? Was it instead, as Schumpeter liked to say, the explicit or implicit discovery of general equilibrium analysis? Or lastly, was it simply the first conscious recognition of constrained maximization as the archetype of all economic reasoning?[57]

In this book we shall answer Blaug's queries and highlight the important similarities in both the form and the content of the works of the marginalist trio from our methodological perspective. We shall argue that the links among the works of the three marginalists are provided by a commonality in the hard core assumptions and core theorems of their respective programmes.

Was the marginalist revolution a rebellion against the then current orthodox labour theory of value? There is common agreement among historians of economic thought that Jevons was reacting to the Ricardo-Mill tradition. This is obvious from even the briefest survey of his writings on value theory and is epitomized by Jevons' now famous line:

When at length a true system of Economics comes to be established, it will be seen that that able but wrong-headed man, David Ricardo, shunted the car of Economic Science on the wrong line — a line, however, on which it was further urged towards confusion by his equally able and wrong-headed admirer, John Stuart Mill.[58]

It is generally recognized that the classical framework did not have the same foothold on the continent that it did in England. For this reason there is some controversy over the exent to which Walras and Menger were reacting to the labour theory of value. We shall argue that Jevons, Menger and Walras all were reacting to the classical framework as all saw their programme of thought as being in contrast to the labour theory of value.

Should the advent of marginalism in the early 1870s be labelled a multiple discovery? Mark Blaug raised this question in a paper given at the Bellagio conference and made a reference to a study of multiple discoveries in the natural sciences by the sociologist Robert Merton. Blaug quotes the following passage from Merton's work:

A great variety of evidence . . . testifies to the hypothesis that, once science has become institutionalized, and significant numbers of men are at work on scientific investigation, the same discoveries will be made independently more than once.[59]

Blaug then asks the question:

Was the state of economic science in the 1860s such as to make the eventual emergence of the marginal utility principle a perfectly predictable phenomenon, in which case it is hardly surprising that Jevons, Menger, and Walras discovered it at just about the same time?[60]

Blaug argues that economics did not, at that time, have the characteristics of a mature science and therefore the answer to the above question "must surely be No."[61] He implies that we should, therefore, not term the marginalist revolution as a multiple discovery. The problem encountered here is whether the marginalist revolution should be labelled as a multiple discovery even if its advent was not a predictable result of mature scientific activity. To a certain extent this is a problem of semantics. In Chapter 10 we shall introduce a distinction between two different types of multiple discoveries and note that the marginalist revolution does fall into one of these categories.

Our next question is: Why did the professionalization of economics take place in the last quarter of the nineteenth century? The rise of marginalism and the professionalization of economics were concurrent. In a reference to the Bellagio conference on the marginalist revolution, A. W. Coats states: "Several conference papers had suggested that the marginal revolution marked the beginning of modern professional economics."[62] Coats also notes: "from the 1870s most of the significant advances in economics were made by academics."[63] Craufurd Goodwin states:

The marginal revolution, in the New World as in the Old, was both coincident with and a significant part of the professionalization of economic science. During the 1880s economists began to meet together in significant numbers, to form associations, to publish journals, and above all to perceive their field of inquiry as a respectable discipline.[64]

It is often intimated that the causality runs from the professionalization of economics to the acceptance of marginalism. We have noted already George Stigler's conjecture that it was the acquired academic tastes that led to the acceptance of marginalism. Another example of this is implicit when Blaug asks:

Why did economics become professionalized in the last quarter of the nineteenth century and why should a professionalized science of economics find the truth of utility theory so self-evident that resistance to it becomes inpossible?[65]

In this book we argue that the causality is mainly in the other direction; it was the rise to dominance of the marginalist programme that led to the academization and professionalization of economics.

Our final question is: Was the rise of marginalism due to dialectic internal or external to the economics discipline? There is a great deal of confusion within the literature on the history of economic thought about what should be considered as an "external" or "exogenous" influence and what should be considered an "internal" or "endogenous" influence. We shall consider a scientific event attributable to the internal dialectic if the event is generated in the attempt to advance the theoretical understanding of phenomena in accordance with a set of scientific principles, formulated in regard to a set of scientific (metatheoretical) rules. Any other influence on the discipline is considered to be attributable to the external dialectic. For example, the influence of changes in the social structure on the *application* of theory (an influence felt in all the sciences) is properly labelled as due to an external dialectic. Furthermore, any influence upon scientific values (i.e., scientific procedure, scientific metaphilosophy, theories of observation, etc.) emanating from a change in the social structure is to be labelled as due to an external dialectic.

To clarify our definitions of the internal and external dialectics we shall make an analogy and then give an example. In the literature on the history of economic thought influences are labelled as external far more than is appropriate. Here is our analogy. If some astronomical observation proved anomalous to the currently held theories of physics, and the physicists responded to this anomaly with a theoretical reformulation, we would label this as the internal development of physics along its own peculiar logic of discovery. We would not argue that the physicist had succumbed to social influence external to the scientific endeavour. Similarly, if an economic phenomenon arises which is anomalous to a dominant economic theory, and economists respond to this anomaly with a theoretical reformulation, then we should label this as an internal development of economics along its own logic of discovery.

For example, many might consider the impact of the Great Depression on economic theory as an example of an external influence. It was actually attributable to the internal dialectic. (By this we do not mean that the Great Depression itself was caused by the state of economic theory, although this is an interesting hypothesis.) The neoclassical economic framework was dominant prior to the Great Depression. A prediction of that framework was that there would *not* be persistent unemployment of factor resources. The large scale of persistent unemployment of labour in the 1920s (in Europe) and in the 1930s provided a counterexample to this prediction. It is not unexpected that the presentation of a counterexample to a prediction of a dominant theory will bring forth a response from scientists. The theoretical reformulations that were developed in an attempt to account for the persistent unemployment of factor resources are exactly analogous to the responses by physicists when confronted by an anomaly. The influence of the Great Depression on economic theory is attributable to its own logic of discovery because the response to this anomaly was wholly within the bounds of the project of developing a scientific understanding of economic phenomena. In the early part of this chapter we considered various endogenous and exogenous explanations for the rise of marginalism. The explanation for the rise of marginalism that we shall put forward in this book is methodologically based and is, therefore, endogenous.

The questions about the marginalist revolution which we have raised in this chapter are interrelated. We shall argue that gaining important insights into their answers is dependent upon consideration of the marginalism of Jevons, Menger and Walras as a research programme. We shall return to these questions in Chapter 10.

NOTES

1. Mark Blaug, *Economic Theory in Retrospect*, 2nd edn. (London: Heinemann Educational Books, 1977), p. 308.
2. deMarchi, "Mill and Cairnes and the Emergence of Marginalism in England," in R. D. Black, A. W. Coats and Craufurd D. W. Goodwin, eds., *The Marginal Revolution in Economics: Interpretation and Evaluation* (Durham, N. C.: Duke University Press, 1973), p. 78.
3. C. Goodwin, "Marginalism Moves to the New World," in Black *et al.*, *op.cit.*, p. 290.
4. For our purposes Jevons' (1862) may be considered as prolegomena to his (1871) as the profession took no notice of his earlier piece. Richard Howey states: "Jevons' first public statement however, was delayed

until October 7, 1862 . . . . On that date, in Cambridge, the Secretary read, to section F of the British Association for the Advancement of Science, Jevons' 'Notice of a General Mathematical Theory of Political Economy.' No one besides the Secretary is known to have heard the paper read. The next year an abstract was printed in *Report of the Thirty-Second Meeting of the British Association for the Advancement of Science* (1863). No one is known to have mentioned this printed abstract in the next ten years." Howey, "The Origins of Marginalism," in Black *et al.*, *op. cit.*, p. 18.

5. Clearly, the terms "internal" and "external dialectic" could be defined in such a manner as to make the latter two conjectures exogenous. The semantics are unimportant; the point is that they are endogenous with respect to the project of understanding economic phenomena using the scientific method.

6. Frank Knight, "Introduction," in Karl Menger, *Principles of Economics*, trans. and ed. James Dingwall and Bert F. Hoselitz (Glencoe, Illinois: The Free Press, 1950), pp. 12–13.

7. *Ibid.*

8. T. W. Hutchison, "The 'Marginal Revolution' and the Decline and Fall of English Classical Political Economy," in Black *et al.*, *op. cit.*, p. 200.

9. *Ibid.*, p. 194.

10. H. Sidgwick, *Principles of Political Economy* (London: Macmillan. 1883), p. 1, quoted in Hutchison, "Decline and Fall," p. 186.

11. Walter Bagehot, *Economic Studies*, ed. R. H. Hutton (London: Longmans, Green, 1902), p. 262, quoted in Hutchison, "Decline and Fall," p. 192.

12. R. L. Meek, "Marginalism and Marxism," in Black *et al.*, *op. cit.*, p. 240. Meek's reference is to Oscar Lange, *Political Economy*, Vol. I, trans. A. H. Walker (New York, 1963), pp. 148–72 and 250–2.

13. E. K. Hunt argues that marginalism became *less* appropriate as a scientific theory during the last quarter of the nineteenth century due to the increased concentration of industry. E. K. Hunt, *History of Economic Thought: A Critical Perspective* (Belmont, California: Wadsworth, 1979), p. 236.

14. Goodwin, "Marginalism Moves," p. 295.

15. *Ibid.*

16. For this and the quotes immediately above see George J. Stigler, "The Adoption of the Marginal Utility Theory," in Black *et al.*, *op. cit.*, p. 311.

17. *Ibid.*, pp. 314–15.

18. *Ibid.*, p. 318.

19. David Ricardo, *On the Principles of Political Economy and Taxation*, Vol. I of *The Works and Correspondence of David Ricardo*, ed. Pierro Sraffa with the collaboration of M. H. Dobb (Cambridge: Cambridge University Press, 1951).

20. Adam Smith, *Adam Smith's Moral and Political Philosophy*, ed. and intro. Herbert W. Schneider (New York: Hafner, 1948); John Stuart

Mill, *Philosophy of Scientific Method*, ed. and intro. Ernest Nagel (New York: Hafner, 1950).

21. Concerning this issue, Coats states: "Despite their keen interest in policy questions, the classical economists had also upheld intellectual values and had formed a kind of quasi-professional self-conscious group or social circle, outside the universities." A. W. Coats, "Retrospect and Prospect," in Black *et al.*, *op. cit.*, p. 347.

22. Piero Sraffa, *Production of Commodities by Means of Commodities* (Cambridge: Cambridge University Press, 1960).

23. Stigler, "The Adoption of the Marginal Utility Theory," p. 315.

24. Goodwin, "Marginalism Moves," p. 302.

25. Mark Blaug, "Was There a Marginal Revolution?" in Black *et al.*, *op. cit.*, p. 13.

26. Hunt, *History of Economic Thought*, p. 269

27. H. W. Spiegel, *The Growth of Economic Thought* (Englewood Cliffs, N. J.: Prentice-Hall, 1971), p. 507.

28. Goodwin, "Marginalism Moves," p. 300.

29. Quoted in T. W. Hutchinson, *On Revolutions and Progress in Economic Knowledge*, (Cambridge: Cambridge University Press, 1978), p. 233. Wicksell, *Lectures on Political Economy on the Basis of the Marginal Principle*, p. 77.

30. Hunt, *History of Economic Thought*, p. 243.

31. Goodwin, "Marginalism Moves," p. 301.

32. T. W. Hutchison, *A Review of Economic Doctrines 1870–1929* (Oxford: Clarendon Press, 1953), p. 227.

33. Meek, "Marginalism and Marxism," p. 244.

34. Joseph A. Schumpeter, *History of Economic Analysis* (New York: Oxford University Press, 1954), p. 869.

35. Goodwin, "Marginalism Moves," p. 287.

36. *Ibid.*, p. 295.

37. Richard Howey states: "Walras estimated, in 1901, that he had spent, from his inherited capital, 50,000 francs (equal to ten times his highest annual salary) to spread his doctrines." Howey, "The Origins of Marginalism," p. 27. Eric Streissler states: "Menger had the status, the institutional position to enforce at least initial concurrence with his opinions." Streissler, "To What Extent Was the Austrian School Marginalist?" in Black *et al.*, *op. cit.*, p. 162. Like Walras and Menger, Jevons was also an ardent promoter of his own ideas.

38. Stigler, "Adoption of the Theory," p. 310.

39. *Ibid.*, pp. 308–9.

40. *Ibid.*, p. 306.

41. Spiegel, *The Growth of Economic Thought*, p. 259.

42. Blaug, "Was There a Marginal Revolution?", p. 6.

43. Nassau William Senior, *Letters on the Factory Act* (London: B. Fellowes, 1837); *Political Economy* (London: C. Griffen, 1863). Henry Spiegel gives an example of Senior's continued employment of the labour theory of value despite his statement of an utility theory. Spiegel states: "In his [Senior's] *Letters on the Factory Act* of 1837

he sharply objected to a statutory ten-hour day since his reduction of working hours would wipe out the manufacturers' profits, which he ascribed to the last two hours of a twelve-hour day, a view more in line with a labor theory of value than with Senior's utility theory." Spiegel, *The Growth of Economic Thought*, pp. 353–4.

44. George J. Stigler, *Essays in the History of Economics* (Chicago: University of Chicago Press, 1965), p. 82.

45. *Ibid.*, pp. 78–9.

46. There is no mention of Gossen's work in the economic literature of his time. His work became known through the efforts of Jevons and only after the marginalist revolution was well on its way to success. Hermann Heinrich Gossen, *Entwickelung der Gestze des menshlichen Verkehrs, und der daraus fliessenden Regeln für menschlichen Handeln* (Berlin: R. L. Prager, 1927).

47. Howey, "The Origins of Marginalism," p. 25.

48. Imre Lakatos and Alan Musgrave, eds., *Criticism and the Growth of Knowledge* (Cambridge: Cambridge University Press, 1970), p. 115.

49. See Chapter 9 of this book.

50. A. W. Coats, "Retrospect and Prospect," in Black *et al.*, *op. cit.*, p. 338.

51. D. Winch, "Marginalism and the Boundaries of Economic Science," in Black, *et al.*, *op. cit.*, p. 59.

52. Thomas S. Kuhn, *The Structure of Scientific Revolutions*, (Chicago: University of Chicago Press, 1970), p. 10.

53. Blaug, "Was There a Marginal Revolution?" p. 8.

54. *Ibid.*, p. 11.

55. Eric Streissler, "To What Extent Was the Austrian School Marginalist?" in Black *et al.*, *op. cit.*

56. R. F. Harrod, *John Maynard Keynes* (Harmondsworth, Middlesex: Penguin, 1972), p. 166.

57. Blaug, "Was There A Marginal Revolution?" pp. 8–9.

58. W. Stanley Jevons, *The Theory of Political Economy*, 2nd edn. (London: Macmillan, 1879), (1st edn., 1871), p. li.

59. Blaug, "Was There a Marginal Revolution?" p. 4. See R. K. Merton, "Singletons and Multiples in Scientific Discovery: A Chapter in the Sociology of Science," *Proceedings of the American Philosophical Society* 105, No. 5 (1961), p. 482.

60. *Ibid.*, p. 5.

61. *Ibid.*, p. 7.

62. Coats, "Retrospect and Prospect," p. 345.

63. A. W. Coats, "The Economic and Social Context of the Marginal Revolution of the 1870s," in Black *et al.*, *op. cit.*, p. 49.

64. Goodwin, "Marginalism Moves", p. 287.

65. Blaug, "Was There a Marginal Revolution?" p. 18.

5 The Newtonian Methodological Vision of the Marginalist Trio

I do not know what I may appear to the world; but to myself I seem to have been only like a boy playing on the seashore, and diverting myself in now and then finding a smoother pebble or a prettier shell than ordinary, whilst the great ocean of truth lay all undiscovered before me.[1]

Isaac Newton

There is potential for rewarding application of the Lakatosian framework to the economics of the marginalist revolution because of the similarity in methodology employed by economists and physicists. This structural similarity is due to the emulation of physics by Walras, Jevons and Menger. This is not meant in some equivocal way; in a sense, all work of the eighteenth and nineteenth centuries can be said to have been under the spell of Newtonian success. We refer, instead, to the specific structure of the research programme. In the first section of this chapter, which is brief, the *intention* of each in the marginalist trio to imitate *this* natural scientific method is established. In the second section, the methodological views of Jevons, Menger and Walras are discussed and then compared with the Lakatosian perspective. Overall, we argue that these marginalists had at least vague (precursive) notions of the Lakatosian concepts of the "research programme" and the "positive heuristic" and that each intended to establish what we would now call a research programme.[2]

A. THE INTENTION TO IMITATE THE NATURAL SCIENTIFIC METHOD

Walras states in his *Elements of Pure Economics*: "this pure theory of economics is a science which resembles the physico-mathematical sciences in every respect."[3] His intention of imitation is clear in the following passage from the *Elements*:

By demonstrating rigorously first the elementary theorems of geometry and algebra, and then the resulting theorems of the calculus and mechanics, in order to apply them to experimental data, we have achieved the marvels of modern industry. *Let us follow the same procedure in economics*, and, without doubt, we shall eventually succeed in having the same control over the nature of things in the economic and social order as we already have in the physical and industrial order."[4](Italics mine)

Throughout the *Elements*, Walras offers analogies with physics. In the following statement, Walras typifies the general enthusiasm among the marginalists of the 1870s for this project of building a Newtonian type of economics:

The law of supply and demand regulates all these exchanges of commodities just as the law of universal gravitation regulates the movements of all celestial bodies. Thus the system of the economic universe reveals itself, at least in all its grandeur and complexity; a system at once vast and simple, which, for sheer beauty, resembles and astronomic universe.[5]

Jevons is equally clear. In the "Preface to the First Edition" of his *Theory of Political Economy*, he states:

The theory of Economy thus treated presents a close analogy to the science of Statistical Mechanics, and the Laws of Exchange are found to resemble the Laws of Equilibrium of a lever as determined by the principle of virtual velocities.[6]

In his *Theory* he states:

As all the physical sciences have their basis more or less obviously in the general principles of mechanics, so all branches and divisions of economic science must be pervaded by certain general principles. It is to the investigation of such principles — to the tracing out of the mechanics of self-interest and utility, that this essay has been devoted. The establishment of such a theory is a necessary preliminary to any definite drafting of the superstructure of the aggregate science.[7]

For Carl Menger an imitation of physics was necessary due to a natural uniformity of method that traversed the science. In his *Grundsätze der Volkswirtschaftlehre*, Menger states:

This method of research, attaining universal acceptance in the natural sciences, led to very great results and on this account came mistakenly to be called the natural-scientific method. It is, in reality, a method common to all fields of empirical knowledge, and should properly be called the empirical method.[8]

Newtonian mechanics provided a prototype for economic theory. It is not surprising that an explication of Newtonian mechanics, that is, the Lakatosian framework, also provides an explication of economic theory.

B. THE METHODOLOGY OF THE MARGINALIST TRIO

In this section Lakatos' framework is compared with the methodological views of Jevons, Menger and Walras. It is argued that these marginalists had at least vague notions of the Lakatosian concepts of the "research programme" and the "positive heuristic" and that each had a reasonable idea of the developmental nature of scientific work.

i. Jevons

The "theory of successive approximations," inspired by Newton and familiar to classical political economists, adumbrates Lakatos' notion of a research programme. This theory is expounded by Jevons in an article in his *Principles of Science* (1874) under the title "Successive Approximations to Natural Conditions." He states:

When we examine the history of scientific problems, we find that one man or one generation is usually able to make but a single step at a time. A problem is solved for the first time by making some bold hypothetical modifications approaching more nearly to the truth. Errors are successively pointed out in previous solutions, until at last there might seem little more to be desired. Careful examination, however, will show that a series of minor inaccuracies remain to be corrected and explained, were our powers of reasoning sufficiently great, and the purpose adequate in importance.[9]

This "theory of successive approximations" is similar to Lakatos' concept of a research programme. Jevons, like Lakatos, turns to the history of science for evidence concerning his methodological hypotheses. The first sentence of the above passage reveals Jevons' recognition that science is a process that involves steps. Lakatos would call these problem shifts. The Jevonian scientist begins with a "bold hypothetical simplification" which leads to the solution of a problem. In the Lakatosian framework this corresponds to an initial model with a hard core from which model core theorems are produced. An error is pointed out. In the Lakatosian framework this corresponds to the recognition of an anomaly. Next, "hypothetical modifications approaching more nearly to the truth" are implemented. In the Lakatosian framework this corresponds to the theoretical adjustment. Jevons observes that a "series of minor inaccuracies remain to be corrected and explained." In the Lakatosian framework this corresponds to the positive heuristic.

To clarify these points Jevons uses the *same key example* that Lakatos uses in his exposition of the concept of a research programme. The example is Newton's planetary programme. Jevons states:

Newton's successful solution of the problem of the planetary movements entirely depended at first upon a great simplification. The law of gravity only applies directly to two infinitely small particles . . . Newton, by a great effort of mathematical reasoning, was able to show that two homogeneous spheres of matter act as if the whole of their masses were concentrated at the centres; in short, that such spheres are centrobaric bodies. He was then able with comparative ease to calculate the motions of the planets on the hypothesis of their being spheres, and to show that the results roughly agreed with observation.[10]

Jevons completes the passage with a further "successive approximation to natural conditions" made by Newton concerning the anomalous fact that "the earth was really a spheroid with a protuberance around the equator." The parallel is striking. Where Jevons states: "Newton's successful solution of the problem of the planetary movements entirely depended at first upon a great simplification . . . two infinitely small particles," Lakatos states: "Newton first worked out his programme for a planetary system with a fixed point-like sun and one single point-like planet,"[11] Where Jevons states: "Then . . . to calculate the motion of the planets on the hypothesis of their being spheres" Lakatos states: "then he worked out the case where the sun and planets were not mass-points but mass-balls."[12] Where

Jevons states: "the earth was really a spheroid with a protuberance around the equator," Lakatos states: "It was then that he started to work on *bulging* planets rather than round planets, etc."[13] (Italics in original).

Here is another example given by Jevons in his *Principles* which highlights his understanding of the developmental nature of scientific research:

It is only, however, under forced hypotheses that we can assert the path of a projectile to be truly a parabola: the path must be through a *perfect vacuum*, where there is no resisting medium of any kind; the force of gravity must be uniform and act in parallel lines; or else the moving body must be either a mere point, or a perfect centrobaric body, that is a body possessing a definite centre of gravity. These conditions cannot be really fulfilled in practice. The *next great step in the problem* was made by Newton and Huyghens, the latter of whom asserted that the *atmosphere would offer a resistance* proportional to the velocity of the moving body, and concluded that the path would have in consequence a logarithmic character.[14] (Italics mine.)

The example could be told in Lakatosian terminology and would have a similar import. If a projectile were observed to *not* move in a parabola this would constitute a global counterexample to the initial model. The assumption of a perfect vacuum provides the corresponding local counterexample. The theoretical adjustment is to replace this assumption by the assumption that the atmosphere offers resistance. Note that the *modus tollens* is used as a criticism of an auxiliary hypothesis (the assumption of a perfect vacuum) and is not directed at any fundamental law. If the new prediction that the motion will have a logarithmic character is corroborated then the acceptance of the new model constitutes empirical progress. "Atmospheric resistance" was the local counterexample for the first model. "Projectiles moving with logarithmic character" was the global counterexample. Note that the counterexamples become corroborations of the adjusted model.

Jevons is no naive falsificationist. He agrees with Lakatos that the facts alone are not enough to overthrow a model or a research programme. He states:

Even at the present day discrepancies exist between the observed dimensions of the planetary orbits and their theoretical magnitudes, after making allowance for all disturbing causes.[15]

It is because the *modus tollens* can always be directed away from the basic principles of a research programme that the hard core cannot be overthrown by the facts. Jevons recognizes the protection of hard core principles and bases this on the fundamental distinction between a theory and that which a theory explains. Jevons states:

In truth men never can solve problems fulfilling the complex circumstances of nature. All laws and explanations are in a sense hypothetical, and apply exactly to nothing which we can know to exist. In place of the actual objects which we see and feel, the mathematician substitutes imaginary objects, only partially resembling those represented, but so devised that the discrepancies are not of an amount to alter seriously the character of the solution . . . . We speak and calculate about inflexible bars, inextensible lines, heavy points, homogeneous substances, uniform spheres, perfect fluids and gases, and we deduce a great number of beautiful theorems, but all is hypothetical . . . . There is no such thing as an inflexible bar, an inextensible line, nor any one of the other perfect objects of mechanical science; they are to be classed with those mythical existences, the straight line, triangle, circle, etc., about which Euclid so freely reasoned. Take the simplest operation considered in statics — the use of a crowbar in raising a heavy stone . . . we neglect far more than we observe.[16]

The *modus tollens* is never directed at fundamental principles of the science such as the law of gravity and the three laws of motion in Newton's programme. Rather it is directed at *auxiliary* assumptions. Jevons clearly understood this.

Jevons intended to found what we would now call a research programme in economics. He notes in *Theory* that economics as a science must be "pervaded by certain general principles" concerning "the mechanics of self-interest and utility."[17] He sets for himself the task of establishing a starting point for such a science. He states: "The establishment of such a theory is a *necessary preliminary* to any definite drafting of the superstructure of the aggregate science"[18] (Italics mine). In other words, a research programme must be established before great strides in theoretical progress may take place. Clearly Jevons had this methodological vision.

ii. Walras

Walras considered the "rational method" of the physico-mathematical sciences, as opposed to the "experimental method," to be appropriate for economics. He decomposed this method into three stages. First, "ideal-type concepts" are formed by a process of abstraction from the "real-type concepts" which are directly observable. Second, these abstractions are used in the construction of a hypothetico-deductive model from which a set of theorems and demonstrations ensue. Third, the theorems are applied to reality. Walras incorporates the Platonic notion of the "universal" through these "ideal-type concepts."[19] He states: "A truth long ago demonstrated by the Platonic philosophy is that science does not study corporeal entities but universals of which these entities are manifestations."[20] For Walras the object of scientific models will be characterized not only by a particular set of "ideal-type concepts" but also by the laws which are conjectured to govern the interaction of these universals. The combination of these "ideal-type concepts" with their governing laws is similar to Lakatos' notion of the hard core. Walras shares with Lakatos and Jevons a view of scientific progress as the development of a series of abstract models with ever-increasing empirical content. Walras describes his own work in exactly these terms. The latter part of the following passage, in which Walras recognizes the fact of production as anomalous to the series of models he has developed, renders clear the meaning of the first sentence:

Any order of phenomena, however complicated, may be studied scientifically provided the rule of proceeding from the simple to the complex is always observed. In formulating our mathematical theory of exchange, we began with the exchange in kind of two commodities for each other and then passed to the exchange of several commodities for one another through the medium of *numéraire.* Thus far, however, we have left out of consideration the fact that commodities are *products* which result from the combination of productive factors such as land, men and capital goods. We have now reached the point where we must take this fact into account.[21] (Initial emphasis mine)

Walras perceives the incorporation of the cited anomaly as part of that movement from "the simple to the complex" which, for both Walras and Lakatos, characterizes scientific study. Each expansion of the empirical base yields an ever-closer approximation to reality. This Lakatosian notion of progress is manifest in Walras' writings. In discussing the problem shift from the two-commodity model to the several-commodity model, Walras states: "It is all the more important to stress the point because the assumption of the use of a *numéraire* brings us closer to the world of reality."[22] In another passage he states: "Finally, in order to come still more closely to reality, we must drop this hypothesis of an annual market period and adopt in its place the hypothesis of a continuous market."[23]

Walras, like Lakatos and Jevons, rejects naive falsificationism. Theories which result from a process of abstraction can only be approximations of reality; they are therefore, not directly refutable. Walras states: "Everyone who has studied any geometry at all knows perfectly well that only in an abstract, ideal circumference are the radii all equal to each other and that only in an abstract, ideal triangle is the sum of the angles equal to the sum of two right angles."[24] This is reminiscent of Jevons' statement. Walras asserts that the predictions of such rational analysis are not to be tested by reality but rather *applied* to reality. In other words, the worth of the theory lies not in its verifiable nature (which is non-existent) but rather in its scope. The scope of a theory is expanded by content-increasing problem shifts. Walras, Jevons and Lakatos place emphasis on the developmental nature of scientific work for this reason. The similarity of Walras' vision of the developmental process to Lakatos' concept of the positive heuristic is evident in the following passage from Walras' *Elements*:

I did it as simply as possible, only to find that practically all the criticisms levelled against me have consisted in calling my attention to complications which I had left to one side. I find it very easy to reply to these criticisms. So far as I am concerned, since I was the first to elaborate a pure theory of economics in mathematical form, my aim has been to describe and explain the mechanism of production in terms of its bare essentials. It is for other economists who come after me *to incorporate one at a time* whatever complications they please. They in their way and I in mine will then, I think, have done what needs to be done.[25] (Italics mine)

These "complications" that other economists may introduce, of which Walras speaks, can only be understood as a positive heuristic in a Lakatosian sense.

Nineteenth-century thinkers were deeply impressed with the success of Newtonian physics. For Walras, the secret of this success lay not in the subject matter but rather in the method. He contended that if the laws of economics were articulated in the same manner as those of Newtonian physics then as an equal degree of success would be attained. He imitated Newtonian physics in the development of his economic ideas because he perceived a unity of method across the rational sciences and considered Newton's programme as science at its best. The series of models developed by Newton is tied together by a hard core of ideas centred upon the law of universal gravitation and his three laws of dynamics. Walras envisioned the laws of utility maximization, uniformity of price, and those of supply and demand as playing the same role in the development of economic science. Walras states:

Maximum effective utility, on the one hand; uniformity of price, on the other hand — be it price of a consumer's good on the final products market, or the price of net income on the capital goods market — these always constitute the double condition by which the universe of economic interests is automatically governed, just as the universe of astronomical movements is automatically governed by the double condition of gravitation which acts in direct proportion to the masses and in indirect proportion to the square of the distances. In one case as in the other, the whole science is contained in a formula two lines in length which serves to explain a countless multitude of particular phenomena.[26]

Walras entertained the idea that his *Elements* and the work of a few others would fulfill the same function in the economics research programme that Newton's *Principia* had in physics. In the *Preface to the Fourth Edition* of the *Elements*, he states:

It is already perfectly clear that economics, like astronomy and mechanics, is both an empirical science and a rational science. And no one can reproach our science with having taken an unduly long time in becoming rational as well as empirical. It took from a hundred to a hundred and fifty or two hundred years for the astronomy of Kepler to become the astronomy of Newton and Laplace, and for the mechanics of Galileo to become the mechanics of d'Alembert and Lagrange. On the other hand, less than a century has elapsed between the publication of Adam Smith's work and the contributions of Cournot, Gossen, Jevons, and myself . . . .

The twentieth century, which is not far off, will feel the need, even in France of entrusting the social sciences to men of general culture who are accustomed to thinking both inductively and deductively and who are familiar with reason as well as experience. Then mathematical economics will rank with the mathematical sciences of astronomy and mechanics; and on that day justice will be done to our work.[27]

In the text of the *Elements* his statements are also direct:

Very few of us are capable of reading Newton's *Philosophiae Naturalis Principia Mathematica* or Laplace's *Mecanique celeste*; and yet, on the word of competent scientists, we all accept the current description of the universe of astronomical phenomena based on the principle of universal gravitation. Why should the description of the universe of economic phenomena based on the principle of free competition not be accepted in the same way? There is no reason why the proof of the system, once established, may not be taken for granted, nor why the assertions involved may not be used in the study of questions of applied or practical economics. For my part, however, I have felt bound to give both the proof and the assertions, in order to present the main outlines of a truly scientific theory of social wealth.[28]

Walras, like Jevons, intended to found what we would now call a research programme.

iii. Menger

Walras, Jevons and Lakatos stress the mathematical character of most scientific developments. Menger, with his anti-mathematical attitude, might appear to be an outlier. Yet Menger himself considered his method to be the same as that of the natural sciences. To repeat an earlier quote:

This method of research, attaining universal acceptance in the natural sciences, led to very great results and on this account came mistakenly to be called the natural scientific method. It is, in reality, a method common to all fields of empirical knowledge, and should properly be called the empirical method.[29]

To the extent that Menger's method involves an heuristic of discovery it is, fundamentally, the same as that employed by Walras, Jevons and Newton and modelled by Lakatos. Menger expresses this method as follows:

In what follows [in his *Grundsätze*] I have endeavored to reduce the complex phenomena of human economic activity to the simplest elements that can still be subjected to accurate observation, to apply to these elements the measure corresponding to their nature, and constantly adhering to this nature, to investigate the manner in which the more complex economic phenomena evolve from their elements according to definite principles.[30]

Menger does not say that "more complex economic phenomena" are *deduced* from initial principles; he posits that they "*evolve* from their elements *according* to definite principles" (italics mine). The meaning of this cryptic assertion becomes clear with the presentation of his economics. The fundamental propositions are embodied in a series of ever more complex stages each of which is constructed by adjusting the previous stage in a manner which transforms anomaly into corroboration. On the one hand, each stage of analysis has an informal deductive character and thus involves a logic of justification. On the other hand, the movement from one stage to the next involves a logic of discovery. An expanding empirical base is guaranteed by this latter "logic" as long as the adjustments do not preclude the retention of previous predictive content. This heuristic power of Menger's work is part of the explanation for the development of the Austrian school as such power is a necessary condition to all progressive research.

In 1871 Menger laid the groundwork for a programme of economic thought in his *Grundsätze der Volkswirtschaftlehre* (*Principles of Economics*). The *Grundsätze* (this term may also be translated as "fundamental propositions") was to be the first of four volumes. Menger embedded the "fundamental propositions" in a form conductive to further development; he never completed the planned work. It was his two disciples, Friedrich von Wieser and Eugen Böhm-Bawerk, who developed and promulgated the fundamental propositions. Menger, like Walras and Jevons, intended (and succeeded) in founding a research programme.

NOTES

1. Quote taken from Howard Eves, *An Introduction to the History of Mathematics*, 4th ed. (New York: Holt, Rinehart and Winston, 1979), pp. 326–7.
2. See Chapter II for definitions of these terms.
3. Leon Walras, *Elements of Pure Economics*, trans. William Jaffe (London: George Allen and Unwin, 1954), p. 71.
4. *Ibid.*, p. 471.
5. *Ibid.*, p. 374.
6. W. Stanley Jevons, *The Theory of Political Economy*, 2nd ed. (London: Macmillan, 1879), p. vii.
7. *Ibid.*, pp. xvii–xviii.
8. Karl Menger, *Principles of Economics*, trans and ed. James Dingwall and Bert F. Hoselitz with an introduction by Frank H. Knight (Glencoe, Illinois: The Free Press, 1950), p. 47.
9. W. Stanley Jevons, *The Principles of Science*, (London: Macmillan, 1874), p. 465.
10. *Ibid.*, p. 466.
11. Imre Lakatos and Alan Musgrave, eds., *Criticism and the Growth of Knowledge* (Cambridge: Cambridge University Press, 1970), p. 138.
12. *Ibid.*, p. 135.
13. *Ibid.*, p. 136.
14. Jevons, *The Principles of Science*, pp. 466–7.
15. *Ibid.*, p. 457.
16. *Ibid.*, p. 458.
17. Jevons, *The Theory of Political Economy*, pp. xvii–xviii.
18. *Ibid.*, p. xviii.
19. Walras, *Elements of Pure Economics*, p. 71.
20. *Ibid.*, p. 61.
21. *Ibid.*, p. 211.
22. *Ibid.*, p. 192.
23. *Ibid.*, p. 380.
24. *Ibid.*, p. 71.
25. *Ibid.*, p. 478.
26. *Ibid.*, p. 305.
27. *Ibid.*, p. 47.
28. *Ibid.*, p. 428.
29. Menger, *Principles of Economics*, p. 47.
30. *Ibid.*, pp. 46–7.

6 Walras

If in the last analysis Walras' system is perhaps nothing but a huge research program, it still is, owing to its intellectual quality, the basis of practically all the best work of our own time.[1]

Joseph A. Schumpeter *History of Economic Analysis*

Walras' emulation of the Newtonian method is unfolded in the concrete form of economic analysis. The sequential development of a set of central ideas within Walras' *Elements of Pure Economics*[2] is underscored by the application of the Lakatosian framework. Our main point is that the Walrasian framework fits well into a Lakatosian scheme; our goal is to make clear Walras' attempt to develop programmatic research in the Newtonian style.

Each of the marginalists presented in their respective texts the foundation for, and first steps of, what would now be called a research programme. By such a presentation they each communicated not only the content of the hard core of ideas around which their programme coalesced, but also the manner in which the implicit impact of that hard core (the positive heuristic) might be articulated. In this chapter, Walras' *Elements of Pure Economics* is examined as a research programme, that is, as a series of interconnected models each of which is developed in response to a confrontation of the previous model with an anomaly. In Chapters 7 and 8, the same approach is taken to Menger's *Principles of Economics* and Jevons' *Theory of Political Economy*.

The material in this chapter, and in Chapters 7 and 8, involves *reconstructed* presentations of the respective economics of Walras, of Menger, and of Jevons. In a reconstruction the basic content of the material remains the same. The types of adjustments that might be involved in a reconstruction are: a different ordering of presentation, a different emphasis, making explicit that which is implicit, making general that which is particular, and making connections and separations which have not been made previously. This process is, of course, not random; a reconstruction entails a selection process based on certain principles.

In this chapter, and in the next two, the Lakatosian framework is used as an explicit theory of historical selection for the purposes of rational reconstruction. The programme of economic theory presented by each of the marginalist trio is traced. The format is roughly as follows: First, an initial model is established. An anomaly is introduced. Through a demonstration analysis, the anomaly is identified as producing either a local alone, or a global and a local counterexample. The theoretical adjustment is noted and the analysis of the new model is briefly summarized. The retention of former content and the introduction of novel content — novel with respect to the programme — is noted. The reconstruction continues in this fashion through a series of models. As each reconstruction progresses, the hard core, protective belt, retreat and consolidation, degree of progressiveness, and core theorems are identified and discussed. Subsequent to these reconstructions, the works of the three marginalists are brought together in Chapter 9 and discussed as the foundation for a broader research programme.

Like both Jevons and Menger, Walras presents his ideas in a series of ever more complicated models based on a hard core of assumptions, with each new model transforming anomalies into corroborations of the programme. The positive heuristic, that is, the series of anomalies to be incorporated, includes, as major stages of development, a movement from two-commodity exchange to three, and then to *m*-commodity exchange, production possibilities, the production of means of production, circulation, and money. Within these stages are further progressive developments which include discontinuous utility functions, initial possession of more than one commodity, arbitrage, the *numéraire* as a means of exchange, the capital goods market, the incorporation of depreciation allowance, insurance premiums, stocks of new capital goods held for sale by producers, stocks of consumers' goods held by consumers, stocks of raw materials held by producers, stocks of consumers' goods and raw materials held for sale by producers, consumers' and producers' cash holdings, money savings, dual monetary standard, fiduciary money, and variable coefficients of production. (The incorporation of the possibility of holding various stocks involves introducing services of availability.)

A. THE INITIAL MODEL

To trace the development of the positive heuristic within Walras' work, it is first necessary to establish the initial model. Walras considers a barter economy of two commodities with many holders of each commodity. No individual holds both commodities initially. Individuals attempt to maximize utility through trading at the one ratio of exchange which prevails in the competitive market. Utility functions are additive and continuous. Walras uses the term *rareté* to "designate the intensity of the last want ('which is or which might have been') satisfied by any given quantity consumed of the commodity."[3] The *rareté* of a commodity diminishes with an increase in the quantity consumed of that commodity. Excess demand (supply) in the market for a commodity will result in a rise (fall) in the price of that commodity.

In this chapter we will be noting that the assumptions of perfect competition, one ratio of exchange, utility maximization, diminishing *rareté*, price rising (falling) with excess demand (supply), and additive utility functions are maintained by Walras throughout the series of models; they constitute the hard core of his programme.

To establish the core theorems and begin the reconstruction, we must review the analysis and predictions of this initial model. It follows from the assumption of uniformity of price that $p_a p_b = 1$, where p_i is the price of good i in terms of the other good. Walras derives the following equations of exchange:

$$O_b = D_a p_a$$
$$D_b = O_a p_a$$
$$O_a = D_b p_b \qquad \text{(W-1)}[4]$$
$$D_a = O_b p_b$$

where O_i is the effective offer of good i and D_i is the effective demand for good i. Walras demonstrates that equilibrium in one market implies equilibrium in the other. Let $D_a = \alpha O_a$ where the variable α incorporates excess supply or excess demand.[5] By substituting for O_a and D_a using the above equations of exchange we obtain: $O_b = \alpha D_b$. If $\alpha = 1$, then $D_a = O_a$. $D_a = O_a$ if and only if $D_b = O_b$. This is Walras' Law as manifested in the two-commodity model; it is one of the core theorems of the programme.

According to Walras' Law, a general equilibrium may be found by solving either the demand and offer equations in the market for good (A), or the demand and offer equations in the market for good (B). The equilibrium solution is provided (if one exists) by the assumption that an excess demand (supply) entails a rise (fall) in price. Walras notes that there is no solution if the demand curve meets the price axis below the price intercept of the offer curve. The possibility of multiple solutions is also discussed.[6]

Using the calculus of maximization under a constraint, Walras demonstrates that:

$$\phi_{a,1}(d_a) = p_a \phi_{b,1}(q_b - d_a p_a) \qquad \text{(W-2)[7]}$$

and that:

$$p_a = \frac{r_{a,1}}{r_{b,1}} \qquad \text{(W-3)[8]}$$

where q_i is income in terms of good i, d_i is the individual demand for good i, $\phi_{i,j}$ is the *rareté* function of individual j for good i, and $r_{i,j}$ is the *rareté* of individual j for good i.

The assumption of diminishing *rareté* (diminishing marginal utility) ensures that this solution will be one of maximum utility. Thus, every maximizing individual sets the ratio of his *raretés* equal to the prevailing ratio of exchange. It also follows that "values in exchange are proportional to *raretés*."[9] Walras puts forward the following related result as the most important core theorem:

The exchange of two commodities for each other in a perfectly competitive market is an operation by which all holders of either one, or of both, of the commodities can obtain the greatest possible satisfaction of their wants consistent with the condition that the two commodities are bought and sold at one and the same rate of exchange throughout the market.[10]

For future reference label this as the Social Welfare Theorem. Concerning the Social Welfare Theorem, Walras states:

The main object of the theory of social wealth is to generalize this proposition by showing, first, that it applies to the exchange of several commodities for one another as well as to the exchange of two commodities for each other, and secondly, that, under perfect competition, it applies to production as well as to exchange.[11]

In the above statement, which captures the essential nature of research programmes which is to extend the range of core theorems through the development of a successively more sophisticated series of models, Walras has outlined some of the early stages of his positive heuristic.

Equation W-2 yields an individual's demand for good (A) as a function of the price of (A). The market demand function for good (A) is the summation of such individual demand functions; $D_a = F_a(p_a)$. The market demand function for good (B) may be similarly derived: $D_b = F_b(p_b)$. Using the equations of exchange $O_a = F_b(1/p_a)1/p_a$ and $O_b = F_a(1/p_b)1/p_b$, the derivation of the offer curves follows immediately.

Using the model, Walras also predicts that if the *rareté* of a commodity increases (decreases), then its price will increase (decrease), and if the quantity possessed of a commodity increases (decreases), then the price of the commodity will decrease (increase). He also predicts that if, after a given change in the data, *raretés* remain unchanged, then prices will not change.[12] For future reference label these as the Comparative Statics Results.

To summarize: this initial model of Walras' programme yields predictions concerning income constraints, individual demand and offer functions, the setting of the ratio of *raretés* equal to price, market demand and offer functions, and the proportionality of values in exchange to *raretés*. Walras' Law, the Comparative Statics Results, and the Social Welfare Theorem are the most important core theorems.

B. DISCONTINUOUS UTILITY FUNCTIONS

The first step of the positive heuristic is delivered by the recognition that, in reality, individuals are sometimes characterized by discontinuous utility functions due to inherent indivisibilities in the commodities. The fact that it will not always be possible to set the ratio of the *raretés* equal to the prevailing price ratio results in global counterexamples to both Equation W-3 and the Social Welfare Theorem. A demonstration analysis reveals that it is the assumption of continuous utility functions, which was imported into the analysis during the calculus, which is the source of the local counterexample.

As a theoretic adjustment, Walras allows for the possibility of discontinuous utility functions. He reconstructs the initial model on this basis and demonstrates that if, due to the discontinuity of an utility function, an individual cannot set the ratio of the *raretés* exactly equal to the prevailing price ratio then a close approximation "of the arithmetical mean of the intensities of the last wants satisfied and of the first wants unsatisfied"[13] will be set equal to the price. This demonstration allows him to retain the core theorems associated with Equation W-3 and the Social Welfare Theorem in suitably amended forms. He demonstrates that an individual demand function for a commodity can be determined for all prices in the case where the utility function is discontinuous.[14] He invokes the "Law of Large Numbers" to argue that a discontinuous market demand curve is not possible. This allows him to retain the earlier comparative statics predictions. Thus, it is clear that there has been a retention of former unrefuted content.

The completion of this progressive problem shift allows Walras to put forward predictions about a new range of phenomena which includes discontinuous utility functions. These could not have been made using the initial model. The theorems concerning situations in which only continuous utility functions are encountered and those related to aggregated demand and offer curves may be derived from the adjusted model. Thus, there has been an expansion of the empirical base.

C. PRE-TRADE POSSESSION OF BOTH COMMODITIES

In reality, individuals might be holders of both commodities before the commencement of trading. The next step in the positive heuristic is provided by the recognition of this anomaly. In this case Equation W-2 provides a global counterexample. Walras states the corresponding local counterexample and theoretic adjustment as follows:

Up to this point we assumed that every party to the exchange was a holder of no more than one commodity, either commodity (A) or commodity (B). We must now take up the particular case where one and the same individual is a holder of two commodities (A) and (B), and we have to express such an individual's trading schedule mathematically.[15]

Walras constructs the next model of the series on this basis. Using $p_a p_b = 1$, the equations of W−2, and the "theorem of maximum satisfaction," Walras derives the following:

$$\phi_{b,1}(q_{b,1} + d_b) = p_b \phi_{a,1}(q_{a,1} - d_b p_b) \qquad \text{(W-4)}[16]$$

and:

$$\phi_{a,1}(q_{a,1} + d_a) = p_a \phi_{b,1}(q_{b,1} - d_a p_a)$$

where $q_{i,j}$ is the income of good i for person j. These two equations encompass that range of phenomena which proved anomalous to W-2. That which proved anomalous to the earlier model becomes a corroboration of the latter model. The equations W-4 reduce to the earlier predictions in the special case in which individuals have only one commodity pre-trade. Walras notes this retention of former unrefuted content. He states:

the second case is the general case, and the case previously studied a special case which can be found by equating one of the quantities possessed in the general case to zero.[17]

Walras arrives at several other novel predictions. Using the equations of W-4 and recalling that $p_a p_b = 1$, he demonstrates that:

If the demand for one of the two commodities is zero at a certain price, the demand for the other commodity is also zero at the corresponding price.[18]

Using the same equations, Walras also demonstrates that:

If the demand for one of the two commodities is positive at a given price, the demand for the other is negative, that is, its offer is positive at the corresponding price.[19]

For much of the analysis the demonstration of the retention of former unrefuted content is manifest. The problem shift to include the possibility that individuals might initially hold more than one commodity is progressive because predictions over a new range of phenomena are put forward while former unrefuted content is retained.

D. THE THREE-COMMODITY MODEL

Exchange often involves more than two commodities. This observation provides the next anomaly to be addressed. When there are more than two commodities available the demand (or offer) of a commodity will be a function of many prices. This provides global counterexamples to both the aggregated and individual demand and supply curves of the earlier models. The corresponding local counterexample is the assumption of a two-commodity barter economy. Walras first introduces a three-commodity model, and then an m-commodity model.

Walras temporarily retreats from the assumption that any individual may initially hold more than one commodity. He states: "all we need to do is to return to the case in which each party to the exchange is a holder of only one commodity and then generalize our formula in a suitable way."[20] This action might preclude the retention of former unrefuted content except for the fact that Walras retrieves this consideration and explicitly consolidates his analysis at a later stage. This temporary simplification does not present an anomaly to the Lakatosian framework.

Assume three commodities: (A), (B), and (C). All markets

are separate in the sense that arbitrage is not possible. This is a protective belt assumption. If the individual demand functions of the holders of each commodity are aggregated, then six equations are obtained:

$$D_{a,b} = F_{a,b}(p_{a,b}, p_{c,b})$$
$$D_{c,b} = F_{c,b}(p_{a,b}, p_{c,b})$$
$$D_{a,c} = F_{a,c}(p_{a,c}, p_{b,c})$$
$$D_{b,c} = F_{b,c}(p_{a,c}, p_{b,c}) \qquad \text{(W-5)}^{21}$$
$$D_{b,a} = F_{b,a}(p_{b,a}, p_{c,a})$$
$$D_{c,a} = F_{c,a}(p_{b,a}, p_{c,a})$$

where $p_{i,j}$ is the price of good i in terms of good j, $F_{i,j}$ is the aggregate demand function for good i in exchange for good j, and $D_{i,j}$ is the aggregate demand for good i in exchange for good j. There will also be six equations of exchange:

$$D_{b,a} = D_{a,b}p_{a,b}$$
$$D_{b,c} = D_{c,b}p_{c,b}$$
$$D_{c,a} = D_{a,c}p_{a,c}$$
$$D_{c,b} = D_{b,c}p_{b,c} \qquad \text{(W-6)}^{22}$$
$$D_{a,b} = D_{b,a}p_{b,a}$$
$$D_{a,c} = D_{c,a}p_{c,a}$$

The two-commodity model is easily seen as a special case of the three-commodity model if the quantity available of one of the commodities is set equal to zero. There is a retention of former unrefuted content; predictions may be derived from the three-commodity model for the special case of the two-commodity world. The equations of W-5 are generalized versions of the aggregated demand functions of the earlier models. The equations of W-6 are generalized versions of W-1.

The expansion of the empirical base is evidenced by the new predictions of W-5 and W-6 over a three-commodity world. Walras observes that there are twelve equations and twelve unknowns in the system, and he takes this as an encouraging indication.

E. THE *M*-COMMODITY MODEL

The three-commodity model acts as a stepping stone between the two-commodity model and the *m*-commodity model. The assumption of only three commodities provides the local counterexample. The global counterexample is provided by, among other things, the equations of offer and demand of the three-commodity model. The equations of demand of the three-commodity model are superseded by the "*m* − 1 equations of effective demand for (B), (C), (D) . . . in exchange for (A)":

$$D_{b,a} = F_{b,a}(p_{b,a}, \ p_{c,a}, \ p_{d,a}, \ \ldots),$$
$$D_{c,a} = F_{c,a}(p_{b,a}, \ p_{c,a}, \ p_{d,a}, \ \ldots),$$
$$D_{d,a} = F_{d,a}(p_{b,a}, \ p_{c,a}, \ p_{d,a}, \ \ldots) \qquad \text{(W-7)}[23]$$

. . . .

plus *m* − 1 similar equations of demand associated with every other good. In total there are $m(m-1)$ equations of demand. There will also be *m* − 1 equations of exchange, similar to those of W-6, of each good for each other good. This yields a total of $m(m-1)$ equations of exchange, and, overall, a total of $2m(m-1)$ equations and $2m(m-1)$ unknowns.

Just as the two-commodity model is easily seen as a special case of the three-commodity model so also is the three-commodity model seen as a special case of the *m*-commodity model. There is a retention of unrefuted content. The equations W-7 are generalized versions of equations of W-5. The new set of equations of exchange are generalized versions of the old set. There has been an expansion of the empirical base with this problem shift because predictions may now be put forward concerning an *m*-commodity world whereas this was not possible before.

F. ARBITRAGE

Thus far, arbitrage has not been allowed in the *m*-commodity model. In reality, arbitrage can occur, and the present stage of the model does not preclude the possibility that arbitrage will be profitable. If profitable arbitrage is possible, then the system of equations does not yield a perfect general equilibrium, and, thus, a global counterexample is produced. The corresponding local counterexample is the arbitrary preclusion of arbitrage. Walras attains a "perfect" general equilibrium by introducing the following system of equations.

$$p_{a,b} = \frac{1}{p_{b,a}} \qquad p_{c,b} = \frac{p_{c,a}}{p_{b,a}} \qquad p_{d,b} = \frac{p_{d,a}}{p_{b,a}} \ \dots$$

$$p_{a,c} = \frac{1}{p_{c,a}} \qquad p_{b,c} = \frac{p_{b,a}}{p_{c,a}} \qquad p_{d,c} = \frac{p_{d,a}}{p_{c,a}} \ \dots \qquad \text{(W-8)}[24]$$

$$p_{a,d} = \frac{1}{p_{d,a}} \qquad p_{b,d} = \frac{p_{b,a}}{p_{d,a}} \qquad p_{c,d} = \frac{p_{c,a}}{p_{d,a}} \ \dots$$

. . . .

Arbitrage will not be profitable with the fulfilment of this system of equations. The empirical defence of the inclusion of these equations is that the existence of arbitrage in the real world should lead to their approximate fulfilment. These restrictions add $(m-1)(m-1)$ equations to the system. However, since arbitrage may now be allowed, the earlier $m(m-1)$ equations of exchange may be replaced by the following m equations:

$$D_{a,b} + D_{a,c} + D_{a,d} + \dots = D_{b,a}p_{b,a} + D_{c,a}p_{c,a} + D_{d,a}p_{d,a} + \dots$$
$$D_{b,a} + D_{b,c} + D_{b,d} + \dots = D_{a,b}p_{a,b} + D_{c,b}p_{c,b} + D_{d,b}p_{d,b} + \dots$$
$$D_{c,a} + D_{c,b} + D_{c,d} + \dots = D_{a,c}p_{a,c} + D_{b,c}p_{b,c} + D_{d,c}p_{d,c} + \dots$$
$$D_{d,a} + D_{d,b} + D_{d,c} + \dots = D_{a,d}p_{a,d} + D_{b,d}p_{b,d} + D_{c,d}p_{c,d} + \dots$$

. . . .

$$\text{(W-9)}[25]$$

Using the price relationships of W-8 Walras demonstrates that one of the equations of W-9 may be eliminated. Thus we have $(m-1)$ equations of exchange. The number of equations equalled the number of unknowns prior to the allowance of arbitrage. The introduction of arbitrage and the system W-8 required the addition of $(m-1)(m-1)$ arbitrage equations, but it also allowed for the elimination of $(m-1)(m-1)$

equations of exchange. The number of equations remains equal to the number of unknowns.

Walras takes meticulous care to ensure the retention of former unrefuted content by consolidating the earlier developments of the heuristic with these new problem shifts of the *m*-commodity model. The possibility that individuals hold more than one commodity prior to the commencement of trade is reintroduced as well as the possibility of discontinuous utility functions. Using the theorem of maximum utility Walras derives a generalized version of W-4. W-4 can be derived from this new set of equations as the special case where $m = 2$. Walras states a generalized Social Welfare Theorem for the *m*-commodity stage. He states:

The exchange of several commodities for one another in a market ruled by free competition is an operation by which all holders of one, several or all of the commodities exchanged can obtain the greatest possible satisfaction of their wants consistent with the twofold condition: (1) that any two commodities be exchanged for each other in one and the same ratio for all parties and (2) that the two ratios in which these commodities are exchanged for any third commodity be proportional to the ratio in which they are exchanged for each other.[26]

He also re-establishes the related result that: "Values in exchange are proportional to *raretés*."[27] The *numéraire* is introduced as a standard measure of value. It is defined as: "the commodity in terms of which the prices of all others are expressed."[28] Walras introduces the process of *tâtonnement* and his auctioneer to argue that a general equilibrium will, in fact, be achieved.

The comparative statics results concerning the variation of prices in the two-commodity model are also surpassed by the new theorems put forward; they are thus "refuted" in a Lakatosian sense. Walras states the new forms of these core theorems as follows:

Given a state of general equilibrium in a market for several commodities where exchanges take place with the aid of a *numéraire*, if the utility of one of these commodities increases or decreases for one or more of the parties, everything else remaining equal, the price of this commodity in terms of the *numéraire* will increase or decrease.

If the quantity of one of the commodities in the hands of one or more holders increases or decreases, all other things remaining equal, the price of this commodity will decrease or increase.[29]

and,

Given several commodities, if both the utility and the quantity of one of these commodities in the hands of one or more parties or holders vary in such a way that the *raretés* remain the same, the price of this commodity will not change.

If the utility and the quantity of all the commodities in the hands of one or more parties or holders vary in such a way that the ratios of the *raretés* remain the same, none of the prices will change.[30]

These new theorems reduce to the old ones in the special case of the two-commodity world if a commodity other than the one under consideration is declared as the *numéraire*.

Walras demonstrates the retention of former unrefuted content with the introduction of this problem shift to the *m*-commodity world. With the new theorems and predictions the shift is observed to be progressive in a Lakatosian sense.

G. THE NUMÉRAIRE AS A MEANS OF EXCHANGE

Walras also develops the positive heuristic one step further while still in the multi-commodity stage. The *numéraire* can serve not only as a standard of value but also as a means of exchange. This is an important development of the positive heuristic because, as Walras states, "the assumption of the use of a *numéraire* (as a means of exchange) brings us closer to the world of reality."[31] This is a particularly convenient problem shift since if all exchanges take place through the medium of a *numéraire*, then the price relations of W-8 are implied and there will be no need for arbitrage operations. Walras states:

the situation of a market in a state of general equilibrium can be completely defined by relating the values of all the commodities to the value of any particular one of them. That particular commodity is called the *numéraire*.[32]

Walras assumes at this stage of the analysis that the use of the *numéraire* as a means of exchange will have no effect on the price of the *numéraire*. Walras realizes that this is not the case in the real world; however, he employs this assumption as part of the protective belt, thus precluding criticism for the moment. He states:

In the real world the matter presents itself quite differently. Every trader keeps available a stock of money for eventual exchange; and, this being the case, the use of a commodity as money does not affect its value in ways that we shall study later on.[33]

Walras notes the retention of former unrefuted content that accompanies the problem shift of "introducing the *numéraire* as a means of exchange." He states: "we can pass from indirect to direct prices at will simply by abstracting from the *numéraire*."[34]

H. PRODUCTION

In reality commodities are not received like manna from heaven; rather, they are produced. Walras recognizes this anomaly. He states:

We have left out of consideration the fact that commodities are *products* which result from the combination of productive factors such as land, men and capital goods. We have now reached the point where we must take this fact into account.[35] (Italics in original)

Walras describes the problem shift as follows:

Having studied the problem of the mathematical determination of the prices of products, we are ready to pose and examine the problem of the mathematical determination of the prices of productive services.[36]

The theorems of the simple multi-commodity world, which become globally anomalous with the recognition of production, will be replaced. The empirical base will be extended by the inclusion of theorems concerning the prices of land services, labour services, and services of capital proper, and the quantities of goods produced. Walras employs the protective belt to preclude, at this stage of the analysis, any consideration of the service of availability of any stores of income goods held by consumers or producers.[37] Consideration of the service of availability is included in a subsequent problem shift. The protective belt is also employed to abstract from considerations of fixed and variable costs. Walras does this by assuming that all manufacturers produce in equal quantities.

Walras defines equilibrium in production as:

A state in which the effective demand and offer of productive services are equal and there is a stationary current price in the market for these services. Secondly, it is a state in which the effective demand and supply of products are also equal and there is a stationary current price, in the products market. Finally, it is a state in which the selling prices of products equal the costs of the productive services that enter into them.[38]

The selling price is brought into line with the costs of production by the forces of the competitive market. Entrepreneurs, who combine the factor of production in an attempt to maximize profits, are free to enter and leave markets.[39] There will be an increase (decrease) in output in those markets where the selling price is greater than (less than) the cost of the factors of production. In equilibrium, entrepreneurs reap zero economic profits.

Suppose a world of m commodities and n productive services. Productive services may also be consumed and therefore the want curves are diminishing. The income constraint of any individual may be written as:

$$o_t p_t + o_p p_p + o_k p_k + \ldots = d_a + d_b p_b + d_c p_c + d_d p_d + \ldots$$
$$(\text{W-10})^{40}$$

where p_t, p_p and p_k are the prices of the services of capital, land, and persons respectively and o_t, o_p, and o_k are the offers of these services. The offer (or demand) for each of the services, the demand for each of the commodities as functions of the prices of services (in terms of the *numéraire*), and the prices of commodities (also in terms of the *numéraire*), may be found for each individual by using this income constraint, and the condition of maximum satisfaction. These individual functions may be aggregated so that the following system of equations results:

$$O_t = F_t(p_t, p_p, p_k, \ldots p_b, p_c, p_d, \ldots),$$
$$O_p = F_p(p_t, p_p, p_k, \ldots p_b, p_c, p_d, \ldots),$$
$$O_k = F_k(p_t, p_p, p_k, \ldots p_b, p_c, p_d, \ldots),$$
$$\ldots\ldots\ldots\ldots\ldots\ldots\ldots\ldots\ldots\ldots\ldots\ldots\ldots\ldots\ldots \quad \text{(W-11)}[41]$$
$$D_b = F_b(p_t, p_p, p_k, \ldots p_b, p_c, p_d, \ldots),$$
$$D_c = F_c(p_t, p_p, p_k, \ldots p_b, p_c, p_d, \ldots),$$
$$D_d = F_d(p_t, p_p, p_k, \ldots p_b, p_c, p_d, \ldots),$$
$$\ldots\ldots\ldots\ldots\ldots\ldots\ldots\ldots\ldots\ldots\ldots\ldots\ldots\ldots$$

The demand for the *numéraire* may be found by rearranging the aggregated income constraint:

$$d_a = o_t p_t + o_p p_p + o_k p_k + \ldots - (D_b p_b + D_c p_c + D_d p_d + \ldots)$$
$$\text{(W-12)}[42]$$

Walras makes the protective belt assumption that the coefficients of production are fixed. The need for equality, between the demand for services and the offer of services, to produce an equilibrium, yields the following system of equations:

$$a_t D_a + b_t D_b + c_t D_c + d_t D_d + \ldots = O_t$$
$$a_p D_a + b_p D_b + c_p D_c + d_p D_d + \ldots = O_p \quad \text{(W-13)}[43]$$
$$a_k D_a + b_k D_b + c_k D_c + d_k D_d + \ldots = O_k$$
$$\ldots\ldots\ldots\ldots\ldots\ldots\ldots\ldots\ldots\ldots\ldots\ldots\ldots\ldots$$

where $a_t, b_t, c_t, \ldots, a_p, b_p, c_p, \ldots$ are coefficients of production. To produce a general equilibrium it is also necessary to have the selling prices of products equal to the cost of production. Walras demonstrates that raw materials are reducible to services, therefore these are not included explicitly in the cost of production equations. Thus:

$$a_t p_t + a_p p_p + a_k p_k + \ldots = 1$$
$$b_t p_t + b_p p_p + b_k p_k + \ldots = p_b$$
$$c_t p_t + c_p p_p + c_k p_k + \ldots = p_c \quad \text{(W-14)}[44]$$
$$d_t p_t + d_p p_p + d_k p_k + \ldots = p_d$$
$$\ldots\ldots\ldots\ldots\ldots\ldots\ldots\ldots\ldots\ldots\ldots$$

There is a total of $2m + 2n$ equations. However, through appropriate manipulations, W-12 may be reproduced from the other equations. To put this algebraic manipulation into words, the equality of the demand for services with the offer of services ensures that the total value of income to consumers equals the total value of the offer of services. The condition that the costs of production equal the prices of commodities ensures that the value of the total offer of products will equal the value of the total offer of services, which equals income. Thus we have W-12. It may therefore be eliminated leaving $2m + 2n - 1$ unknowns.

The thought experiment of *tâtonnement* is more treacherous in a world of production. Random prices are introduced, and offer is compared to demand. If a general equilibrium results, then the process is complete. If, however, a general equilibrium does not result (which is likely), and price adjustments are needed, then products must be remanufacturable if we are to avoid path dependence. Walras handles this difficulty by introducing tickets. Tickets stand in lieu of the products and services during *tâtonnement* until the equilibrium is established. Production occurs only after the establishment of the equilibrium and is instantaneous. Walras invokes the protective belt to abstract from the time necessary for the actual production process.

Walras demonstrates the retention of unrefuted content and the novelty of this latest model. He establishes his "double law of supply and demand, and of the cost of production":

Given several services by means of which various products can be manufactured and assuming that these services are exchanged for their products through the medium of a *numéraire*, for the market to be in equilibrium, or for the prices of all the services and all the products in terms of the *numéraire* to be stationary, it is necessary and sufficient (1) that the effective demand for each service and each product be equal to its effective supply at these prices; and (2) that the selling prices of the products be equal to the cost of the services employed in making them. If this twofold equality does not exist, in order to achieve the first it is necessary to raise the prices of those services or products the effective demand for which is greater than the effective supply and to lower the price of those services or products the effective supply of which is greater than the effective demand; and in order to achieve the second, it is necessary to increase the output of those products the selling price of which is greater than the cost of production and to decrease the output of those products of which the cost of production is greater than the selling price.[45]

Walras demonstrates that "values in exchange are proportional to *raretés*,"[46] and the Social Welfare Theorem is also retained:

Production in a market ruled by free competition is an operation by which services can be combined and converted into products of such a nature and in such quantities as will give the greatest possible satisfaction of wants within the limits of the double condition, that each service and each product have only one price in the market, namely the price at which the quantity supplied equals the quantity demanded, and that the selling price of the products be equal to the cost of the services employed in making them.[47]

It is clear that the content of the theorems of the earlier models is retained in the production model. Walras states:

We may also generalize the law of the variation of prices in the following terms:

Given several products of services and given a state of general equilibrium in a market where exchange is effected with the aid of a *numéraire*, if, all other things remaining equal, the utility of one of these products or services increases or decreases for one or more of the parties to the exchange, the price of this product or service in terms of the *numéraire* will increase or decrease.

If, all other things being equal, the quantity of one of these products or services in the hands of one or more holders increases or decreases, the price of this product or service will decrease or increase.

Given several products or services, if both the utility and the quantity of one of these products or services in the hands of one or more parties or holders vary in such a way that the *raretés* remain the same, the price of this product or service will not change.

If the utilities and the quantities of all the products or services in the hands of one or more of the parties or holders vary in such a way that the ratios of the *raretés* remain the same, the prices of these products or services will not change.[48].

There are also new theorems. Walras states:

If, all other things being equal, the quantity of a service owned by one or more individuals increases or decreases (its effective offer then increasing or decreasing so that its price falls or rises), the prices of those products in the production of which this service is employed will fall or rise.

If, all other things being equal, the utility of a product increases or decreases for one or more consumers (its effective demand then increasing or decreasing so that its price rises or falls), the prices of the services employed in its production will rise or fall.[49]

The shift to a production model was rational in a Lakatosian sense because with that model predictions over a new range of phenomena could be put forward and there was a retention of unrefuted content.

I. CAPITAL GOODS

The next major problem shift concerns the determination of the prices of capital goods themselves. Thus far the marketing of capital goods has been abstracted from, and it is this abstraction that provides the local counterexample. Walras states: "In the preceding pages we have determined the prices of various types of income, but we have not yet determined the prices of the capital goods yielding these incomes in the form of uses and services."[50] The global counterexamples are provided by any of the predictions in which the price of capital goods might be expected to play a role. Walras introduces the capital goods market to the analysis.

Capital goods are demanded because of the stream of services which they yield. It follows that the price of a capital good will depend on the price of the services it yields. The term "income" will henceforth refer to the value of this stream of services. If a depreciation allowance and an insurance premium are taken into consideration the value of net income for the capital good can be determined. The rate of net income will be π/P where π is the return per period and P is the price of the capital good. The rate of net income for different capital goods must be the same in equilibrium, otherwise there would be a redistribution of expenditure upon capital. It follows that, in equilibrium, for any capital good:

$$P = \frac{p}{i + u + v} \qquad \text{(W-15)}[51]$$

where P is the price of the capital good, p is the return per period, i is the rate of net income, u is the rate of depreciation, and v is the insurance rate.

Heretofore, the income from services has been spent on consumption. In such a world there can be no prices of capital as there is no motive to exchange existing capital goods. When a difference arises between aggregate income and consumption, then a capital market will arise. Walras only considers the case of an excess of income over capital. This excess of income must equal the aggregate expenditure on capital. The price of capital goods must equal the costs of production. Since the quantity of land does not respond to price, the price of land is determined by the ratio of the price of its services over the rate of net income:

$$P_t = \frac{p_t}{i} \qquad \text{(W-16)}^{52}$$

The factors which determine the population are beyond the scope of analysis, thus:

$$P_t = \frac{\pi_p}{i} \qquad \text{(W-17)}^{53}$$

Since the price of capital goods must equal the costs of production, we have:

$$k_t p_t + \ldots + k_p p_p + \ldots + k_k p_k + k_{k'_1} p_{k'} + k_{k''} p_{k'} + \ldots = P$$
$$k'_t p_t + \ldots + k'_p p_p + \ldots + k_{k'} p_k + k'_{k'} p_{k'} + k'_{k''} p_{k''} + \ldots = P_{k'}$$
$$k''_t p_t + \ldots + k''_p p_p + \ldots + k''_k p_k + k''_{k'} p''_{k'} + k''_{k''} p''_{k''} + \ldots = P_{k''}$$

$$\cdots\cdots\cdots\cdots\cdots\cdots\cdots\cdots\cdots\cdots\cdots\cdots\cdots\cdots\cdots\cdots\cdots$$

$$\text{(W-18)}^{54}$$

where k_t, k_p, k_k, $k_{k''}$, ... are the coefficients of production for capital good K of, respectively, the services of land, persons, a first capital good, a second capital good, etc.

Let us examine the total system of equations that Walras employs at this stage in the development of his programme. In addition to W-16 through to W-18 above there are n offer equations in the system:

$$O_t = F_t(p_t \ldots p_p \ldots p_k, p_{k'}, p_{k''} \ldots p_b, p_c, p_d \ldots p_e),$$

$$O_p = F_p(p_t \ldots p_p \ldots p_k, p_{k'}, p_{k''} \ldots p_b, p_c, p_d \ldots p_e),$$

$$O_k = F_k(p_t \ldots p_p \ldots p_k, p_{k''}, p_{k''} \ldots p_b, p_c, p_d \ldots p_e), \qquad \text{(W-19)}[55]$$

$$O_{k'} = F_{k'}(p_t \ldots p_p \ldots p_k, p_{k'}, p_{k''} \ldots p_b, p_c, p_d \ldots p_e),$$

$$O_{k''} = F_{k''}(p_t \ldots p_p \ldots p_k, p_{k'}, p_{k''} \ldots p_b, p_c, p_d \ldots p_e),$$

where p_e is the price of a unit of perpetual income (E). It is through the introduction of the good (E) (which has a diminishing want curve) that Walras allows for the possibility of differences between the level of income and of consumption of an individual. In other words, the possibilities of saving and dissaving are introduced.

There will be m equations of aggregate demand:

$$D_b = F_b(p_t \ldots p_p \ldots p_k, p_{k'}, p_{k''} \ldots p_b, p_c, p_d \ldots p_e),$$

$$D_c = F_c(p_t \ldots p_p \ldots p_k, p_{k'}, p_{k''} \ldots p_b, p_c, p_d \ldots p_e),$$

$$D_d = F_d(p_t \ldots p_p \ldots p_k, p_{k'}, p_{k''} \ldots p_b, p_c, p_d \ldots p_e),$$

$$D_a = O_t p_t + \ldots + O_p p_p + \ldots + O_k p_k + O_{k'} p_{k'} + O_{k''} p_{k''}$$
$$+ \ldots - (D_b p_b + D_c p_c + D_d p_d + \ldots + E) \quad \text{(W-20)}[56]$$

and:

$$E = D_e p_e + F_e(p_t \ldots p_p \ldots p_k, p_{k'}, p_{k''} \ldots p_b, p_c, p_d \ldots i) \quad \text{(W-21)}[57]$$

We also have n equations of exchange setting equal the demand and offer of services:

$$a_t D_a + b_t D_b + c_t D_c + d_t D_d + \ldots + k_t D_k + k_t D_{k'} + k_t D_{k''} + \ldots = O_t$$

$$a_p D_a + b_p D_b + c_p D_c + d_p D_d + k_p D_k + k_p D_{k'} + k_p D_{k''} \ldots P_p$$

$$a_k D_a + b_k D_b + c_k D_c + d_k D_d + \ldots$$
$$+ k_k D_k + k'_k D_{k'} + k''_i D_{k''} + \ldots = O_k$$

$$a_{k'} D_a + b_{k'} D_b + c_{k'} D_c + d_{k'} D_d + \ldots$$
$$+ k_{k'} D_k + k'_{k'} D_{k'} + k''_{k'} D_{k''} + \ldots = O_{k'}$$

$$a_{k''} D_c + b_{k''} D_b + c_{k''} D_c + d_{k''} D_d + \ldots$$
$$+ k_{k''} D_k + k'_{k''} D_{k'} + k''_{k''} D_{k''} + \ldots = O_{k''}$$

$$\text{(W-22)}[58]$$

There are also the following n cost of production equations for consumer goods:

$$a_t p_t + \ldots + a_p p_p + \ldots + a_k p_k + a_{k'} p_{k'} + a_{k''} p_{k''} + \ldots = 1$$
$$b_t p_t + \ldots + b_p p_p + \ldots + b_k p_k + b_{k'} p_{k'} + b_{k''} p_{k''} + \ldots = p_b$$
$$c_t p_t + \ldots + c_p p_p + \ldots + c_k p_k + c_{k'} p_{k'} + c_{k''} p_{k''} + \ldots = p_c$$
$$d_t p_t + \ldots + d_p p_p + \ldots + d_k p_k + d_{k'} p_{k'} + d_{k''} p_{k''} + \ldots = p_d$$

$$(\text{W-23})[59]$$

There are L cost of production conditions for capital goods:

$$k_t p_t + \ldots + k_p p_p + \ldots + k_k p_k + k_{k'} p_{k'} + k_{k''} p_{k''} + \ldots = p_k$$
$$k_t p_t + \ldots + k_p p_p + \ldots + k'_{k} p_k + k'_{k'} p_{k'} + k'_{k''} p_{k''} + \ldots = p_{k'}$$
$$k_t p_t + \ldots + k_p p_p + \ldots k''_{k} p_k + k''_{k'} p_{k'} + k''_{k''} p_{k''} + \ldots = p_{k''}$$

$$(\text{W-24})[60]$$

There are the the following L equations from W-15:

$$P_k = \frac{p_k}{i + u_k + v_k}$$

$$P_k = \frac{p_{k'}}{i + u_{k'} + v_{k'}} \qquad (\text{W-25})[61]$$

$$P_k = \frac{p_{k''}}{i + u_{k''} + v_{k''}}$$

And, finally, there is:

$$D_k P_k + D_{k'} P_{k'} + D_{k''} P_{k''} + \ldots = E \qquad (\text{W-26})[62]$$

This yields $2n + 2m + 2L + 2$ equations. One equation may be eliminated leaving an equality between the number of equations and the number of unknowns. Walras again uses tickets and abstracts from production in time. He again goes into a detailed discussion of *tâtonnement*. Also the capital goods produced cannot be used for production in the period under consideration. This is a protective belt assumption.

Walras derives the following results:

If, all other things being equal, the utility of net income increases or decreases for one or more parties to the exchange when the market is in a state of general equilibrium, the rate of net income will decrease or increase.

If the quantity of net income increases or decreases for one or more holders, the rate of net income will increase or decrease.

If (both) the utility and the quantity of net income vary from one or more parties or holders in such a way that the *raretés* remain unchanged, the rate of net income will not change.[63]

He also makes the following predictions:

In a market for capital goods, the equilibrium prices of these goods in terms of the *numéraire* are equal to the ratios of the prices of their net incomes to the rate of net income.

If, all other things being equal, the price of the gross income of a capital good increases or decreases, the price of the capital good itself will increase or decrease.

If the rate of depreciation on the premium rate of insurance increases or decreases, the price of the capital good will decrease or increase.

If, all other things equal, the rate of net income increases or decreases, the prices of all capital goods will decrease or increase.[64]

It should be clear that the shift to the model which incorporates capital markets is rational in a Lakatosian sense. Predictions over a new range of phenomena, that is, the pricing of capital goods, may not be put forward. Note that the inclusion of the prices of capital goods as endogenous variables affects most of the equations in the system. It is clear also that the cost of production equations, the equations of exchange, and the demand and offer equations of the earlier models are special cases of this latter model. Thus, there is a retention of unrefuted content.

The Lakatosian structure of Walras' programme should be evident by this time. There is, therefore, no need to go into great detail concerning Walras' development, and further articulation of the series of models.

Walras lays out the next stages of the positive heuristic. He states:

In the course of establishing and solving the equations of production and capital formation . . . we deliberately abstracted . . . from the following seven categories ...: (7) *new capital goods* which producers hold for sale in the form of products; (8) stocks of *income goods* consisting of *consumers' goods* in the homes of consumers; (9) stocks of *income goods* consisting of raw materials held (for future use) by producers; (10) new income goods consisting of *consumers' goods* and *raw materials* held for sale by the producers of these goods; (11), (12) and (13) consumers' *cash* holdings, producers' *cash* holdings, and *money savings*. The time has now come to introduce these elements in order to complete our general problem of economic equilibrium.[65]

Walras incorporates category (7) by including the services of availability of a capital good in the coefficient of production for a commodity. He incorporates categories (9) and (10) by including the services of availability of raw materials in the coefficient of production for a commodity.

Thus far, Walras has abstracted from the existence of money and circulating capital. The protective belt has been used to preclude consideration of cash holdings and stocks of income or new capital goods held for future sale or use.[66] The formal recognition of these omissions provides global counterexamples which, *inter alia*, include the cost-of-production functions, the equation of the aggregate exchange of services for final products, and all functions of the total price vector (because new prices, those of circulating capital, must be introduced). The assumption of a barter economy, and the abstraction from the services of availability provided by stocks of income goods and money, provide the corresponding local counterexamples. Walras calls this problem shift the "problem of circulation."[67]

In the next step of the heuristic Walras incorporates money. It is assumed that time is needed for the flow of products and services and that payments are spread over the interval. Individuals will hold a certain amount of cash and income goods for the services of availability they render and will hold them in proportions consistent with the maximization of utility given their want curves. Producers will hold the quantities of income goods and cash determined by the coefficients of production given the condition of equality between the selling price and the cost of production. In this manner Walras introduces a transactions and a credit demand for money. There is no speculative or precautionary demand for money. Walras states:

> There may be a small element of uncertainty which is due solely to the difficulty of foreseeing possible changes in the data of the problem. If, however, we suppose these data constant for a given period of time and we suppose the prices of goods and services and also the dates of their purchase and sales to be known for the whole period, there will be no occasion for uncertainty. [68]

Walras employs the "hypothesis of constant data during the period under consideration" [69] as a protective belt to preclude the existence of uncertainty and, thereby to remove the possibility of a speculative or precautionary demand for money. Nor do newly produced capital goods join into the production process in the period under consideration. In this manner, Walras continues to abstract from the possibility of growth.

Walras' theoretic adjustment to handle the "problem of circulation" is to treat stocks of income goods, raw materials, and money as *capital* insofar as they provide a service of availability. These circulation-capital goods, labelled (A'), (B'), (C'), ... (M) ..., are physically the same as the goods and raw materials previously considered; however, because they are valued for their services of availability, they are considered as capital. This explains the necessity of distinct variables for their prices and quantities. Individuals are assumed to have *rareté* functions for these services of availability and producers are assumed to encounter coefficients of production which call for their employment.

The coefficients of production of raw materials for produced goods are defined to include "two sorts of services of availability: that rendered by the raw material while it is held *in stock* for future use and that rendered while it is placed *on display* for sale." [70] The direct contribution of raw materials is *not* included in the cost of production of a good because that contribution can always be decomposed into the contributions of particular productive services. However, the value of the *services* of availability rendered by stocks of raw materials is included. This theoretic adjustment includes, in addition to the above factors, a reinterpretation of earlier constructs so that the anomaly of "stocks of new capital goods held for future sale" may be incorporated. The coefficients of production of capital goods for produced goods are redefined to include, not only the direct contribution to production by the use of the capital good itself, but also the services of availability conveyed. The quantity of a capital service effectively demanded and offered at equilibrium now includes the demand for stocks of new capital goods to be held for sale by producers.

Walras assumes that transactions must be made in money. A quantity of cash is necessary for the realization of transactions because receipts and payments are spread across time and are not coordinated. Money (U) is considered as a circulating capital good which has no direct utility but does provide a service of availability. Individuals are assumed to have *rareté* functions for the services of availability of products *in the form of money*. Similarly, producers are assumed to encounter coefficients of production which demand the retention of stocks of money for transaction purposes. An initial distribution of circulating capital and money is assumed.

The income constraint faced by an individual in this expanded model includes, not only the return to services provided by the land, labour and capital possessed, but also the return from quantities of circulating capital possessed.

Given the condition of utility maximization, the *rareté* functions for the services of availability of products can be determined as a function of the total price vector (which now includes the prices of these services). The aggregation of these individual offer curves yields the total offer of each service as a function of the total price vector. Label these: $O_{a'}$, $O_{b'}$, ... Setting the offer of these services by owners equal to the demand for these services by producers, we have the following equilibrium conditions:

$$O_{a'} = a_{a'}(D_a + D_{a'}) + b_{a'}(D_b + D_{b'}) + \ldots$$
$$+ m_{a'}D_m + \ldots + k_{a'}D_k + \ldots$$
$$O_{b'} = a_{b'}(D_a + D_{a'}) + b_{b'}(D_b + D_{b'}) + \ldots$$
$$+ m_{b'}D_m + \ldots + k_{b'}D_k + \ldots$$
$$\ldots\ldots\ldots\ldots\ldots\ldots\ldots\ldots\ldots\ldots\ldots\ldots\ldots\ldots\ldots\ldots\ldots\ldots\ldots\ldots\ldots\ldots$$

$$(W\text{-}27)^{71}$$

where letting $i = a, b, \ldots$ and $j = a, b, \ldots$ we have $i_{j'}$ as the coefficient of production of the service (J') for the production of good (I) and D_i as the demand for good (I).

The services of raw materials offered will equal the quantity possessed as the *rareté* of raw materials for consumers is zero. Setting the offer of the new raw materials equal to the demand, we have:

$$a_m(D_a + D_{a'}) + b_m(D_b + D_{b'}) + m_m D_m + \ldots + k_m D_k + \ldots = Q_m$$

$$(\text{W-28})^{72}$$

where i_m is the coefficient of production of raw materials for good (I) for $i = a, b, \ldots m \ldots k \ldots$

Given *rareté* functions for the services of the availability of products in the form of money, the new income constraint, and the condition of maximum satisfaction, an effective quantity demanded for each of these services in the form of money will obtain for each individual. The summation of price of each service times this quantity yields the individual demand for money balances, which Walras calls the *encaisse désirée*. The total quantity of money initially possessed by the individual minus this desired cash-balance equals the quantity of money effectively offered. Aggregating across individuals yields the total effective offer of money. Label this O_u. Producers face coefficients of production which call for the services of (A'), $(B') \ldots (M) \ldots (k) \ldots$ in the form of money. The summation of the demands for each of these services in the form of money times their respective prices yields the demand for money by producers. Label this D_u. The money market equilibrium condition is: $O_u = D_u$.

In equilibrium, the price of a commodity which provides a service of availability will equal the price of its service divided by the general rate of return. This is because any such commodity must be treated as a capital good. Thus, for good (B), $p_{b'} = p_b i$ where p_b is the price of (B), $p_{b'}$ is the price of the service of availability of (B), and i is the general rate of return. There is a similar equation for each circulating capital good. These constitute novel predictions.

The $3m + 2s + 3$ additional equations of this adjusted model match the $3m + 2s + 3$ additional unknowns. Walras next concerns himself with the practical solution of these equations. The prices of circulating capital goods and the prices of their sevices are determined exactly like the prices of fixed capital goods and the prices of their services, described in Walras' earlier passage on *tâtonnement*. Offer, demand, market equilibrium equations, and additional variables are included to account for (A'), (B')...(M)...(U). The previous solution is found to be totally adequate, *mutatis mutandis*, except for the offer and market equilibrium equations for (U). If the price of the services of money is held constant at a random value during the *tâtonnement* process in the equation for production and capital formation, then the equation of equality between the price of the *numéraire* and unity, and the equation of monetary equilibrium remain. At this stage the price of the service of money is adjusted so that money market equilibrium is attained. A change in the price of the service of money changes virtual income and therefore upsets the equations of production and capital formation. In turn this may result in a renewed disequilibrium in the money market. However, this influence is small because the effect of the initial change in the price of the service of money on income is small. Equilibrium will be reached within a small number of iterations.

Walras states this prediction of the model: "The *rareté* or value of the service of money is directly proportional to its utility and inversely proportional to its quantity."[73] Walras introduces the option of having one commodity serve both as the *numéraire* and as money. He derives the following result:

In the case of a commodity that serves both as money and as *numéraire* the uniform and identical price of its service as circulating capital and as money is established by a rise or fall according as the demand is greater or less than the (total existing) quantity; and this price is maintained (the same in both uses) by minting or melting according as the price of its service as money is greater or less than the price of its service as circulating capital.[74]

It follows from this that the general price level will be directly related to the quantity of money. Walras states:

What is most remarkable, in the case of a commodity which serves both as money and as *numéraire*, is the manner in which all prices rise or fall in terms of (A) in response to an increase or decrease in the *rareté* or value of this commodity in its monetary use when there is a decrease or increase in its quantity.[75]

Walras also notes the increased price of the money commodity when it has direct utility due to the cumulative demand.

Many former predictions are superseded by the predictions of this expanded model. All equations which had the total price vector as an argument will now have $p_{a'}, p_{b'}, \ldots, p_{m'}, \ldots, p_{u'}$ as additional arguments. Cost of production functions will now include the costs of services of availability of circulating capital and money. A new equation is put forward which states that the value of the aggregate excess of income over consumption must equal the value of new fixed capital goods plus the value of new circulating capital goods. The redefining of the coefficients of capital for products leads to a concomitant reinterpretation of the predictions of the model. The former model may be viewed as a special case where all the services of availability are set equal to zero. Thus, there has been an expansion of the empirical base.

Walras takes his programme through a few more models in his *Elements*. He makes an extension to include the possibility of a dual monetary standard so that he might address the bimetallist controversy of his own day. (Walras was a bimetallist.) He also incorporates fiduciary money, and he extends his analysis to cover variable coefficients of production.

NOTES

1. Joseph A. Schumpeter, *A History of Economic Analysis* (New York: Oxford University Press, 1954), p. 1026.
2. Leon Walras, *De la nature de la richesse et de l'origine de la valeur* (Paris: Felix Alean, 1938).
3. *Ibid.*, p. 119.
4. *Ibid.*, p. 88. "W-1" is a label for the set of equations.
5. *Ibid.*, pp. 89–99.

6. *Ibid.*, pp. 108–9.
7. *Ibid.*, p. 127.
8. *Ibid.*, p. 143.
9. *Ibid.*, p. 145.
10. *Ibid.*, p. 143.
11. *Ibid.*
12. *Ibid.*, pp. 146–7.
13. *Ibid.*, p. 144.
14. *Ibid.*, p. 131.
15. *Ibid.*, p. 136.
16. *Ibid.*, p. 138.
17. *Ibid.*, p. 137.
18. *Ibid.*, p. 139.
19. *Ibid.*
20. *Ibid.*, p. 153.
21. *Ibid.*, p. 155.
22. *Ibid.*
23. *Ibid.*, p. 156.
24. *Ibid.*, p. 161.
25. *Ibid.*, p. 162.
26. *Ibid.*, p. 173.
27. *Ibid.*, p. 175.
28. *Ibid.*, p. 161.
29. *Ibid.*, p. 180.
30. *Ibid.*
31. *Ibid.*, p. 192.
32. *Ibid.*, p. 185.
33. *Ibid.*, p. 290.
34. *Ibid.*, p. 191.
35. *Ibid.*, p. 211.
36. *Ibid.*
37. *Ibid.*, p. 214.
38. *Ibid.*, p. 224.
39. *Ibid.*, p. 225.
40. *Ibid.*, p. 238.
41. *Ibid.*, p. 239.
42. *Ibid.*
43. *Ibid.*, p. 240.
44. *Ibid.*
45. *Ibid.*, p. 253.
46. *Ibid.*, p. 258.
47. *Ibid.*, p. 255.
48. *Ibid.*, p. 260.
49. *Ibid.*
50. *Ibid.*, p. 267.
51. *Ibid.*, p. 272.
52. *Ibid.*, p. 270.
53. *Ibid.*, p. 271.

54. *Ibid.*
55. *Ibid.*, p. 279.
56. *Ibid.*
57. *Ibid.*
58. *Ibid.*, p. 280.
59. *Ibid.*
60. *Ibid.*
61. *Ibid.*, p. 281.
62. *Ibid.*
63. *Ibid.*, p. 307.
64. *Ibid.*, pp. 309–10.
65. *Ibid.*, p. 315.
66. *Ibid.*
67. *Ibid.*
68. *Ibid.*, p. 317.
69. *Ibid.*
70. *Ibid.*, p. 315.
71. *Ibid.*, p. 322.
72. *Ibid.*
73. *Ibid.*, pp. 328–9.
74. *Ibid.*, p. 331.
75. *Ibid.*, p. 333.

7 Menger

It is entirely indifferent to me whether the name Austrian School be preserved. The important thing is that every economist worthy of the name has now virtually adopted every essential thing that I stood for.[1]

Carl Menger, 1923

In 1871 Carl Menger laid the groundwork for a programme of economic thought in his *Grundsätze der Volkwirtschaftslehre* (*Principles of Economics*).[2] The *Grundsätze* (this term may also be translated as "fundamental propositions") was to be the first of four volumes. Although Menger had placed the fundamental propositions in a form conducive to their further development, he never completed the planned work. It was his two disciples, Friedrich von Wieser and Eugen Böhm-Bawerk, who developed and promulgated the fundamental propositions.

Menger's *Grundsätze* may be thought of as a presentation and initial development of the hard core of that specific programme as well as a contribution to the development of the broader marginalist research programme. The concern of this chapter is to capture the elements of this intellectual endowment.

Our presentation of Menger's economic theory is not simply a replication of Menger's work but is, rather, a rational reconstruction. Our emphasis is on the interconnectedness of the analysis and the heuristic growth within the text. This emphasis has warranted certain changes. For example, in those cases where Menger gives a concrete example as the only exposition of a general point, we give a general argument. Furthermore, the order of presentation has been altered so as to highlight the heuristic character of the work and also to avoid getting bogged down in definitions at the start. All changes in our reconstruction are only changes of form. The content of the original work has not intentionally been superseded at any point.

The fundamental propositions are embodied in a series of ever more complx stages, each of which is constructed by adjusting the previous stage in a manner which transforms anomaly into corroboration. On the one hand, each stage of analysis has an informal deductive character and, thus, involves a logic of justification. On the other hand, the movement from one stage to the next involves a logic of discovery. An expanding empirical base is guaranteed by this latter "logic" as long as the adjustments do not preclude the retention of previous unrefuted predictive content. The heuristic power of Menger's work is part of the explanation of the rapid development of an Austrian school. Such heuristic power is a necessary condition for all progressive research.

A series of abstract models is presented by Menger in his central and longest chapter "The Theory of Price."[3] Here we trace the tacit logic of discovery of this series of models. Menger introduces certain principles and develops them in what we shall call the Robinson Crusoe (RC) model of an isolated individual. These principles, in combination with some additional ones, also shed light upon the case of isolated exchange, (we shall call this the IE model) which involves two individuals. In this model, the case of one commodity being exchanged for another is examined. The analysis is then expanded to include: a quantity of each good being exchanged at a ratio of one-to-one (instead of being restricted to an exchanged quantity *equal* to one for each individual), a quantity of each good being exchanged at a set ratio of exchange (perhaps different than one-to-one), divisible goods, and the case of exchange without a pre-set ratio. The possibility of many holders of one of the commodities is next introduced. This we shall call the monopoly (M) model. The possibility of many holders of both commodities is then introduced. This we shall call the competitive (C) model. Menger further expands the empirical base through a progressive reinterpretation of the terms used in the development of this series of models (that is, he employs concept stretching in a progressive manner). Production, substitutes in production, and degree-of-marketability of commodities are introduced in this manner. Degree-of-marketability of commodities is introduced as a lead to the discussion of money.

The introductions of most of these complications involves extensions of the term value.

The unrefuted content of the earlier models is observed to be retained in the latter models. For example, the implications of economizing activities and the theorem of gains from trade are valid throughout the analysis. These are the core theorems. Menger's work is progressive in the sense that theorems are demonstrated to apply over an ever-broadening empirical base. It is the core theorems which are retained in the shift from the monopoly model to the competitive model. Many of the theorems of the monopoly model are refuted by the introduction of competitive cases; however, this should not be cited as an objection to the progressiveness of the series of models. It is the retention of the *unrefuted content* in the examination of a *new range* of phenomena that characterizes scientific progress in a Lakatosian sense. Thus the empirical base has been expanded *with respect to the core theorems*, but not with respect to other results (these other results being refuted in the competitive case). Menger's recognition and introduction of the competitive case renders the monopoly model a special case to which one can return if its special characteristics are desired.[4] Menger presents the RC model:

To begin with the simplest case, suppose that an isolated economizing individual inhabits a rocky island in the sea, that he finds only a single spring on the island, and that he is exclusively dependent upon it for satisfaction of his need for fresh water.[5]

It is from this model, the simplest in which the principles may be expounded, that Menger develops a more complex analysis to account for a large range of phenomena. It is chosen as the starting point to demonstrate that the principles are not based on a particular social arrangement but rather are inherent to the human condition.

The theoretical terms, with their attendant ineluctable maze of implicit assumptions, are introduced. They are a part of the hard core. A *good* is anything which is useful in the fulfillment of needs. The *requirement* for a good is the quantity that is necessary to achieve total satiation of the needs for the good during a designated period of time. If the requirement is greater (less) than the available quantity then the good is an *economic* (*non-economic*) *good*. The *value* of a good is the importance attached to the need that it fulfills.

The lemmas are introduced. An isolated individual is characterized by an array of needs. Different needs maintain different levels of importance. Their importance depends on their duration and intensity, and decreases at the margin. These needs can be fulfilled through the acquisition of a sufficient quantity of a particular good. A limited quantity of this good is granted by Nature for each time period and cannot be transferred from one time period to the next. The individual can rank his needs in order of importance, and he attempts to achieve the highest level of satisfaction.

Menger's analysis is informal. The good may be either economic or non-economic in character, although this characteristic is not an inherent quality, as the relationship between the requirements and the available quantity may change. The good is non-economic in character if the available quantity is greater than the individual's requirement. In this case the value of any small portion of the good is zero because the individual's needs would continue to be fulfilled totally if some small portion were lost. Goods obtain value when it is recognized that the loss of any amount will result in the deprivation of a formerly satisfied need. The good is economic in character if the available quantity is less than the individual's requirement. It follows that only economic goods have value. When dealing with economic goods, which have value, the individual seeking the highest level of satisfaction possible will engage in economizing activity which involves efficiency and choice. He is forced to choose between needs because some needs must go unfulfilled. He will choose to fulfill his needs in a descending order of importance, that is, he will continue to contribute quantities of the scarce good toward the fulfilment of a particular need only as long as the incremental contribution to that need is considered as more important than its potential incremental contribution to any other need. Otherwise the highest level of satisfaction will be obtained. Efficiency implies not using more of the good than is necessary to meet a particular need. The economizing individual will be efficient because, for any portion of the economic good that is lost, some need that could have been fulfilled would go unfulfilled. As a result of economizing activity, needs which go unfulfilled are necessarily of lesser importance than those which are fulfilled. The least important needs go unfulfilled if a small portion of the good is valued at the importance attached to the least important needs fulfilled.

Scientific language highlights certain aspects of reality and abstracts from others. The definitions of requirement, economic and non-economic goods, and value have been established. The individual has been put forward as the unit of analysis. Three hard core assumptions presented are: (1) individuals seek the highest possible level of satisfaction, (2) individuals can and do rank their needs, and (3) the importance of a need decreases at the margin. Four conclusions of the analysis are: (1) individuals seeking the highest possible level of satisfaction will engage in economizing activity with respect to economic goods; this implies efficiency and choice in the use of these goods, (2) economizing individuals, when using an economic good to satisfy needs, will fulfill those needs in a descending order of importance so as to ensure maximum satisfaction, (3) the value of any small portion of an economic good is equal to the importance of the least important needs fulfilled, and (4) the value of any small portion of a non-economic good is equal to zero. It would be inappropriate to focus criticism on this "model" as being a mere collection of tautologies. It is on this simple foundation that Menger extends his analysis to produce predictions that are far from self-evident.

An exposition of the essential features of exchange is impossible within the confines of the RC model. The "existence of more than one person" presents itself as a counterexample to the "Robinson Crusoe" lemma of the isolated individual. A second economizing individual is introduced as a theoretic adjustment to allow for an expansion of content. There is neither coercion nor affinity. Property is respected. There are no barriers to trade. The new lemmas allow for an expansion of content that includes "Isolated Echange" (IE). We temporarily retreat from the assumption that each individual possesses a given quantity of a good and instead posit that each possesses one (different) indivisible economic good. The broader assumption is reinstated at the next stage.

There is no incentive to trade if the value of the good possessed is greater than the value of the good not possessed. Trade will not commence if this condition prevails for either individual. The value of the good possessed may be less than the value of the good not possessed. Trade will commence if this condition prevails for both individuals and is recognized.

A higher level of satisfaction is always attained through trade because individuals trade only if the value of the received good is greater than the value of the traded good. This implies that needs of a greater importance to the individual are being fulfilled. This increase in welfare is called the gains from trade.

The lemma of one indivisible good limits the range of the model. A situation in which each individual possesses a number of discrete units of a good provides a local counterexample. The theoretic adjustment is to delete the lemma and assume instead that individual A has n discrete units of economic good I and individual B has m discrete units of economic good II. Recall that needs for these goods vary in inverse proportion to the degree of satisfaction. In other words, the greater the number of units consumed by an individual of a particular good per unit of time, the less value is attached to the last unit consumed. If individual A values his nth unit of good I more than he values a first unit of good II, or individual B values his mth unit of good II more than a first unit of good I, then there can be no trade. If each individual values a first unit of the other good more than the last unit of his own good, then trade will proceed. There is potential for further trade if individual A values his $(n - 1)$th unit of good I less than a second unit of good II; however, note that the value of the $(n - 1)$th unit, and the value of a second unit of good II is less than the value of the first unit of that good. Further trade will commence if individual B is in a similar position with respect to the relationship between his $(m - 1)$th unit of good II and a second unit of good I. Trade will continue up to the point where either individual places greater value on the last unit of his own good than on the next unit of the other good.

A situation in which the goods are continuously divisible provides a counterexample to the lemma that goods come in discrete units. The above prediction concerning the point of trading equilibrium provides a corresponding global counterexample. The theoretic adjustment is to introduce the divisibility of goods I and II. The lemma of a ratio of exchange of one-to-one is restrictive. It is replaced by the slightly broader assumption of an exogenously given ratio of exchange (not necessarily one to one). Following the analysis based on these new lemmas, the prediction which had produced the global counterexample is replaced by the new prediction that trade will continue until one individual values the last minute increment of his own good that would be exchanged at the given ratio of exchange.

A situation of isolated exchange in which the ratio of exchange is not exogenously fixed provides a local counterexample. The corresponding lemma is deleted. Menger introduces the asssumption that the two individuals possess equal bargaining ability. This gives the problem determinacy. To simplify the exposition, assume that prices are in terms of good II. Also assume that for individual A the last unit of good I is worth x units of good II, where x is a positive number. This implies that the needs fulfilled by the final unit of good I are of equal importance to the needs that would be fulfilled by x units of good II. Individual A will be willing to trade if and only if the price is greater than x units of good II per unit of good I. For individual B assume that the last unit of good II is worth y units of good I, where y is a positive number. Individual B will be willing to trade if and only if the price is less than $1/y$. Trade will commence if and only if x is less than $1/y$ and the ratio of exchange falls between x and $1/y$. The exact price depends, among other things, on the relative bargaining ability of the traders and cannot be strictly determined by economic analysis. Since it has been postulated that the two individuals possess equal bargaining ability then the average of these two bounds, $\frac{x + \frac{1}{y}}{2}$, should prevail as the price. Four hard core lemmas introduced in the IE model are (1) the option of exchange, (2) a lack of coercion, (3) an absence of affinity and (4) the non-existence of barriers to trade.[6] There were three minor problem shifts within the IE model, each of which was progressive. The analysis began with each individual in possession of one indivisible good. The possibility of holding a number of discrete units was introduced, complete divisibility was then postulated, and finally, the ratio of exchange was no longer determined exogenously. New theorems were derived concerning (1) the conditions of trade and (2) the gains from trade. More precisely, it was demonstrated that the existence of trade implies gains from trade. This is because an individual will not engage in trade unless there are benefits to be derived. The result held for each model; it remains valid throughout the analysis. It was demonstrated that trade will continue until one individual attaches a higher value to the last minute increment of his own good than he attaches to the last minute increment of the other good which would be exchanged at the prevailing ratio of exchange. The range over which the ratio of exchange may vary was demonstrated to be determined by economic conditions. This theorem will also remain valid through the remainder of the analysis. The possibility that economic conditions might preclude exchange was also observed.

The three hard core lemmas and the four theorems listed in the summary of the RC model continue to hold in the IE model. The only lemma of the RC model that does not continue to hold is the heuristically refuted assumption of a single isolated individual. The "existence of more than one individual" was an anomaly for the RC model, but has now become a corroboration for the series of models. The adjustments to the RC model acquire importance because they allow for a set of novel predictions the formulation of which was impossible in the unadjusted model. Thus, a new range of phenomena has been encompassed.

Seldom are markets limited to two participants; another local counterexample is thus provided. As a theoretic adjustment an additional holder of good II is introduced. This may be called the Monopoly (M) model as there is only one holder of good I. To retrace the earlier analysis in the light of this complication a retreat is made by assuming that individual A possesses only one unit of good I. Ultimately there is no loss of content, as the assumption that individual A possesses a quantity of good I is reintroduced later. (This is a case of retreat and consolidation.) Individual A values one unit of good I at x units of good II. Individual B_2 values one unit of good II at z units of good I. Assume z is greater than y. It follows that $1/z$ is less than $1/y$ since z and y are both positive. Individual A will not trade unless the price is greater than x units (the price is assumed to be in terms of good II.) Individual B_1 will not trade unless the price is less than $1/y$. Individual B_2 will not trade unless the price is less than $1/z$. Trade will commence only if x is less than $1/y$. This guarantees that a ratio of exchange exists at which A and B_1 find an exchange to their advantage. If the ratio of exchange is less than $1/z$ then both B_1 and B_2 will find it in their economic interest to trade for good I. However, there is only one unit of good I. Individual B_1 will offer a higher price than $1/z$ to exclude individual B_2, thus ensuring for himself the acquisition of the only unit of good I. The IE model is reduced to the special case in which $1/z$ is less than x, but $1/y$ is greater than x. Thus content has been retained. The empirical base has been expanded since predictions may now be made concerning cases where two individuals possess one of the traded commodities.

Menger extends the analysis of the M model to include more individuals in possession of good II. He deletes the assumptions of only two holders of good II. The new auxiliary hypothesis is that individuals B_1 and B_w possess a quantity of good II. Some individual, label him B_q, values a unit of good I at a higher quantity of good II (label this as $1/y$ units of good II) than any other B-type individual. Another individual, label him B_r, values a unit of good I at the next highest (label this as $1/z$ units of good II). Trade will commence if and only if x (the value of good I to A in terms of good II) is less than $1/y$. If trade takes place then the price must fall between $1/z$ and $1/y$ as individual B_q economically excludes individual B_r and the others, thus ensuring the acquisition of the unit of good I for himself.

The earlier stage of the M model is reduced to the special case where B_q is equivalent to B_1, and B_r is equivalent to B_2. Thus, the shift within the M model has been progressive as the former unrefuted content is retained and predictions may now be made concerning exchange situations where there are multiple holders of one of the commodities.

The assumption that individual A has a quantity of good I is reintroduced to consolidate the analysis and thus ensure retention of earlier refuted content. If individual A trades only one unit of the quantity, then the analysis immediately above is to be applied to this special case. The price, label it P^*, that is associated with the trade of one unit of good I will be such that only individual B_q finds it in his economic interest to enter the market. If individual A desires to trade a larger quantity of good I at P^* then individual B_q is the only possible buyer. Recall that the level of importance and therefore the value of a good varied in inverse proportion to the quantity of the good possessed. Thus, for individual B_q the value of each further increment of good I is lower then the value of any earlier increment. The value for individual B_q of additional increments of good I must eventually fall below P^*. The quantity that individual B_q will buy at P^* is therefore limited. If individual A desires to trade more units of good I than this limit, then he must lower the price so that either the price falls below the value of an additional increment of good I for individual B_q or for some other individual. The greater quantity that individual A desires to trade, the lower must be the price.

If a particular quantity of good I is to be traded and cleared from the market then there exists both an upper and a lower bound on the price. The upper bound is equal to the lowest value of good I to be found among the purchasers of that particular quantity of the good. If the price were to rise above this bound then that individual who valued good I the lowest would no longer find it in his economic interest to purchase that last unit and, therefore, the total quantity of good I would no longer be purchased. The price is bounded from below by the fact that those who do enter the market will have to offer a high enough price to economically exclude others who have still lower valuations of good I. Thus the lower bound on the price is set by the highest value of good I among those not participating in the exchange of a particular quantity of good I. Implications are that: (1) those individuals who purchase good I place a higher value on good I (in terms of good II) than those who are excluded from the purchase of good I, (2) the more units of good I that individual A would like to trade the lower must be the price, (3) purchasers of good I will continue to increase their quantity of purchase up to the point at which the value of good I for them falls below its selling price and (4) if individual A chooses to market a particular quantity of good I then the price must fall within a particular range; if he chooses to set a particular price then the quantity that will be purchased is determined; he can choose to set either the price or the quantity but not both. In line with the assumption of maximum satisfaction, individual A will choose to market good I at the price/quantity combination that will yield him the greatest economic gain. Menger points out that the monopolist must be aware of how responsive the purchasers will be to changes in price in this decision.

The M model was produced by allowing for the possibility of multiple holders of good II. The hard core lemmas and core theorems of both the RC and the IE models have been retained. For example the theorem of gains from trade is retained throughout. The M model may be reduced to the IE model simply by setting the number of holders of good II equal to one. The novel predictions made possible by the auxiliary assumptions of the M model are listed in the paragraph above. The shift is progressive.

Particular series of anomalies, belonging to the positive heuristic, may be foreseen and prepared for by a suitable flexibility of the theoretical terms. Both Jevons and Menger recognize the value of including explicitly a provision for such alternative interpretations of theoretical terms so as to take advantage of isomorphisms. Menger states:

By imagining the symbols B_1, B_2, etc., to stand, not for single individuals, but for groups of the population of a country (using B_1 to designate the group of economizing individuals who are most eager and in the strongest competitive positions to exchange grain for the monopolized good, B_2 to designate the group of economizing individuals who are next in eagerness and in competitive strength, and so on) we obtain a model of monopoly trade as it actually appears under the conditions of everyday life.[7]

Further on he states:

If our example is extended as before, and we imagine the symbols, B_1, B_2, B_3, etc., to represent groups of competitors who differ in purchasing power and their desire to trade.[8]

Instead of recognizing "B_1, B_2, B_3,..." as referring to individuals, they may be interpreted as representing groups. This same "do-it-yourself" positive heuristic, which may be used to expand the empirical scope of the series of models as new situations are confronted, is encountered in Jevons' *Theory of Political Economy* in the form of "trading bodies."

A situation of many holders of both commodities may be encountered. In such cases the former assumption of a single holder of good I provides a local counterexample. The price and quantity predictions provide global counterexamples. As a theoretic adjustment Menger at first introduces two holders of good I and then moves on to the more general case of multiple holders of good I. He notes that if the holders collude then the M model may be applied. He assumes that they do not collude but rather that they compete just as the holders of good II do. Call this the competitive (C) model. Under these circumstances no one individual can affect significantly the marketed quantity of good I. This implies that the holders of good I will also not be able to affect the price significantly. The total available quantity is likely to be marketed since, in these circumstances, it is unlikely that there would be an economic incentive for any individual to restrict the available quantity of good I. This model is likely to yield a lower price than under the monopoly. The higher marketed quantity implies that the price must be lowered so as to attract a broader base of purchasers whose valuation of good I is lower at the margin.

The possibility of production may be introduced through a semantical adjustment and the whole series of models re-applied. If the terms *good*, *requirement*, *economic* and *noneconomic*, and *value* are re-interpreted then factors of production may be considered. *Goods of first order* are those "that serve our needs directly." *Goods of second (or Nth) order* are those that serve needs through their capacity to be used in the production of goods of first (or $(N-1)$th) order.

Goods of higher order are called into action by economizing individuals for the purpose of increasing the available quantity of economic goods of first order. The goods character of a good of second order is dependent upon its usefulness in the production of a good of first order. If the good of first order loses its goods-character, or if the complementary goods required for the production of the good of first order are not available, then the good of second order will lose its goods-character unless it has an alternative use which leads to the production of some good of first order. Goods of higher order than two retain their goods-character only if complementary goods are available for the production of a good of the next lower order and that good of the next lower order retains its own goods-character. Whether goods of higher order are economic or noneconomic depends upon the relationship between requirements and available quantities just as for goods of first order. Goods of higher order are required because they lead ultimately to the production of goods of first order which have economic character.

The valuation of goods of higher order is based on the same principle as the valuation of goods of first order, that is, value is equal to the importance placed on the needs that would go unfulfilled if the good were lost. This is unlikely to be equivalent to the value of the total product in which the good of higher order participates. Menger explains:

the value of a given quantity of a particular good of higher order is not equal to the importance of the satisfactions that depend on the whole product it helps to produce, but is equal merely to the importance of the satisfactions provided for by the portion of the product that would remain unproduced if we were not in a position to command the given quantity of the good of higher order.[9]

Menger stresses the substitutability among factors of production. He states an important consideration in the valuation of goods of higher order:

an insufficiency of fertilizer can be compensated for by the employment of a larger amount of land or better machines, or by the more intensive application of agricultural labor services. Similarly, a diminished quantity of almost every good of higher order can be compensated for by a corresponding greater application of the other complementary goods.[10]

Menger examines the extreme case of what we would now

call a Leontief production function, which he describes as "the production process in fixed proportions."[11] Even in this case the value of one factor is less than the value of the total product because the other factors are likely to have alternative uses. Thus, the value of this factor would be the difference between the initial level of satisfactions and the satisfaction derived from the other factors in their next best alternative uses.

With these adjustments to the theoretical terms, production may now be included in the empirical scope of the series of models RC through to C. Thus, this semantic change is progressive in a Lakatosian sense.

Goods that fulfill the same need but with a qualitative difference are substitutes in consumption. These cases provide local counterexamples to the assumption that needs stand in a direct relation to particular goods. (See the third lemma of the RC model.) The lemma is deleted and Menger extends his value principle to account for this range of phenomena. There is a corresponding global counterexample. The valuation of a good is affected by the existence of substitutes. He supposes that two goods can be used to fulfill the same need although they are of a different quality. Formerly the value of the good would have been equal to the importance of any small quantity of it in fulfilling the particular need. Now, however, the loss of the superior unit implies its replacement by the inferior unit. It follows that the value of the superior quality good is equal to the satisfactions directly foregone by losing the unit for its application plus the satisfactions directly foregone in the former use of the inferior quality good minus the benefits derived from the application of the inferior good to the initial need. With this extention of the value concept predictions concerning goods which are substitutes in consumption may now be made. Thus, the semantic adjustment is progressive, as all former unrefuted content is retained.

Menger discusses the marketability of commodities in an attempt to incorporate the special characteristics of money into the analysis. He states:

the obvious differences in the marketability of commodities is a phenomenon of such far-reaching practical importance ... that science cannot, in the long run, avoid an exact investigation of its nature and causes. Indeed, it is also clear that a complete and satisfactory solution to the still controversial problem of the origin of money, the most liquid of all goods, can emerge only from an investigation of this topic. [12]

Menger introduces money as a commodity with the special characteristic that it is perfectly liquid. Money becomes the means of exchange because it aids individuals in their efforts to achieve their ultimate ends by allowing them to separate the act of buying from selling, which avoids the need for a coincidence of wants. The essential characteristic of money is that it is a means of exchange. Menger recognizes a transaction demand for money. Money may play either the role of store-of-wealth or measure-of-value but these are not essential features. The intimate link between the theoretical role that Menger gives to money and its definition is evident. If a consideration of marketability is incorporated, then money may be treated as other commodities and the earlier analysis extended in this direction. The shift is progressive.

We may now review the hard core of Menger's theory, that is, those propositions and terms that connect and unify this series of models. The foremost proposition is that individuals attempt to maximize their levels of satisfaction by fulfilling them through the use of goods. Menger states: "The leading idea in all the economic activity of men is the fullest possible satisfaction of their needs." [13] This principle runs throughout the analysis. It plays a leading role in the explanation of economizing activity, the origin of property, value and money, and the determination of price and exchange activity. The second aspect of the hard core is the recognition of scarcity and the necessity for choice. Menger postulates that individuals can order their needs from greatest to least importance. He argues that value is the importance we place on the needs which are fulfilled by a good (or, the importance of the needs that would go unfulfilled should the good be lost). These hard core principles were augmented by many auxiliary hypotheses, theoretical terms, etc. The most important core theorem, reinforced at each stage of the analysis, was the prediction of gains from trade. To conclude this chapter, we reiterate that this is a rational reconstruction of this part of Menger's work designed to highlight its programmatic structure and is not a synopsis pure and simple.

NOTES

1. Menger, 1923. Translated in *Origins of Sociology* by Albin W. Small (Chicago: University of Chicago Press, 1924). Quoted in *The Year of Economists, 1980–1981* compiled by George J. Stigler and Claire Friedland (Chicago: University of Chicago Press, 1980).
2. Karl Menger, *Principles of Economics*, trans. and ed. James Dingwall and Bert F. Hoselitz with an introduction by Frank H. Knight (Glencoe, Illinois: the Free Press, 1950).
3. *Ibid.*, pp. 191–225.
4. Menger's shift from the monopoly model to the competitive model is roughly analogous to the introduction of an *n*-planet solar system (as opposed to a one planet/one sun system) introduced into a physics research programme. If a situation is encountered in the real world which actually has only one sun and one planet then the earlier simpler model may be used. It should be noted that some of the results of this earlier model would not have been retained in the shift to an n-planet model although, of course, the core theorems would have been retained. Similarly, Menger does not retain all results in his shift from the monopoly model to the competitive model; however, his core theorems are retained. (That these other results are not retained is clearly a good thing since they are refuted when faced with a competitive world.) It should also be noted that Menger's inclusion of the monopoly model as an integral step in the development of his hard core is an unusual step as far as work in the neoclassical tradition is concerned. On the one hand, it is testimony to the strength and versatility of the hard core of his programme. On the other hand, it is clear why this step is usually avoided as it acts as a funnel through which only a limited number of core results may proceed.
5. Menger, *Principles of Economics*, p. 133.
6. Some might confuse these with protective belt assumptions; they are not. All hard core assumptions delimit the range of analysis and the universe of discourse. For example, one would not apply the law of universal gravitation to ideas, nor would one apply the law of utility maximization to a rock. The four hard core assumptions listed in the text above delimit Menger's analysis to an exchange world without coercion, affinity and barriers to trade. The reason these are not protective belt assumptions is because Menger did not allow for the possibility that they should be the receptors of the *modus tollens*. In other words, it is not permitted that they provide a local counterexample to correspond to some global counterexample in the development of the positive heuristic. (This is permitted for protective belt

assumptions only.) This is not to say that an attempt might not be made by later researchers to move these assumptions into the positive heuristic.

7. Menger, *Principles of Economics*, p. 206.
8. *Ibid.*, p. 209.
9. *Ibid.*, p. 164.
10. *Ibid.*, p. 163.
11. *Ibiud.*, p. 162.
12. *Ibid.*, p. 242.
13. *Ibid.*, p. 230.

8 Jevons

I have discovered someone whom I had not realized to be very good — namely Jevons. I am convinced that he was one of *the* minds of the century. He has the curiously exciting style of writing which one gets if one is good enough .... At the age of twenty-two he came to himself and realized how eminent he was; he became quite clear that his brain was full of original thoughts. He threw up his post and all his cash and came back to England for further education: it was not long before he bloomed: but he suffered from sleeplessness and depression, and was drowned while bathing at the age of forty odd.[1]

Letter from J. M. Keynes (age 22) to G. L. Strachey, 8 July 1905

In this chapter we highlight the Lakatosian aspects of the work of Jevons. The immediate task is to demonstrate the expansion of the empirical base that Jevons achieves through the development of a series of models. Jevons presents a model involving the allocation of a stock of commodity between two alternative uses. He introduces the law of utility maximization and the law of the variation of utility.[2] Utility in each use is assumed to be a continuous function and the utility function is additive.[3] Let:

x_i; $i = 1, 2$ quantities applied to use i
u_i utility derived from x_i

Jevons predicts that:

$$\frac{du_1}{dx_1} = \frac{du_2}{dx_2} \qquad \text{(J-1)[4] will obtain.}$$

In reality a commodity may be applied to more than two alternative uses. Thus J-1 provides a global counterexample. The assumption of two alternative uses provides the corresponding local counterexample. Jevons generalizes the model to include the possibility of multiple alternative uses by replacing the assumption of two alternative uses with an assumption of multiple alternative uses. Jevons states: "the same reasoning which applies to uses of the same commodity will evidently apply to any two uses, and hence to all uses simultaneously, so that we obtain a series of equations less numerous by a unit than the number of ways of using the commodities."[5] The following prediction over a new range of phenomena is obtained:

$$\frac{du_1}{dx_1} = \frac{du_2}{dx_2} = \ldots = \frac{du_n}{dx_n} \qquad (J-2)$$

Thus, the new model is theoretically progressive. The case of two alternative uses may be considered as a special use of the more general model. If there are only two alternative uses the J-2 reduces to J-1. Thus, former unrefuted content is retained and the theoretical adjustment is demonstrated to be rational in a Lakatosian sense.

The next theoretic adjustment is an example of a semantic change through concept stretching. If commodities may be allocated across time periods then J-2 provides a global counterexample. The corresponding local counterexample is the implicit assumption of a single time period. This assumption is deleted and the term "alternative uses" is re-interpreted to include alternative uses in different time periods.[6] The result is a sophisticated re-interpretation of J-2 which yields a new prediction concerning the allocation of a commodity across different time periods. Clearly former unrefuted content is retained.

If the probability that a commodity will remain employable is not equal to unity, then a rational individual would not behave as the sophisticated J-2 predicts. The corresponding local counterexample is provided by the implicit assumption of certainty. The law of utility maximization is ill-defined in a world of uncertainty. Jevons replaces the assumption of utility maximization with an assumption of expected utility maximization.[7] He makes the additional assumption that probabilities are available to the optimizing agent and he deletes the assumption of certainty. Let:

$v_a; a = 1, 2, \ldots, n$ the final degree of utility of the commodity in period a.[8]

$p_a; a = 1, 2 \ldots, n$ probability that the commodity will remain usable.

Jevons predicts that:

$$v_1p_1 = v_2p_2 = \ldots = v_np_n \qquad \text{(J-3)}^9$$

will obtain. This constitutes a prediction over a new range of phenomena as it concerns the allocation of a commodity across alternative uses in a world of uncertainty. If $p_i = 1$ for all i's, the J-3 reduces to J-2 and former unrefuted content is demonstrated to be retained.

With regard to J-3 Jevons states: "the distribution of commodity described is that which should be made and would be made by a being of perfect good sense and foresight ... no human mind is constructed in this perfect way."[10] Jevons explains this global counterexample by providing the local counterexample to which it corresponds. He states: "So far we have taken no account of the varying influence of an event according to its propinquity or remoteness."[11] To incorporate propinquity into the analysis Jevons replaces his assumption of expected utility maximization with an assumption of expected discounted-utility maximization.[12] Implicitly he makes the additional assumption that the information concerning the rate(s) for discounting utility is (are) available to the optimizing agent. Let:

$q_a; a = 1, 2, \ldots, n$ "the undetermined fractions which express the ratios of present pleasures or pains to those future ones from whose anticipation they arise."[13]

Jevons predicts that:

$$v_1p_1q_1 = v_2p_2q_2 = \ldots = v_np_nq_n \qquad \text{(J-4)}^{14}$$

will obtain. Thus the introduction of the discounting of utility with respect to time has transformed the anomaly of one model into the corroboration of the next. If the q_i's are equated to one another, then J-4 reduces to J-3 and former corroborated content is demonstrated to be retained.

The discounting of utility with respect to time must be considered as irrational if rationality consists in always choosing a condition of greater utility over a condition of lesser utility. J-3 obtains if an individual is maximizing expected utility. J-4 does not equal J-3 when the q_i's of J-4 are not equated to one another. It follows that expected utility is not being maximized in these cases. Jevons recognizes this. He states:

> To secure a maximum of benefit in life, all future events, all future pleasures or pains, should act upon us with the same force as if they were present, allowance being made for their uncertainty. The factor expressing the effect of remoteness should have no influence.[15]

Jevons salvages the law of utility maximization from this apparent contradiction. In his model, utility is not maximized with respect to a moment of time. Considerations of the future influence action only because utility is produced at the present moment from the mere anticipation of future utility. Jevons' meaning is evident from his definition of the q_i's as: "the ratios of present pleasures or pains to those future ones *from whose anticipation they arise*"[16] (italics mine). Thus, the individual is still "rational" in the sense that he obeys the law of utility maximization; however, Jevons feels that his utility function does not display "perfect good sense."[17]

Jevons introduces major theoretic adjustments to develop his theory of exchange. Exchange provides a global counterexample to earlier predictions because it cannot exist as an alternative use of commodity if only one individual and one commodity have been posited. (These are the corresponding local counterexamples.) Jevons supposes two "trading bodies";[18] each of which is in possession of a different commodity. Let:

A, B	trading bodies
a, b	quantity of different commodities held by A and B respectively
x, y	quantity that A trades out of a and that B trades out of b respectively
$\phi_i(z)$; $i = $ A, B	final degree of utility of commodity originally held by A for individual i.
$\Psi_i(z)$; $i = $ A, B	final degree of utility of commodity originally held by B for individual i.

By force of argument Jevons concludes that:

$$\frac{\phi_A(a - x)}{\Psi^A(y)} = \frac{dy}{dx} \tag{J-5}$$

and;

$$\frac{\phi_B(x)}{\Psi^B(b-y)} = \frac{dy}{dx} \qquad \text{(J-6)}$$

will obtain.[19] He introduces the law of indifference which states that 'when two objects or commodities are subject to no important difference as regards the purpose in view, they will either of them be taken instead of the other with perfect indifference by a purchaser."[20] He then demonstrates that:

$$\frac{\phi_A(a-x)}{\psi_A(y)} = \frac{y}{x} = \frac{\phi_B(x)}{\psi_B(b-y)} \qquad \text{(J-7)[21]}$$

will obtain. The laws of supply and demand are an immediate result. They are revealed by the symmetry of J-7. B is the supplier and A is the purchaser from A's point of view. A is the supplier and B is the purchaser from B's point of view.[22]

The linkage with the initial series of models is clear if the term "alternative uses" is expanded to include exchange as a possibility. In this case

$$\frac{du_1}{dx_1} = \frac{\psi_A(y)dy}{dx_2} \qquad \text{(J-8)}$$

obtains for individual A, and is simply a sophisticated variant of J-1. The consolidation of the earlier analysis with the theory of exchange is simple and former corroborated content is retained.

Jevons defines a "trading body" as "any number of people whose aggregate influence in a market, either in the way of supply or demand, we have to consider."[23] He states:

The trading body may be a single individual in one case; it may be the whole inhabitants of a continent in another; it may be the individuals of a trade diffused through a country in a third. England and North America will be trading bodies if we are considering the corn we receive from America in exchange for iron and other goods. The continent of Europe is a trading body as purchasing coal from England. Farmers of England are a trading body when they sell corn to millers, and the millers both when they buy corn from the farmers and sell flour to the bakers.[24]

Jevons defines the term "trading body" in the most general manner[25] to allow for progressive shifts in his programme.

This clever device for speeding the development of the series of models allows for the expansion of the theory to encompass a wide range of phenomena through appropriate manipulation of the term "trading body" as long as the general laws of the theoretic framework apply.[26] This do-it-yourself positive heuristic is simply the explicit recognition of the possibility of isomorphisms, which is a possibility of any mathematical analysis. Clearly Jevons used the term "trading body" as a pedagogic device to impart this message to his not-so-mathematically-inclined colleagues.

If transport cost is significant then trading bodies will not trade in accordance with J-7, and we are provided with a global counterexample. The corresponding local counterexample is the implicit assumption that transport cost is zero. Jevons states:

We have hitherto treated the theory of exchange as if the action of exchange could be carried on without trouble or cost. In reality, the cost of conveyance is almost always of importance, and it is sometimes the principal element in the equation.[27]

The theoretic adjustment is to introduce a transport cost factor. Jevons states: "In whatever mode the changes are payable, they may be conceived as paid by the surrender on importation of a certain fraction of the commodity received."[28] Let:

m, n; where $0 < m < 1$ the proportion of the commodity
$\qquad\qquad 0 < n < 1$ received by individual B and A respectively after the deduction of the cost of transport.

With the transport cost factor, J-7 becomes:

$$\frac{\phi_A(a-x)}{n\psi_A(ny)} = \frac{y}{x} = \frac{m\phi(mx)}{\psi_B(b-y)} \qquad (J-9)^{[29]}$$

With J-9 the range of phenomena in which transport cost is significant falls within the scope of the theory. If $m = 1$ and $n = 1$ then J-9 reduces to J-7 and zero transport cost is demonstrated to be a special case. Thus, former corroborated content is retained.

In cases where there are more than two trading bodies or

more than two commodities J-7 proves to be inaccurate and thus provides a global counterexample. The corresponding local counterexample is the presupposition of only two commodities and trading bodies. A theoretic adjustment permitting three trading bodies and three commodities allows predictions to be made about a new range of phenomena. The resultant predictive equations reduce to J-7 if the stock of commodity held by one of the individuals is set equal to zero.

Jevons gives directions for expanding the predictive scope of the programme to include cases with any number of trading bodies, cases with any number of commodities, and cases in which trading bodies each possess more than one commodity. He states:

> We might proceed in the same way to lay down the conditions of exchange between more numerous bodies, but the principles would be exactly the same. For every quantity of commodity which is given in exchange something must be received; and if portions of the same kind of commodity be received from several distinct parties, then we may conceive the quantity which is given for that commodity to be broken up into as many distinct portions. The exchanges in the most complicated case may thus always be decomposed into simple exchanges, and every exchange will give rise to two equations to determine the quantities involved. The same can also be done when there are two or more commodities in the possession of each trading body.[30]

The empirical base is expanded with each adjustment as new predictions can be made and former corroborated content is retained. Some of the earlier progress, such as the incorporation of transport costs, is not retained formally although the deletion is only for pedagogical reasons. This is a case of retreat and the implicit consolidation.

Jevons lists particular boundary solutions as anomalous.[31] He also lists three cases of indivisibility as providing anomalies to the equations of exchange; the trade of one indivisible commodity for another, the trade of an indivisible commodity for a divisible one, and the exchange of finitely divisible commodities.[32] Jevons does not incorporate these anomalies into the programme although, in subsequent years, they were incorporated into the orthodox-economics programme by other authors as the appropriate mathematical tools became available.[33] Instead of progressively incorporating these anomalies Jevons collects them under the rubric "Failure of the Equations of Exchange."[34] Thus, Jevons uses the exception-barring technique to restrict the range of the theory. The equations of exchange are accepted as valid *except* when confronted with one of the listed anomalies. Jevons reaches several conclusions concerning the cases of indivisibility, but the analysis is *ad hoc*.

Substitutes also prove anomalous to the theory.[35] The local counterexample is provided by the assumption of the additive utility function which precludes interdependence of utility among commodities. In this case Jevons does not eliminate the local and global counterexample. Instead substitutes are re-interpreted as one homogeneous commodity of variable strength which brings them within the domain of the theory.[36] Thus we have the cultivation of consistency through monster-adjustment as it is the empirical base that is re-interpreted. In subsequent years Edgeworth incorporated the anomalies of substitutes and complements through the introduction of the generalized utility function.[37]

J-5 and J-6 may provide global counterexamples when discommodities are considered. The local counterexample is the implicit assumption that exchange involves commodities. The theoretic adjustment consists in allowing discommodities as a unit of analysis and manipulating the signs of the differentials according to whether the commodity in question is received or traded and the signs of the degree of utility functions according to whether the quantity in question yields a positive or negative utility at the margin. Jevons develops the following general equation of exchange to allow for the possibility of discommodities:

$$\phi(a \pm x)dx + \psi(b \pm y)dy = 0 \qquad \text{(J-10)}[38]$$

Jevons analyzes various possible situations: (1) both commodities yield utility, (2) both commodities yield disutility, and (3) one commodity yields disutility and the other yields utility.[39] The first case demonstrates the retention of former corroborated content. Of the second, Jevons states:

It is possible to conceive yet a . . . case in which people should be exchanging two discommodities, that is to say, getting rid of one hurtful substance by accepting in place of it, what is felt to be less hurtful, though still possessing disutility.[40]

In case (3) above, the possessor of the discommodity must pay to have one thing removed. This allows for a major extension in the predictive content of the theory as cost may now be considered. Jevons states:

Any obstacle, however, may be regarded as so much discommodity, whether it be a mountain which has to be bored through to make a railway, or a hollow which has to be filled with an expensive embankment.[41]

The equations of exchange are incorrect as predictions if production possibilities are present. The corresponding local counterexample is the presumed pre-trade possession of commodities at zero cost. The theoretic adjustment is to introduce the possibility of production through the expenditure of labour which the individuals are presumed to have at their disposal. Thus Jevons develops his theory of production. Let:

$\dfrac{dx}{dt}$ "the rate of production"

$\dfrac{dL}{dt}$ "the degree of painfulness of labour"

$\dfrac{du}{dx}$ "the ratio of the increment of utility to the increment of commodity"[42]

He introduces the law of the variation of the painfulness of labour which states that as the duration of labour increases further increments to labour become increasingly more painful.[43] $\frac{dx}{xt}\frac{du}{dx}$ is the reward to labour.[44] $\frac{dx}{dt}\frac{du}{dx} = \frac{du}{dt}\cdot\frac{du}{dt}$ decreases as the quantity of labour is increased because both $\frac{dx}{dt}$ and $\frac{du}{dx}$ decrease with increases in the quantity of labour. $\frac{dL}{dt}$ increases as the quantity of labour is increase. Jevons predicts that the individual will labour up to the point where $\frac{dL}{dt}=\frac{dx}{dt}\frac{du}{dx}$.[45] (Call this equation J-11.) If labour is to be allocated across different possible productive activities then let:

$$\frac{dx}{dL_1} = w_1$$ the increment of commodity x from additional labour in activity one.

$$\frac{dy}{dL_2} = w_2$$ the increment of commodity y from additional labour in activity two.

The individual will allocate his labour so that:

$$\frac{du_1}{dx} w_1 = \frac{du_2}{dy} w_2 \quad \text{(J-12) obtains.}[46]$$

$$\frac{du_1}{dx} = \phi(x). \frac{du_2}{dy} = \psi(y).$$

By substitution we have:

$$\frac{\phi(x)}{\psi(y)} = \frac{w_1}{w_2} \qquad \text{(J-13).}[47]$$

If an individual were to receive the quantity x_1 of the first commodity for quantity y_1 of the second commodity through exchange then the equation of exchange:

$$\frac{\phi(x+x_1)}{\psi(y-y_1)} = \frac{x_2}{y_1}$$

would obtain.[48] In accordance with J-13, the individual's equation of production would be:[49]

$$\frac{\phi(x+x_1)}{\psi(y-y_1)} = \frac{w_2}{w_1}.$$

By substitution we have:

$$\frac{w_2}{w_1} = \frac{y_1}{x_2} \qquad \text{(J-14)}$$

Jevons summarizes:

Let it be observed that, in uniting the theories of exchange and production, a complicated double adjustment takes place in the quantities of commodity involved. Each party adjusts not only its consumption of articles in accordance with their ratio of exchange, but it also adjusts its production of them. The ratio of exchange governs the production as much as the production governs the ratio of exchange.[50]

Labour may be allocated across different pieces of land.[51] Let:

x	output from a piece of land
$P(L)$	output as a function of the quantity of labour
$\dfrac{dx}{dL}$ or $\dfrac{dP(L)}{dL}$	final rate of production

Jevons predicts:

$$\frac{dx_1}{dL} = \frac{dx_2}{dL} = \ldots = \frac{dx_n}{dL} \qquad \text{(J-15)[52]}$$

must obtain. By force of argument, Jevons concludes that sufficient compensation for the final increment of labour to be called forth is $\frac{dx}{dL}$.[53] Therefore sufficient compensation for the total labour expended is $L\ P'(L)$. Therefore $P(L) - LP'(L)$ is the amount of compensation above that necessary to call fourth the quantity of labour L. This excess is rent. Jevons states:

This expression represents the advantage he derives from the possession of land in affording him more profit than other methods of employing his labour. It is therefore the rent which we would ask before yielding it up to another person, or equally the rent which he would be able and willing to pay if hiring it from another.[54]

If the labourer is working on two pieces of land, then the rent may be calculated as:

$$P_1(L_1) + P_2(L_2) - (L_1 + L_2)\, P'(L_1) \qquad \text{(J-16).[55]}$$

J-16 can be generalized to account for n pieces of land. A new range of phenomena has been brought within the predictive scope of the theory. Equations 11, 13, 14 and 16 constitute such predictions. If a commodity is already in one's possession or the cost of acquisition for the individual is zero then the earlier model is adequate. Thus, former corroborated content is retained.

The theory of production is a large step in predictive content,[56] but a small step heuristically. There is an analogy between the role that the initial allocation of labour plays at this stage of the analysis and the role played by the initial allocation of commodities in the earlier models. In the earlier model the commodity is allocated among alternative uses from which utility is gained directly; in the latter model labour-time is allocated among alternative production processes from which utility is gained indirectly.

$$\frac{\phi(x)}{\psi(y)} = \frac{w_2}{w_1} \text{ implies}$$

$$\frac{du_1}{dx}\frac{dx}{dL_1} = \frac{du_2}{dL_2} \text{ which implies}$$

$$\frac{du_1}{dL_1} = \frac{du_2}{dL_2} \qquad\qquad\qquad \text{(J-17)}.$$

The similarity of J-17 to J-1 is evident.

Jevons notes that some commodities are "not produced by separate processes, but are the concurrent or joint results of the same operation."[57] If production processes are not separate then J-12 provides a global counterexample. The corresponding local counterexample is the implicit assumption that production processes are disjoint. The theoretic adjustment is to allow for joint production processes. Consider an operation which always produces two commodities, x and y, in a proportion of m to n. $\frac{dx+dy}{dL}$ is the extra production given an increment to the labour allocated to this process.[58] Let:

$\frac{du_1}{dx}$ extra utility from an increment of x

$\frac{du_2}{dy}$ extra utility from an increment of y

The "aggregate ratio of utility to labour"[59] will be:

$$\frac{du_1}{dx}\frac{dx}{dL} + \frac{du_2}{dy}\frac{dy}{dL}$$

In a two-commodity world with a joint production process there is no derived equation from the sphere of production.[60] A third commodity, z, may be brought into the analysis and an alternative production process introduced. Jevons predicts:

$$\frac{du_1}{dx}\frac{dx}{dL} + \frac{du_2}{dy}\frac{dy}{dL} = \frac{du_3}{dz}\frac{dz}{dL} \qquad \text{(J-18).}[61]$$

The degree of utility would still have to be considered to determine the exact ratios of exchange that would prevail between x, y, and z.[62] Jevons introduces the possibility of multiple joint products. He predicts:

$$du_1 + du_2 + \ldots = du_n + du_{n+1} + \ldots$$

must obtain between any two alternative processes for the optimizing individual.[63] The possibility of negative utility may be accommodated by attaching the appropriate sign to the differential.[64] Thus, Jevons has expanded the empirical base to include the possibility of multiple processes where both commodities and discommodities are produced jointly and the earlier model is seen as a special case of the latter. This concludes the development of the positive heuristic.[65]

In *Criticism and the Growth of Knowledge* Lakatos states:

Most, if not all, Newtonian "puzzles," leading to a series of new variants superseding each other, were foreseeable at the time of Newton's first naive model and no doubt Newton and his colleagues *did* foresee them: Newton must have been fully aware of the blatant falsity of his first variants. Nothing shows the existence of a positive heuristic of a research programme clearer than this fact: this is why one speaks of "models" in research programmes. A "model" is a set of initial conditions (possibly together with some of the observational theories) which one knows is *bound* to be replaced during the further development of the programme, and one even knows, more or less, how.[66]

If, in the above passage, we replace "Newton" with "Jevons" and "Newtonian" with "Jevonian," then the statements remain valid. Certainly, Jevons did see the blatant falsity of the first variants within his programme. We have traced the series of models within Jevons' *Theory* to highlight particularly the positive heuristic. The Lakatosian analysis underlines the Newtonian structure of Jevons' theoretic framework. The incorporation of a series of anomalies marked the progress of Jevons' programme. These anomalies included multiple alternative uses of a commodity, the allocation across different time periods, uncertainty, propinquity, exchange as an alternative use, transport cost, discommodities, production possibilities, multiple alternative production possibilities, and joint products. Each of these anomalies provided a global counterexample at one stage of the analysis. Each became a corroboration of the theory after an appropriate theoretic adjustment and expansion of the theoretical base. Some of the anomalies adduced by Jevons were not managed by the strategy of progressive shifts. Cases of indivisibility were handled by exception-barring and perfect substitutes through monster-adjustment. The progress noted was theoretical progress.

NOTES

1. R. F. Harrod, *John Maynard Keynes* (Harmondsworth, Middlesex,: Penguin, 1972), p. 124.
2. W. Stanley Jevons, *The Theory of Political Economy*, 2nd edn. (London: Macmillan, 1879), (1st edn., 1871), pp. 43–4. The law of the variation of utility takes modern form in the guise of diminishing marginal utility.
3. These assumptions are implicit.
4. "J-1" is simply a label for the equation. Jevons, *The Theory of Political Economy*, p. 60. In this chapter an attempt has been made to use symbols coincident with those used by Jevons. Some changes have been made for typographical reasons and for the sake of clarity.
5. *Ibid.*
6. Jevons does not actually re-interpret the term "alternative uses" but rather the development of his work can be logically understood in such a manner. Whether such an interpretation was in Jevons' consciousness is not a question for the present forum as this is a rational reconstruction.
7. This is implicit.
8. The modern term for "final degree of utility" is marginal utility.
9. Jevons, *The Theory of Political Economy*, p. 72.
10. *Ibid.*
11. *Ibid.*
12. Jevons does not use the term "expected discounted-utility maximization."
13. Jevons, *the Theory of Political Economy*, pp. 72–3.
14. *Ibid.*, p. 73.
15. *Ibid.*, p. 72.
16. *Ibid.*, pp. 72–3.

17. *Ibid.*, p. 72.
18. *Ibid.*, p. 88.
19. *Ibid.*, pp. 99–100.
20. *Ibid.*, p. 92.
21. *Ibid.*, p. 100.
22. *Ibid.*, p. 101. Also implicit here is the assumption that traders are price takers. Jevons' formulation does not give a determinate answer although it is unlikely that Jevons realized this. An Edgeworth box diagram can be used to show that there are many possible solutions.
23. *Ibid.*, p. 88.
24. *Ibid.*, pp. 88–9.
25. *Ibid.*, p. 88.
26. It is clear in the light of modern work on social welfare functions that some of the extensions of the term trading body were not valid in the sense that the general laws of the theoretical framework did not continue to apply.
27. Jevons, *The Theory of Political Economy*, p. 106.
28. *Ibid.*, p. 107.
29. *Ibid.*, p. 108.
30. *Ibid.*, p. 116–17.
31. *ibid.*, p. 119.
32. *Ibid.*, pp. 121–7.
33. See Gerard Debreu, *Theory of Value* (New Haven: Yale University Press, 1959) and Tjalling C. Koopmans, *Three Essays on the State of Economic Science* (New York: McGraw-Hill, 1957).
34. Jevons, *The Theory of Political Economy*, p. 118.
35. Ibid., p. 134. "Much confusion is thrown into the statistical investigation of questions of supply and demand by the circumstances that one commodity can often replace another, and serve the same purposes more or less perfectly."
36. *Ibid.*, pp. 134–7.
37. F. Y. Edgeworth, *Mathematical Physics* (London: Kegan Paul, 1881). On p. 104 Edgeworth states: "The utility is regarded as a function of two variables, not the sum of two functions of each."
38. Jevons, *The Theory of Political Economy*, p. 130.
39. *Ibid.*, pp. 130–4.
40. *Ibid.*, p. 131.
41. *Ibid.*, p. 129.
42. *Ibid.*, p. 175.
43. *Ibid.*, p. 171.
44. *Ibid.*, p. 176.
45. *Ibid.*
46. *Ibid.*, p. 187.
47. *Ibid.*
48. *Ibid.*
49. *Ibid.*
50. *Ibid.*, pp. 187–8.
51. The theory of rent is presented. *Ibid.*, pp. 215–21.

52. *Ibid.*, p. 216.
53. *Ibid.*, p. 217.
54. *Ibid.*, p. 218.
55. *Ibid.*, p. 219.
56. See Chapter II.
57. *Ibid.*, p. 197.
58. *Ibid.*, p. 200.
59. *Ibid.*
60. *Ibid.*
61. *Ibid.*, p. 201.
62. *Ibid.*
63. *Ibid.*
64. *Ibid.*, p. 202.
65. Jevons puts forward a number of predictions concerning capital. However, we need not concern ourselves with these passages because they are *not* included in the heuristic development. Jevons considers the study of capital to be a distinct branch of the discipline (*The Theory of Political Economy*, p. 241). "In considering the nature and principles of Capital, we enter a distinct branch of our subject. There is no close or necessary connection between the employment of capital and the processes of exchange." Capital is precluded from the formal analysis by Jevons' statement of the problem of economics in his conclusion (*ibid.*, p. 289). "Given a certain population, with various needs and powers of production, in possession of certain lands and other sources of material: required, the mode of employing their labour which will maximize the utility of the produce."
66. Imre Lakatos and Alan Musgrave, eds., *Criticism and the Growth of Knowledge* (Cambridge: Cambridge University Press, 1970), p. 136.

9 The Marginalist Research Programme

We are apt to smile at Gossen's boast of having accomplished a Copernican feat. But this boast was less unreasonable than it may seem at first sight. The replacement of the geocentric by the heliocentric system and the replacement of the "classic" by the marginal utility system were performances of the same kind: they were both essentially simplifying and unifying reconstructions. The comparison strikes us as ridiculous only because of the different intellectual standings of astronomy and economics. [1]

Joseph A. Schumpeter

The works of Jevons, Menger and Walras taken together constitute what may be viewed as an overall research programme. In this chapter we note the similarity of the hard cores, around which each of the marginalists based his programme, and the similarity in core theorems and core demonstrations. We will also find that the *differences* in the works of the three marginalists are fruitful for the overall programme in that they assist in the development of the positive heuristic. The marginalists recognized themselves as belonging to what we would now call the same research programme.

Chapters 5, 6, 7, and 8 constitute the "empirical base" of this study. In Chapter 5 the imitation of physics which yielded a structural similarity across the separate works of the marginalists was established. In Chapters 6, 7 and 8 the Lakatosian structure of each of the separate programmes was highlighted through reconstructions. In this chapter, the striking similarity of content across the three programmes of thought, in exactly those areas that are important for programmatic research, is presented. The similarity of content, when combined with the similarity of form, ensured the coherence as a research programme of the works of the marginalists.

A. THE HARD CORE OF THE OVERALL PROGRAMME

The hard core is the set of central ideas which unites the series of models of a programme and which is inviolable. The most important elements of the hard cores of the three separate marginalist frameworks were common to all three. These elements are: (a) the individual as a key unit of analysis, (b) the law of utility maximization, (c) the marginal utility/total utility distinction, (d) the law of diminishing marginal utility, (e) the prevalence of competition and (f) the potency of the equilibrating mechanism. We designate these assumptions as the hard core of the overall programme.

The first four assumptions of this hard core embody what had been formulated prior to the 1870s. However, the marginalists of the 1870s were unique in their inclusion of these ideas in the hard core of a research programme made available to the discipline. The employment of these four assumptions created a chasm between the marginalist framework and classical political economy, although the fifth and sixth assumptions do not separate the programmes.

i. The Individual as Key Unit of Analysis
In the works of the three marginalists there is an emphasis on the individual as the key economic agent. This is particularly true of Jevons and Menger who even try to explain production from an individual perspective. Walras allows for the firm as an economic agent.

ii. The Law of Utility Maximization
The law of utility maximization states that individuals will attempt to maximize their level of utility. Each of the three marginalists places this law at the basis of his science of economics. Jevons states:

To satisfy our wants to the utmost with the least effort — to procure the greatest amount of what is desirable at the expense of the least that is undesirable — in other words, to *maximize pleasure*, is the problem of Economics.[2] (Italics in original)

Menger states: "The leading idea in all the economic activity of men is the fullest possible satisfaction of their needs."[3] Walras states: "Each party to an exchange seeks the greatest possible satisfaction of his wants."[4] Jevons takes the law of utility maximization through several variations. As Jevons' programme progresses within his text we move from a law of utility maximization to a law of expected utility maximization and, finally, to a law of discounted utility maximization. The existence of these variations of the law should not be considered as evidence that the *modus tollens* has been directed at the hard core or that theoretic adjustments to the hard core have occurred. Such a conclusion would imply that the law of utility maximization was not a member of the hard core. There is a connecting similarity among these variations of the law. It is this connecting similarity, which is evident upon inspection, that is inviolable within the programme and that constitutes part of the hard core. A scrutiny of the various forms of a law is of assistance in obtaining a more precise specification of what it is that is "hard" in the various statements of the law.

Jevons' and Menger's use of this law is different than that of Walras. Jevons and Menger consider the law to be universal in the sense that it applies to all human behaviour. Walras, on the other hand, separates the sphere of production from the sphere of consumption when he introduces entrepreneurs who maximize profits instead of utility. Walras states:

We now see that the desire to avoid losses and to make profits is the mainspring of the entrepreneur's actions in demanding productive services and offering products for sale, just as we saw earlier that the desire to obtain maximum satisfaction was the mainspring of the actions of landowners, labourers and capitalists in offering productive services and in demanding products.[5]

Walras has a dual law of utility and profit maximization whereas Jevons and Menger employ a single universal principle of utility maximization. To a large extent, the discipline followed Walras with his dual law of "profit and utility" maximization rather than following Jevons' and Menger's use of one catholic law of utility maximization. It has often been written of Jevons and Menger that they were brilliant on demand aspects of economic phenomena but ignored supply aspects. To a large extent this accusation stems not from a failure on their part so much as from the fissure within the modern theoretic framework caused by the dual law of utility and profit maximization. Developing a programme based on one universal law of utility maximization was a path not taken. Jevons attempted to explain activity in the sphere of production completely within the pleasure/pain principle. As much of Menger's text is concerned with the sphere of production as is concerned with consumption. Some modern economists have recognized the mildly schizophrenic character inherent in modern analysis of having a law of utility maximization and a law of profit maximization both as explanations of human behaviour, but little work has been done. Clearly, the research programme that developed subsequent to the marginalism of the 1870s accepted the dual law of utility and profit maximization.

iii. The Marginal Utility/Total Utility Distinction

Total utility is the whole benefit received from a quantity of a good consumed, and marginal utility is the extra benefit received from the last minute increment of the good consumed. This distinction between total and marginal utility is one of the "marginal ideas" which had appeared before the 1870s but which had not been placed in the hard core of an available research programme prior to that time. All three of the marginalists make this distinction and agree on its fundamental importance. Jevons employs the terms "total utility" and "degree of utility." He states: "We are now in a position to appreciate perfectly the difference between the *total utility* of any commodity and *the degree of utility* of the commodity at any point"[6] (italics in original). Jevons uses mathematical terminology to make the distinction. He defines "u" as the utility function in terms of the quantity of the good "x" and states: "*The degree of utility is*, in mathematical language, *the differential coefficient of u considered as a function of x*, and will itself be another function of x"[7] (italics in original). Menger uses an example to communicate the distinction. He states:

The lives of men depend on satisfaction of their need for food in general. But it would be entirely erroneous to regard all food they consume as being necessary for the maintenance of their lives or even their health .... The separate concrete acts of satisfying the need for food accordingly have very different degrees of importance.[8]

It is clear from the passages surrounding this quote that by "degree of importance associated with each concrete act of satisfaction" Menger means marginal utility. Walras makes the distinction as follows:

let the term *effective utility* designate the sum total of wants satisfied by any given *quantity consumed* of a commodity . . . let the term *rareté* designate the intensity of the last want satisfied by any given quantity consumed.[9] (Italics in original)

iv. The Law of Diminishing Marginal Utility

The law of diminishing marginal utility states that as the quantity of a good consumed increases, the marginal utility decreases. Jevons states the law thus: "We may state as a general law, that the degree of utility varies with the quantity of commodity, and ultimately decreases as that quantity increases."[10] Menger states the law as follows:

We see now, in addition, that the satisfaction of any one specific need has, up to a certain degree of completeness, relatively the highest importance, and that further satisfaction has a progressively smaller importance, until eventually a stage is reached at which a more complete satisfaction of that particular need is a matter of indifference.[11]

Walras' statement of the law is succinct: "*rareté* increases as the quantity possessed decreases, and vice versa."[12] Each of the marginalists presented this law as one of the great discoveries of the science. In this regard, Jevons states: "The final degree of utility is that function upon which the theory of Economics will be found to turn."[13] The law of diminishing marginal utility is another "marginalist idea" that had been formulated prior to the 1870s but had never before been made available as part of a hard core.

v. The Prevalence of Perfect Competition

Perfect competition may be said to prevail in a particular market when there is perfect information, a large number of competitive (non-colluding) buyers and sellers, a standardized desirable good, and a single price. It is difficult to be precise in this context because each of the marginalists handles perfect competition differently and none of the three gives an explicit definition. This amorphousness is due to the fact that the marginalists were *not in substantive disagreement* with the classical political economists over this assumption.

Walras' conception of perfect competition must be gleaned from his description of markets in the real world, although our above formulation provides a relatively accurate description of his conception. He concludes a descriptive passage with the statement:

> The whole world may be looked upon as a vast general market made up of diverse special markets where social wealth is bought and sold. Our task then is to discover the laws to which these purchases and sales tend to conform automatically. To this end, we shall suppose that the market is perfectly competitive, just as in pure mechanics we suppose, to start with, that machines are perfectly frictionless. [14]

Jevons' emphasis is on perfect knowledge and non-collusive behaviour. He avoids the need to assume large numbers by postulating that a single price will prevail. He introduces his assumption of perfect competition through the definition of a market. He states:

> By a market I shall mean two or more persons dealing in two or more commodities, whose stocks of those commodities and intentions of exchanging are known to all. It is also essential that the ratio of exchange between any two persons should be known to all the others. It is only so far as this community of knowledge extends that the market extends. Any persons who are not acquainted at the moment with the prevailing ratio of exchange, or whose stocks are not available for want of communication, must not be considered part of the market. Secret or unknown stocks of a commodity must also be considered beyond stocks of a market so long as they remain secret and unknown. Every individual must be considered as exchanging from a pure regard to his own requirements or private interests, and there must be perfectly free competition, so that anyone will exchange with anyone else for the slightest apparent advantage. There must be no conspiracies for absorbing and holding supplies to produce unnatural ratios of exchange. [15]

Jevons sums up his definition as follows: "A market, then

is theoretically perfect only when all traders have perfect knowledge of the conditions of supply and demand, and the consequent ratio of exchange." [16]

Menger, along with Jevons and Walras, is concerned with explaining economic phenomena in a competitive world. He emphasizes the development within a progressing society of large numbers of competitive buyers and sellers and of an increase in the flow and availability of information. (In contrast to Jevons' and Walras' single price, Menger argues that, in a stable situation, price will vary over a very narrow range.) Menger justifies the use of a competitive model by arguing that competition is the state towards which society tends. He states: "the need for competition itself calls forth competition, provided there are no social or other barriers in the way." [17]

There are no patently clear real-world anomalies to the "marginalist ideas" presented here as the first four hard core laws of the programme. On the other hand there is an obvious anomaly to the fifth hard core assumption — the prevalence of perfect competition — which is provided by the existence of monopolies. It is interesting to compare how each marginalist treats this anomaly. Walras uses lemma-incorporation. In other words, he makes it clear that his theory is meant to apply only to the universe of phenomena where perfect competition applies, by associating with each theorem the statement that perfect competition has been assumed. Walras chastises other economists in this regard. He states:

Once a principle has been scientifically established, the first thing that one can do is to distinguish immediately between the cases to which the principle applies and those to which it does not apply. Conversely, the fact that economists have often extended the principle of free competition beyond the limits of its true applicability is proof positive that the principle has not been demonstrated. [18]

Walras investigates the case of monopoly but keeps this framework analytically separate from the main body of his programme. Jevons uses the monster-barring technique to manage the anomaly of monopoly. This is done by introducing the assumption of perfect competition *through a definition*. With Jevons the anomaly of monopoly cannot arise, since his theory deals only with markets and markets are, by his definition, perfectly competitive. With the exception of this act of monster-barring, Jevons ignores the problem of monopolies in his *Theory*. Walras' employment of lemma-incorporation is clearly preferable to Jevons' convoluted definition of a market. Menger asserts that the logical development of the economic forms within his text parallels the actual historical development of these economic forms in society. With regard to monopoly, Menger states:

> Monopoly, interpreted as an actual condition and not as a social restriction on free competition, is therefore, as a rule, the earlier and more primitive phenomenon, and competition the phenomenon coming later in time. Anyone wishing to expound the phenomena prevailing under competition will therefore find it to his advantage to begin with the phenomena of monopoly trade.[19]

Within the sweep of his programme Menger arrives at a monopoly model and then transforms it into a competitive model. The shift from one model to the next within any programme can be judged as rational or otherwise only in the light of the target of the research. (To use an analogy, the appropriateness of an adjustment to a map is dependent both upon the terrain which one is attempting to chart and the purpose of the map.) Upon examination it is clear that the shift from the monopoly model to the competitive model within Menger's programme is rational (in a Lakatosian sense) *given that it is a perfectly competitive world which he is attempting to capture*. This may seem puzzling since there is a gain as well as a loss in content in the shift from the monopoly to the competitive model. The important point to note is that if we are attempting to model a competitive world then the loss is of *refuted* content. The advantage of Menger's approach is that it displays the power of certain parts of his hard core to cover diverse cases. A retreat may be made to the monopoly model, where this is judged useful. The disadvantage of his approach is that the target of theoretical activity has been shifted (from monopoly to competition) in the midstream of the programme. This has the potential to cause confusion. Walras' technique of using lemma-incorporation and of providing a separate framework for examining monopolies appears to have been the best alternative at this stage of economic theorizing.

vi. The Potency of the Equilibrating Mechanism

The assumption of the potency of the equilibrating mechanism is that markets clear rapidly through price and quantity adjustments. There are two aspects to Walras' equilibrating mechanism. He postulates that an excess demand will increase price and an excess supply will decrease price. He also postulates that productive capacity will move into venues where revenues exceed costs and move out where costs exceed revenues. Walras describes the equilibrium which is approached through this dual mechanism as follows:

The current equilibrium prices are those at which the demand and the supply of each service or product are equal and at which the *selling price* of each product is equal to the *cost of production*, i.e., the cost of the productive services employed.[20] (Italics in original)

Walras goes into extraordinary detail in his description of the equilibrating process and introduces the now famous "Walrasian auctioneer." With each successive stage in his series of models he describes the process through which equilibrium may be achieved in the more articulated model. Some of these descriptions consume the whole chapter.

Jevons, like Walras, assumes that markets approach equilibrium rapidly through both price and quantity adjustments. Unlike Walras, Jevons does not engage in an extended discussion of the mechanism. He suggests that the complexity of the equilibrating mechanism places it almost beyond the reach of words. He states:

Let it be observed that, in uniting the theories of exchange and production, a complicated double adjustment takes place in the quantities of commodity involved. Each party adjusts not only its consumption of articles in accordance with their ratio of exchange, but it also adjusts its production of them. The ratio of exchange governs the production as much as the production governs the ratio of exchange .... It is not easy to express in words how the ratios of exchange are finally determined. They depend upon a general balance of producing power and of demand as measured by the final degree of utility.[21]

Jevons' absolute rejection of the possibility of overproduction is evidence of his confidence in the power of the equilibrating mechanism. He states:

Early writers on Economics were always in fear of a supposed glut, arising from the powers of production surpassing the needs of consumers, so that industry would be stopped, employment fail, and all but the rich would be starved by the superfluity of commodities. The doctrine is evidently absurd and self-contradictory.[22] (Italics in original)

Menger's conception of the equilibrating mechanism is basically the same as Walras' and Jevons' although it is the most primitive of the three. Like Jevons and Walras, he postulates that markets clear rapidly through an equilibrating mechanism. However, Menger's equilibrating mechanism involves only price adjustments which, he argues, usually take place "from above." Menger presents a demand function which is inversely related to price and a supply function with zero elasticity. It is evident that quantity adjustments were not considered by Menger because he was trying to capture the elements of the very short run.

B. CORE THEOREMS AND CORE PROOFS

As mentioned above, there is a set of core theorems with attendant demonstrations which is common among the marginalist trio. Although conjectures become more refined as a programme shifts from one model to the next, there remains an identifiable continuity within a given series of theorems associated with the series of models. This identifiable continuity within a series of theorems is called a *core theorem*. There is also an identifiable continuity within a research programme with regard to the argument which supports a core theorem. This is called a *core demonstration*. The core demonstrations of a programme link the hard core to the core theorems. A research programme is identified not only by its hard core but also by its core theorems and core demonstrations. In this section we will identify four core theorems of the marginalist research programme. These four theorems are: (a) the social welfare theorem, (b) the equimarginal theorem,[23] (c) the bond between marginal utility and value, and (d) the theorem that factor services obtain their marginal product. We shall also give a brief discussion of the attendant core demonstrations.

i. The Social Welfare Theorem

The social welfare theorem states that completely free trade will result in a maximum of utility for each individual and for society given the initial distribution of wealth. This is the most important theorem which connects the three marginalists. Jevons states this theorem as follows: "so far as is consistent with the inequality of wealth in every community, all commodities are distributed by exchange so as to produce the maximum of benefit."[24] Jevons derives this result from a combination of the assumptions of no coercion and no affinity with the hard core assumption of utility maximization. The core demonstration which links the hard core to the social welfare theorem is simple. Jevons states as follows: "No one is ever required to give what he more desires for what he less desires, so that perfect freedom of exchange must be to the advantage of all."[25]

Any *effective* restriction on trade will prevent some trades from taking place that would have occurred in the absence of the restriction. If individuals are utility maximizers and they are being prevented by a restriction from making a trade in which they would otherwise have engaged, then they are being forced by the restriction to a lower level of utility than they would otherwise have enjoyed. Jevons retains the core theorem of social welfare through each stage of the programme and the core demonstration supports it throughout the series of models.

At an early stage in the development of his programme Walras states the social welfare theorem:

The exchange of the two commodities for each other in a perfectly competitive market is an operation by which all holders of either one, or, of both, of the two commodities can obtain the greatest possible satisfaction of their wants consistent with the condition that the two commodities are bought and sold at one and the same ratio of exchange throughout the market.[26]

Walras places the greatest possible emphasis on this theorem; he centres the development of pure economic theory around it. In reference to the social welfare theorem he states:

The main object of the theory of social wealth is to generalize this proposition by showing, first, that it applies to the exchange of several commodities for one another as well as to the exchange of two commodities for each other, and secondly, that, under perfect competition, it applies to production as well as to exchange .... We may say, therefore, that his proposition embraces the whole of pure and applied economics.[27]

According to Walras, the *Elements* may be thought of as a series of "proofs" demonstrating the validity of the social welfare theorem over an ever-broadening empirical base. Walras employs the same core demonstration as does Jevons.

Menger presents the social welfare theorem in two separate steps. In the first step he points out the gains from trade. He states:

if command of a certain amount of A's goods were transferred to B and if command of a certain amount of B's goods were transferred to A, the needs of both economizing individuals could be better satisfied than would be the case in the absence of this reciprocal transfer.[28]

In the second step he demonstrates that economizing individuals will engage in trade right up to the limit of their advantage so that their gains are maximized Menger describes this limit:

Above all we would find, in each instance and at any given point in time, a limit up to which two persons can exchange their goods to their mutual economic advantage ... this limit is reached when one of the two bargainers has no further quantity of goods which is of less value to him than a quantity of another good at his disposal of the second bargainer who, at the same time, evaluates the two quantities of goods inversely.[29]

The concatenation of these two steps yields the social welfare theorem. Menger's core demonstration is fundamentally the same as Jevons' and Walras'.

ii. The Equimarginal Theorem

The second common core theorem is the equimarginal theorem, which states that the utility maximizing consumer will purchase that bundle of commodities which sets the ratio of the marginal utility to the price for each commodity equal across all commodities. Walras states the theorem as follows:

Given two commodities in a market, each holder attains maximum satisfaction of wants, or maximum effective utility, when the ratio of the intensities of the last wants satisfied (by each of these goods), or the ratio of their *raretés*, is equal to the price.[30]

Walras reformulates this core theorem at each stage of the development of his programme. In another place Walras states the theorem more simply: "Values in exchange are proportional to *raretés*."[31] This core theorem follows from the hard core assumptions of utility maximization and diminishing marginal utility. The core demonstration associated with this theorem involves the simple problem in calculus of maximizing a utility function under an income constraint. Walras uses the theorem of maximum satisfaction to derive the laws of supply and demand.

Jevons states the equimarginal theorem as follows: "The ratio of exchange of any two commodities will be the reciprocal of the ratio of the final degrees of utility of the quantities of commodity available for consumption after the exchange is completed."[32] Jevons, like Walras, derives from this theorem the laws of demand and supply which he calls the "equations of exchange." We have Walras' word that Jevons' core theorem of maximum satisfaction is identical to his own. In the Preface to the first edition of the *Elements* Walras states: "Mr. Jevons . . . founds the whole application of mathematics to economics on a fundamental formula which serves as my point of departure and which I call the condition of maximum satisfaction."[33] Jevons also uses the same core demonstration as does Walras. Menger's statement of the condition of maximum satisfaction is as follows:

The end result of this procedure is that the most important of the satisfactions that cannot be achieved have the same importance for every kind of need, and hence that all needs are being satisfied up to an equal degree of importance of the separate acts of satisfaction.[34]

For this formulation of the equimarginal theorem to be precisely the same as Jevons' and Walras', Menger would have to have said that "the most important of the satisfactions that cannot be achieved have the same importance for every kind of need" for each extra dollar spent on them. However, this aspect of the theorem was implicit in the example which Menger discussed. Menger's core demonstration, although verbal, is the same as Jevons' and Walras'.

iii. The Bond between Marginal Utility and Value

The third common core theorem is the bond between marginal utility and value. All three marginalists emphasize that prices are determined by marginal utility, and that the values of productive services follow from the values of products rather than the other way around. Jevons states: "Value depends solely on the final degree of utility."[35] On the next page he states: "I hold labour to be *essentially variable*, so that *its value must be determined by the value of the produce, not the value of the produce by that of the labour*" (italics in original).[36] Walras makes the same point: "It is not the cost of the productive services that determines the selling price of the product, but rather the other way around."[37] Walras realizes that in a general equilibrium model all of the variables are dependent upon one another. Simultaneously, he insists on this sequential causality. He asserts that it is the *raretés* which determine the values of products and it is the value of products which determines the values of productive services. He defends this apparent inconsistency by arguing that some influences on a variable may be of a higher order of magnitude than others. In such cases, he argues, the influence of the variable of the higher magnitude may be considered as the cause. Walras' sequential causality is to be interpreted in this light.

Menger discusses the bond between marginal utility and value. (Recall that for Menger the term "goods of higher order" refers to productive services of raw materials and the term "goods of lower order" refers to products that are directly consumable.) Menger states:

We therefore have the principle that the value of goods of higher order is dependent upon the expected value of the goods of lower order they serve to produce. Hence goods of higher order can attain value, or retain it once they have it, only if, or as long as, they serve to produce goods that we expect to have value for us. If this fact is established, it is clear also that the value of goods of higher order cannot be the *determining* factor in the prospective value of the corresponding goods of lower order. Nor can the value of the good of lower order be the determining factor in its present value. On the contrary, the value of goods of higher order is, in all cases, regulated by the prospective value of the corresponding goods of lower order to whose production they have been or will be assigned by economizing men.[38]

iv. The Theorem that Factor Services Obtain the Value of Their Marginal Product

Our fourth common core theorem is that factor services obtain the value of their marginal product. This core theorem states that each factor service obtains a return which is exactly equivalent to its contribution to the productive process. The marginalists directed this principle particularly at the return to labour. Jevons states: "the competition to obtain proper workmen will strongly tend to secure to the latter all legitimate share in the ultimate produce."[39] And he states:

Every labourer ultimately receives the due value of his produce after paying a proper fraction to the capitalist for the remuneration of abstinence and risk. At the same time, workers of different degrees of skill receive very different shares according as they contribute a common or a scarce kind of labour to the result.[40]

Menger's statement of the same principle is more emotive:[41]

It may well appear deplorable to a lover of mankind that possession of capital or a piece of land often provides the owner a higher income for a given period of time than the income received by a laborer for the most strenuous activity during the same period. Yet the cause of this is not immoral, but simply that the satisfaction of more important human needs depends upon the services of the given amount of capital or piece of land than upon the services of the laborer. *The agitation of those who would like to see society allot a larger share of the available consumption goods to laborers than at present really constitutes, therefore, a demand for nothing else than paying labor above its value.* For if the demand for higher wages is not coupled with a program for the more thorough training of workers, or if it is not confined to advocacy of freer competition, it requires that workers be paid not in accordance with the value of their services to society, but rather with a view to providing them with a more comfortable standard of living, and achieving a more equal distribution of consumption goods and of the burdens of life. A solution of the problem on this basis, however, would undoubtedly require a complete transformation of our social order.[42] (Italics mine)

Walras states the theorem in more nearly modern terminology:

In a state of equilibrium, when cost of production and selling price are equal, the prices of the services are proportional to their marginal productivities, i.e. to the partial derivatives of the production function.[43]

This theorem, in combination with the minimization of cost of production, Walras calls the "theory of marginal productivity."[44] Concerning this theory, Walras states that it is:

a cardinal theory in pure economics . . . because it shows the underlying motive of the demand for services and the offer of products by entrepreneurs, just as the *theory of final utility* shows the underlying motive of the demand for products and offer of services by landowners, workers, and capitalists.[45]

Walras recognized that Jevons' concept was similar. Referring to the theory of marginal productivity, Walras states: "the germ of which is to be found in Chapters VI and VII of Jevons's *Theory of Political Economy*."[46]

C. THE POSITIVE HEURISTIC

The positive heuristic of the overall programme has four sources. First, there are those aspects of individual positive heuristics which some of the founders successfully incorporated and others did not. There will be an attempt to secure the position of these corroborations of the programme. Second, there will be those parts of individual positive heuristics which have not yet been incorporated into any of the individual programmes. The overall programme will turn its attention to these anomalies which can be identified through an examination of the protective belt. Third, new techniques of analysis may allow some formerly hard core assumption to be moved to the protective belt and, thereby, eventually, become a part of the positive heuristic. Finally, there may be an attempt by the overall programme to explain anomalies that had not been foreseen by the founders. We shall mention examples of all these. One thing is clear. Those aspects of the positive heuristic which all of the founders had in common and successfully incorporated will *not* become a part of the positive heuristic of the overall programme. They will be considered corroborations of the programme and no reason would be seen to repeat their work. It is also important to note that the ordering of the positive heuristic of the overall programme is not fixed. The particular direction into which some normal scientist takes the programme is to some extent arbitrary as long as the anomaly which he addresses is a part of the positive heuristic. For example, it is arbitrary whether the introduction of a generalized utility function or the introduction of uncertainty takes precedence.

First, let us examine those aspects of the positive heuristic which all three founders managed to incorporate or bypassed as an obvious, and therefore implicit, step in the development of their programme. It is this series of models which we would expect *not* to remain a part of the active research of the overall programme but rather to be relegated to the textbooks. All of the marginalists developed their exchange model through the two-commodity phase and then to the N-commodity phase. The following possibilities were thoroughly explored: multiple alternative uses of a commodity, exchange as an alternative use of a commodity, each individual initially holding a bundle of many different commodities, the exchange of one commodity for another, exchange of a quantity of commodity at a ratio of one-to-one, exchange at any given ratio of exchange, and many holders of different commodities. These possible applications for the overall programme having been thoroughly established, they become corroborations in at least a theoretical sense and do not consitute part of the overall positive heuristic.

Next let us examine those aspects of the individual positive heuristic which were not incorporated by all of the founders or, perhaps, were not incorporated at all but rather recognized and then managed in an *ad hoc* fashion. These shall become part of the overall programme's positive heuristic. The fact that some of the founders manage to incorporate some aspect of an individual positive heuristic while others fail to incorporate that same aspect does not constitute sufficient grounds for removing this aspect from the overall programme's positive heuristic and, thus, for considering it as a corroboration of the overall programme. The reason for this is that the overall programme will not only be attempting to incorporate anomalies which one founder succeeded in incorporating into his own programme while others failed, but also trying to incorporate anomalies which those other programmes successfully incorporated which the initial founder ignored. Thus, it must be demonstrated that all of these anomalies, some having been incorporated in one individual programme, some having been incorporated in another, can consistently be incorporated into one overall programme. This is an area for active research and belongs in the positive heuristic. Some of the elements of individual positive heuristics which fall into this category and some of which we shall discuss presently are: production, substitution in production, prices of capital goods, time periods, uncertainty, propinquity, transport costs, discommodities, joint products, the *numéraire*, money, degree of marketability, depreciation and insurance on capital goods, new capital goods held for sale by producers in the form of products, stocks of income goods in the homes of consumers consisting of consumers' goods, stocks of income goods held by producers consisting of raw materials held for future use, new income goods consisting of consumers' goods and raw materials held for sale by the producers of these goods, and monopoly.

Walras deals with production problems through the introduction on the law of profit maximization whereas both Jevons and Menger attempt to manage production under the universal law of utility maximization. The overall programme, in fact, picked up on Walras' technique. Thus, those anomalies which Menger and Jevons had incorporated concerning the sphere of production would have to be reexamined by the overall programme. For example, Jevons had incorporated time periods, uncertainty, propinquity, transportation costs, discommodities and joint products. Walras had looked at none of these explicitly. These, therefore, need to be reincorporated by the programme as a whole. This does not mean that Jevons' work was wasted. On the contrary, most of these anomalies will be able to be incorporated through the same or very similar theoretic adjustments as those Jevons used. Thus, the hard part of the research is done. It is this work which lays the foundation for the overall programme. As the anomalies which had been incorporated by Jevons or Menger are dealt with, there must be an ongoing re-examination of those incorporated by Walras to ensure compatibility. Those anomalies separately incorporated by Walras include: substitutes in production (Menger handles these also, but very poorly), prices of capital goods, depreciation and insurance on capital goods, and capital and income goods held in stocks by households or producers.

Walras uses the *numéraire* and the concept of services of availability to introduce money. Menger uses degree of marketability to introduce money. Jevons ignores money in his *Theory*. The incorporation of money would be expected to become an outstanding problem for the programme as a whole. Walras' notion of "services of availability" constitutes a transaction demand for money and relies on a predictable future. It is not immediately clear that his formulation is adequate with the incorporation of uncertainty into a dynamic framework. Menger's degree-of-marketability perhaps allows for a wider scope. Modern macroeconomics uses a concept very similar to Menger's degree-of-marketability by its manifold definition of money as M^1, M^2, M^3, . . ., M_∞. The incorporation of money into the modern marginalist framework as anything other than a superfetation has proved to be difficult. To a large extent, this is the problem of the microfoundations of macroeconomics.

Our three marginalists handle monopoly differently. Jevons uses the classic monster-adjustment technique to eliminate the possibility. He defines a market in such a way as to exclude anything which is not competitive from the category. Walras' solution is to separate monopoly from competition; perhaps this is the best solution here. Walras avoids monopoly in the mainstream of his programme through lemma-incorporation. In other words, the condition of competition is included in the statement of each result. Walras' results are not meant to refer to monopoly. He provides a separate analysis. This is preferable to Jevons' technique because monster-adjustment hides the anomaly whereas lemma-incorporation highlights it as a restriction and simultaneously maintains the validity of the theory. Menger incorporates monopoly as an early stage in the development of his series of models. This is not a bad alternative, although it can be confusing in a pedagogical sense. The source of possible confusion is in the shift from the monopoly model to the competitive model as some predictions of the monopoly model, such as the particular determined price, will not hold for the competitive model. Thus, in the shift to the competitive model there may be thought to have been a loss of content producing an ambiguous, and not necessarily progressive, shift in the programme. This is an incorrect view because it is that very recognition of competition in the real world as the new goal of theoretical activity that now refutes those theorems which were only true for the monopoly model but are not true for the competitive model. If you are trying to model a competitive world, such a shift is progressive. The advantage of handling monopoly as an integral step in the development of the programme is that it emphasizes the universality of the hard core. Menger saw the further advantage that a logical programme developed in this manner paralled the actual historical development. The disadvantage is the possible confusion stated above.

Next we examine that part of the positive heuristic which had not yet been incorporated by any marginalists but was either promised as a part of the future development or hinted at in the formulation of the protective belt. One aspect of the positive heuristic promised but not developed to any significant degree was the move to a dynamic model. By a dynamic model we mean, among other things, that newly produced capital goods become active in the production process during the period under consideration. Jevons states:

We must carefully distinguish, at the same time, between the Statics and Dynamics of this subject. The real condition of industry is one of perpetual motion and change . . . . If we wished to have a complete solution of the problem in all its mutual complexity, we should have to treat it as a problem of motion in a problem of dynamics.[47]

Jevons, however, does not take this step. Walras also tells us of his concern for the dynamic. As he approaches the last steps of his own heuristic, he states:

Our economy will then be ready to function, and we shall be in a position, if we so desire, to pass from the static to the dynamic point of view. In order to make this transition we need only suppose the data of the problem, viz. the quantities possessed, the utility of want curves, etc., to vary as a function of *time*. The fixed equilibrium will then be transformed into a *variable* or *moving* equilibrium, which re-establishes itself automatically as soon as it is disturbed.[48]

And then he states:

Finally, in order to come wtill more closely to reality, we must drop the hypothesis of an annual market period and adopt in its place the hypothesis of a continuous market. Thus, we pass from the static to the dynamic state.[49]

Walras discusses the dynamic situation but only through an arithmetical example which is reminiscent of Quesnay's *Tableau Économique*. He does not successfully incorporate the dynamic aspects of the programme nor could he, given his mathematical training. This problem had to wait for the normal scientists of the programme. Menger often alludes to dynamic topics, such as growth, in his discussion, but does not bring this into his programme in a manner that would warrant the term incorporation.

Another aspect of reality all but ignored by the three marginalists in the development of their respective programmes is the distinction between fixed and variable costs. Walras brings this into his protective belt. He states: "In making this assumption (fixed coefficients of production), we are neglecting another matter, namely that of the distinction between fixed and variable costs in business."[50] This is an anomaly that we would expect the overall programme to adopt as a part of its positive heuristic. Walras mentions but does not incorporate two more anomalies. He states:

> In our description of the mechanism of exchange, production and capital formation, we have not only assumed perfect freedom of competition in the markets for products, services and capital goods, but we have also abstracted from two: first, the method of appropriation of services concerning which we made no special assumptions, and, second, the role of the State, its services and its needs. It is manifest, however, that an economy cannot function without the intervention of an authority empowered to maintain order and security, to render justice, to guarantee national defence, and to perform many other services besides.[51]

The method of appropriation of services and the role of the state were not properly incorporated into the series of models. Walras discusses taxation but he keeps this analysis separate from the main body. Jevons also discusses the method of appropriation of services. He states:

> It is obvious, however, that there are many intricacies in a matter of this sort. It is not always possible to graduate work to the worker's liking; in some businesses a man who insisted on working only a few hours a day would soon have no work to do. In the professions of law, medicine, and the like, it is the reputation of enjoying a large practice which attracts new clients.[52]

The lumpiness of some services and the role of the state might be expected to be on the overall programme agenda.

Next we look at those aspects of reality which the founding marginalists had avoided, but which with the advance of technique, mainly mathematical, could be incorporated into the analysis. The most important example of this was the additive utility function which was part of the hard core for each of the individual marginalists and which precluded them from explaining complements and substitutes in consumption in anything but an *ad hoc* manner. As more sophisticated mathematics became available to the profession it became possible to shift the additive utility function out of the hard core and to the protective belt. With the shift to a generalized utility function, substitutes and complements in consumption and production become corroborations of the overall programme. Other anomalies which become handled in a much more satisfactory manner with the introduction of more sophisticated mathematics include discontinuous utility functions, divisible goods, and particularly the development of dynamic analysis.

Finally, there is an attempt by the overall programme to explain anomalies that the founders did not foresee as a part of the positive heuristic. The most obvious cases of this are the attempts to explain monetary crises, persistent disequilibrium in the labour market, and disequilibria more generally. Walras certainly recognized the existence of such possibilities but he did not see any possibility of incorporating these phenomena. He states:

> The diversion of productive services from enterprises that are losing money to profitable enterprises takes place in various ways, the most important being through credit operations, but at best these ways are slow. It can happen in the real world, that under some circumstances a selling price will remain for long periods of time above cost of production and continue to rise in spite of increases in output, while under other circumstances a fall in price, following upon this rise, will suddenly bring the selling price below cost of production and force entrepreneurs to reverse their production policies. For, just as a lake is, at times, stirred to its very depths by a storm, so also the market is sometimes thrown into violent confusion by crises, which are sudden and general disturbances of equilibrium. The more we know of the ideal conditions of equilibrium, the better we shall be able to control or prevent these crises.[53]

Menger also recognizes the possibilities of such crises. Jevons discounts the possibility of general underconsumption. Persistent general disequilibria still remain to be explained within the modern marginalist research programme, and research in this area is active.

D. THE SELF-RECOGNITION OF A RESEARCH PROGRAMME

The works of the three marginalists (and of Gossen) were recognizable, to those familiar with the material, as belonging to what we would now call a research programme. When Walras encountered the works of Jevons, Gossen and

Menger, he immediately recognized the strong similarity to his own work. He admitted their precedence as far as the discovery of the basic principles of the science was concerned. He felt compelled to proclaim that he had no knowledge of their existence when constructing his own framework.

Jevons, when confronted with the work of Gossen, recognized the similarity, gave credit to Gossen for the earliest discovery of the fundamental principles, and also felt compelled to deny knowledge of the work prior to the development of his own. Jevons recognized Walras' work as belonging to the same programme; the two men became regular correspondents. Howey quotes a letter from Jevons to Walras; "'It is satisfactory to me to find that my theory of exchange,' he [Jevons] wrote on May 12, 1874, 'which, when published in England, was either neglected or criticized, is practically confirmed by your researches.'"[54] Howey quotes another letter from Jevons to Walras: "In 1875 Jevons wrote to Walras, whom he regarded as an ally. 'I have no doubt whatever about the ultimate success of our efforts, but it will take some fighting.'"[55] Jevons did not know of Menger's work but there can be little doubt that he would have agreed with Walras' assessment that it belonged to the same programme. Menger learned of Walras' work through a third party. It took some time for the Austrians to recognize the similarities in the works. One may presume that this delay was due to the mathematical intricacies in Walras' presentation.

NOTES

1. Joseph A. Schumpeter, *History of Economic Analysis* (New York: Oxford University Press, 1954), p. 919.
2. W. Stanley Jevons, *The Theory of Political Economy*, 2nd edn. (London: Macmillan, 1879), (1st edn., 1871), p. 37.
3. Karl Menger, *Principles of Economics*, trans. and ed. James Dingwall and Bert F. Hoselitz with an introduction by Frank H. Knight (Glencoe, Illinois: The Free Press, 1950), p. 240.
4. Leon Walras. *Elements of Pure Economics*, trans. William Jaffe (London: George Allen and Unwin 1954), p. 143.

5. *Ibid.*, p. 225.
6. Jevons, *The Theory of Political Economy*, p. 49.
7. *Ibid.*, p. 51.
8. Menger, *Principles of Economics*, p. 124.
9. Walras, *Elements of Pure Economics*, p. 119.
10. Jevons, *The Theory of Political Economy*, p. 52.
11. Menger, *Principles of Economics*, p. 125.
12. Walras, *Elements of Pure Economics*, p. 120.
13. Jevons, *The Theory of Political Economy*, p. 52.
14. Walras, *Elements of Pure Economics*, p. 84.
15. Jevons, *The Theory of Political Economy*, pp. 85–6.
16. *Ibid.*, p. 87.
17. Menger, *Principles of Economics*, p. 217.
18. Walras, *Elements of Pure Economics*, pp. 256–7.
19. Menger, *Principles of Economics*, p. 217.
20. Walras, *Elements of Pure Economics*, p. 42.
21. Jevons, *The Theory of Political Economy*, pp. 187–8.
22. *Ibid.*, p. 207.
23. Mark Blaug, *Economic Theory in Retrospect*, 2nd edn. (London: Heinemann Educational Books, 1977), p. 301. Blaug employs the phrase "equimarginal principle" to label this core theorem.
24. Jevons, *The Theory of Political Economy*, p. 153.
25. *Ibid.*
26. Walras, *Elements of Pure Economics*, p. 143.
27. *Ibid.*
28. Menger, *Principles of Economics*, pp. 177–8.
29. *Ibid.*, p. 187.
30. Walras, *Elements of Pure Economics*, p. 125.
31. *Ibid.*, p. 145.
32. Jevons, *The Theory of Political Economy*, p. 95.
33. Walras, *Elements of Pure Economics*, p. 36.
34. Menger, *Principles of Economics*, p. 131.
35. Jevons, *The Theory of Political Economy*, p. 165.
36. *Ibid.*, p. 166.
37. Walras, *Elements of Pure Economics*, p. 400.
38. Menger, *Principles of Economics*, p. 150.
39. Jevons, *The Theory of Political Economy*, p. 294.
40. *Ibid.*, pp. 295–6.
41. This quote should be useful to students of the external dialectic.
42. Menger, *Principles of Economics*, p. 174.
43. Walras, *Elements of Pure Economics*, p. 385.
44. *Ibid.*
45. *Ibid.*
46. *Ibid.*
47. Jevons, *The Theory of Political Economy*, p. 93.
48. Walras, *Elements of Pure Economics*, p. 318.
49. *Ibid.*, p. 380.
50. *Ibid.*, p. 240.

51. *Ibid.*, p. 447.
52. Jevons, *The Theory of Political Economy*, pp. 196–7.
53. Walras, *Elements of Pure Economics*, pp. 380–1.
54. Howey, "The Origins of Marginalism," in R. D. Collison Black, A. W. Coats and Craufurd D. W. Goodwin, eds., *The Marginal Revolution in Economics: Interpretation and Evaluation* (Durham, N. C.: Duke University Press, 1973), p. 28. Quoting from Jaffé, *Correspondence of Leon Walras*, Vol. 1, p. 393.
55. *Ibid.*, p. 26, quoting from Jaffe *Correspondence*, Vol.1, pp. 474–475.

10 Marginalist Puzzles Reconsidered

According to a familiar tradition from which it is convenient to start, this revolution centered in the rise of the marginal utility theory of value that is associated with the names of three leaders: Jevons, Menger, and Walras. We pause to salute them. [1]

Joseph A. Schumpeter

The marginalists viewed their programme and the classical framework as competitors. Contrary to a popular view, not only Jevons, but also both Walras and Menger, were reacting stalwartly to classical political economy. All three contrasted their research programme *en bloc* with the classical framework. All three called for a rejection of classical political economy *in toto* and for its replacement with their own programmes. Their respective arguments for making the choice of their marginalist programme over classical political economy were almost identical and were rational in a Lakatosian sense. It is clear the the discipline accepted their reasoning. In this chapter we re-examine the questions about the marginalist revolution raised in Chapter 4 with the expectation that our Lakatosian approach to the economics of Jevons, Menger and Walras will provide some new insights. To begin, we address the question of Jevons', Menger's and Walras' reactions to the then orthodox labour theory of value.

The three marginalists shared the same line of argument, as regards classical political economy, which runs as follows. First, they establish that everything that can legitimately be explained by classical political economy can also be explained by their own programme. Second, they point out anomalies which cannot be explained by classical political economy and which can be explained by their own programme. They are highly critical of the classical framework for its excessive exception-barring. They point to the advantage of their programme in bringing all phenomena of the economic universe under a unified framework. Third, they point out any incoherency in classical political economy. It is claimed that the classical theory does not really constitute an explanation at all. Fourth, the progressiveness of their own programme is noted in opposition to the degenerativeness of the classical framework. In examining the specific line of argument offered by each of the marginalists we shall see that they fit this pattern closely.

Jevons addresses his criticisms to the classical framework *en bloc* as a research programme. He states:

I believe it is generally supposed that Adam Smith laid the foundations of this science; that Malthus, Anderson, and Senior added important doctrines; that Ricardo systematised the whole; and, finally, that Mr. J. S. Mill filled in details and completely expounded this branch of knowledge.[2]

Jevons sees the introduction of a marginalist programme of thought as a revolution. He does not call for piecemeal changes in the classical framework but rather for a rejection of key parts of what we would now call its hard core. He states:

The conclusion to which I am ever more clearly coming is that the only hope of attaining a true system of Economics is to fling aside, once and forever, the mazy and preposterous assumptions of the Ricardian School.[3]

Jevons attacks the idea of labour as the cause of value. He states:

Economists have not been wanting who put forward labour as the *cause of value*, asserting that all objects derive their value from the fact that labour has been expended on them; and it is thus implied, if not stated, that value will be proportional to labour.[4]

Jevons notes that there are many counterexamples to the proposition that value will be proportional to labour. He is critical of the fact that Ricardo handles these anomalies through exception-barring. Jevons states:

This is a doctrine which cannot stand for a moment, being directly opposed to facts. Ricardo disposes of such an opinion when he says: "There are some commodities, the value of which is determined by their scarcity alone."[5]

Jevons stresses the unsatisfactory nature of such exception-barring and observes that there are counter-examples even within the supposed scope of the exception-barred proposition. He states:

The mere fact that there are many things, such as rare ancient books, coins, antiquities, etc., which have high values, and which are absolutely incapable of production now, disperses the notion that value depends on labour. Even those things which are producible in any quantity by labour seldom exchange exactly at the corresponding values.[6]

Jevons asserts that it is unreasonable to found a theory of value on labour because labour itself is a variable quantity. He states:

Ricardo, by a violent assumption, founded his theory of value on quantities of labour considered as one uniform thing. He was aware that labour differs infinitely in quality and efficiency, so that each kind is more or less scarce, and is consequently paid at a higher or lower rate of wages.[7]

Jevons argues that historical cost is irrelevant in the pricing of goods because economic agents make their decisions with an eye to the future. (As we shall see, both Menger and Walras also emphasize this point.) Jevons states:

The fact is, that *labour once spent has no influence on the future value of any article*: it is gone and lost forever. In commerce, by-gones are forever by-gones; and we are always starting clear at each moment, judging the values of things with a view to future utility.[8]

Jevons is concerned that the number of equations does not exceed the number of unknowns in the classical framework and that therefore the explanatory power of the programme must be questioned. His spirited attack on the Wage Fund theory is succinctly summarized in the following passage:

This theory pretends to give a solution of the main problem of the science — to determine the wages of labour; yet, on close examination, its conclusion is found to be a mere truism, namely, that the average rate of wages is found by dividing the whole amount appropriated to the payment of wages by the number of those between whom it is divided.[9]

Later in the *Theory* Jevons follows up on this attack. In reference to the Wage Fund doctrine he states: "such a doctrine is radically fallacious; *it involves the attempt to determine two unknown quantities from one equation*"[10] (italics in original). Jevons emphasizes that his theory retains the unrefuted explanatory content of the classical labour theory of value. Of his own theory he states: "This theory is in harmony with facts; and, wherever there is any apparent reason for the belief that labour is the cause of value, we obtain an explanation of the reason."[11] Jevons suggested that his programme offered not only the retention of former unrefuted content but also the incorporation of new content. He attacked the classical framework for its employment of disparate laws in the determination of the values of different kinds of factors of production. Specifically, he argued that the analysis associated with the determination of rent should also be applied to labour. Jevons stressed the advantage of a unified approach which could incorporate these formerly disparate areas and which was, in fact, provided by the marginalist programme. He declared the progressiveness of his programme. He states:

I feel sure that when, casting ourselves free from the Wage-Fund Theory, the Cost of Production doctrine of Value, the Natural Rate of Wages, and other misleading or false Ricardian doctrines, we begin to trace out clearly and simply the results of a correct theory, it will not be difficult to arrive at a true doctrine of wages.[12]

It is a common opinion that the marginalists on the continent were *not* reacting to the classical framework in their formulation of a new theory of value and in their presentation of that new theory. (This view is attributable to the obviously higher degree of dominance of the classical framework in England.) Nonetheless, a careful reading of Menger's *Principles* shows that this is incorrect. After the long and thorough exposition of each main point in the *Principles* Menger returns to the labour theory of value for a comparative critical discussion. In fact, the twenty-five pages written on "The Laws Governing the Value of Goods of Higher Order"[13] constitute a polemic directed against the labour theory of value. Menger meticulously sets forward his arguments on value and then culminates that chapter with a rapid-fire attack on the classical framework. There can be no doubt that Menger was concerned with its refutation. Let us examine his arguments.

Menger tells us that his purpose in setting up an economic theory was both to establish a framework that was in correspondence with the facts and to clear up some misunderstandings in the field. Here Menger is intimating that the importance of his theory is its excess corroborated content when compared with the classical framework. He states:

I have devoted special attention to the investigation of the causal connections between economic phenomena involving products and the corresponding agents of production, not only for the purpose of establishing a price theory based upon reality and placing all price phenomena (including interest, wages, ground rent, etc.) together under one unified point of view, but also because of the important insights we thereby gain into many other economic processes heretofore completely misunderstood.[14]

Menger's assault on the labour theory of value is multi-pronged. For the first prong of the assault, he argues that you cannot explain the value of lower order goods in terms of the value of higher order goods (as the labour theory of value attempts to do) unless you can explain the value of the higher order goods. To explain the value of the higher order goods one must obtain the value of even higher order goods. An infinite regress is produced and the argument fails. Menger states this "infinite regress" argument as follows:

The economic character of a good thus cannot be a consequence of the circumstances that it has been produced from economic goods of higher order, and this explanation would have to be rejected in any case, even if it were not involved in a further internal contradiction. The explanation of the economic character of goods of lower order by that of goods of higher order is only a pseudo-explanation, and apart from being incorrect and in contradiction with all experience, it does not even fulfill the formal conditions for the explanation of a phenomenon. If we explain the economic character of goods of first order by that of goods of second order, the latter by the economic character of goods of third order, this again by the economic character of goods of fourth order, and so on, the solution of the problem is not advanced fundamentally by a single step, since the question as to the last and thus cause of the economic character of goods always still remains unanswered. [15]

For the second prong of the assault, Menger provides a methodological attack, similar to Jevons' attack, on the method of exception-barring employed in the classical framework. Menger states:

That a large and important group of phenomena cannot be fitted into the general laws of a science dealing with these phenomena is telling evidence of the need for reforming the science. It does not, however, constitute an argument that would justify the most questionable methodological procedure of separating a group of phenomena from all other objects of observation exactly similar in general nature, and elaborating special highest principles for each of the two groups. [16]

The lack of a unified framework is one of Menger's main points of contention with the classical framework. In reference to the labour theory of value he states: "this argument . . . [does not provide] . . . a formally correct solution . . . to the problem of discovering a universally valid explanation of the value of goods." [17]

For the third prong of the assault, Menger highlights the anomalies in the classical framework which can be explained by a marginalist framework. He states:

Nor can the fact that some goods are products of labour while others are given us by nature without labour be represented with any greater justice as the criterion for distinguishing economic from non-economic character, in spite of the fact that a great deal of clever reasoning has been devoted to attempting to interpret actual phenomena that contradict this view in a sense that does not. For experience tells us that many goods on which no labor was expended (alluvial land, water power, etc.) display economic character whenever they are available in quantities that do not meet our requirements. Nor does the fact that a thing is a product of labor by itself necessarily result in its having goods-character let alone economic character. Hence the labor expended in the production of a good cannot be the criterion of economic character. On the contrary, it is evident that this criterion must be sought exclusively in the relationship between requirements for and available quantities of goods. [18]

Menger discusses the anomaly to the classical framework that the value of land cannot be explained in terms of labour content. He, like Jevons, stresses the unimportance of historical cost. He states:

Such items of its past history are of interest in judging its *natural* fertility, and certainly also for the question of *whether the application of economic* goods to this piece of land (improvements) *were appropriate and economic*. But its history is of no relevance when its general economic relationships, and especially its *value*, are at issue. For these have to do with the importance goods attain for us solely because they assure us future satisfactions.[19] (Italics in original)

Menger takes care to show that each of the counter-examples which he cites to the classical framework can be explained by a marginalist programme. Menger emphasizes that with his framework he can bring a larger range of phenomena under one set of laws. In reference to land, for example he states: "The value of services of land is therefore not subject to different laws than the value of the services of machines, tools, houses, factories, or any other kind of economic good."[20]

Menger asserts that his programme provides a solution to the problem of finding a universally valid explanation for price phenomena. He states:

The fact that the *prices* of the services of land, capital, and labor, or, in other words, rent, interest, and wages, cannot be reduced without the greatest violence (as we shall see later) to quantities of labor or costs of production, has made it necessary for the proponents of these theories to develop principles of price formation for these three kinds of goods that are entirely different from the principles that are valid for all other goods. In the preceding sections, I have shown with respect to goods of all kinds that all phenomena of *value* are the same in nature and origin, and that the magnitude of value is *always* governed according to the same principles.[21] (Italics in original)

It is clear that Menger has incorporated the Lakatosian criterion of progressiveness into the above statement. In the *Principles* he cites counterexamples to the classical theories of rent, interest and wages and then shows how with his one set of principles a theory may be developed which not only maintains the unrefuted content of the classical framework but also leads to an expansion of theoretical content. It is, as

Schumpeter states concerning Menger's work, that "the influence of Smith, Ricardo, and expecially J. S. Mill is ... unmistakable."[22]

Walras spends three chapters in the articulated version of his *Elements* controverting the classical framework. His purpose is quite clear from the titles of these chapters: "Exposition and Refutation of the English theory of the Price of Products," "Exposition and Refutation of the English Theory of Rent," and "Exposition and Refutation of the English Theories of Wages and Interest."[23] Walras opens the first of these chapters with a quotation from Ricardo where the classicalist is listing exceptions to his labour theory. Ricardo states that those commodities which cannot be increased in quantity will provide exceptions to his analysis. Walras points out both a local and a global counter-example in Ricardo's analysis. The local counterexample is that "there are no products that can be multiplied without limit."[24] In other words, all commodities belong to Ricardo's list of exceptions. The global counterexample is that there is not:

> any one value of costs of production, which, having itself been determined, determines in turn the selling pices of products. The selling prices of products are determined in the market for products by reason of their utility and their quantity. There are no other conditions to consider, for these are the necessary and sufficient conditions. It does not matter whether the products cost more or less to produce than their selling prices.[25]

We see that Walras places the same emphasis on the irrelevance of historical cost as is placed by Menger and Jevons. Also in common with Jevons and Menger, Walras stresses the benefit of having a unified theory of rent, interest and wages. He states: "We may ask ... why this school does not try to formulate a unified general theory to determine the prices of all productive services in the same way."[26] Walras asserts that with his marginalist programme he can place economic phenomena under a unified framework. Furthermore, with his programme he can also explain that which is anomalous to the classical framework.[27]

Walras makes the same complaint as Jevons concerning the lack of equality between the equations and the unknowns within the classical world. He states:

I feel constrained to have always as many equations as there are unknowns in my problems, while the illustrious authors of the theories cited in Lesson 40 [the chapter critical of the classical wage theory] allow themselves sometimes to determine one and the same unknown by means of two equations and sometimes to use a single equation to solve for two, three, and even four unknowns.[28]

Walras also formulates Menger's infinite regress criticism. He states that merely to cite counterexamples is a shallow criticism of the labour theory of value. A more important question to ask is: Why does labour itself have value? He states:

In either case why is labour worth anything? Why is it exchangeable? That is the question before us. Adam Smith neither asked it nor answered it. Surely, if labour has value and is exchangeable, it is because it is both useful and limited in quantity, that is to say because it is scarce. Value, thus, comes from scarcity. Things other than labour, provided they are scarce, have value and are exchangeable just like labour itself. So the theory which traces the origin of value to labour is a theory that is devoid of meaning rather than too narrow, an assertion that is gratuitous rather than inacceptable.[29]

Each of the marginalists viewed the marginalist framework as what we would now call a research programme. There was a striking similarity in the arguments they put forward concerning this competition.

The second question we address is: Was the rise of marginalism due to dialectic internal or external to the economics discipline? Our answer is that the rise of marginalism was mainly due to an internal dialectic, that is, due to endogenous influence of the scientific attractiveness to the discipline of a research programme with a powerful positive heuristic in the face of an alternative degenerative framework. It was in the 1870s that the marginalist ideas first became available in the form of a research programme. The new programme appeared to be progressive; the classical framework appeared to be degenerative. As noted just above these were exactly the grounds upon which Jevons, Menger and Walras argued for the acceptance of marginalism, and we conjecture that the programme was, in fact, accepted on these grounds. The rise of marginalism was a development *within* the scientific project of constructing theoretical structures to explain economic phenomena and so it is proper to say that this ascendency was attributable to an internal dialectic.

Lakatos suggests that programmes of thought are never refuted "by the facts." They are never rejected until there is an alternative progressive programme.[30] The marginalist revolution provides a corroboration of this Lakatosian conjecture. Classical political economy (particularly the Wage Fund doctrine) was in a crisis prior to the 1870s. Yet it was not until the marginalist research programme appeared that the classical framework lost its dominance.

Next we shall address the question: What were the links between the works of Jevons, Menger and Walras? Note that in answering this question we shall not be collecting similarities at random but rather taking note of those which our Lakatosian metatheory indicates to be important. The similarities which link the works of Jevons, Menger and Walras include elements of their hard cores, the core theorems with their attendant core demonstrations, the form of the analysis, and the methodological vision. Many of the differences among the works of the marginalist trio may be attributed to differences in their respective positive heuristics. Such differences add to rather than detract from the potential for viewing their works *en masse* as the foundation for a broad research programme as it is the interaction of these differences which would lead to the construction of the overall programme's heuristic.

As was noted in Chapter 8, the common elements in the hard cores of the individual works are: (1) the individual as a key unit of analysis, (2) the marginal utility/total utility distinction, (3) the law of utility maximization, (4) the law of diminishing marginal utility, (5) the prevalence of perfect competition, and (6) the potency of the equilibrating mechanism. These six points might be considered as the hard core of the overall marginalist research programme.

Also, as noted in Chapter 8, there are four common core theorems. These are: (1) the social welfare theorem, (2) the equimarginal theorem, (3) the bond between marginal utility and value, and (4) the theorem that factor services obtain their marginal product.

A further link between the marginalists, which also should be clear from Chapters 5, 6, and 7, is that all three put their ideas into the form of a research programme. It is this form that led to the rise of marginalism and the fact that the works of all three authors shared this form certainly increased the speed and probability of the overall programme's acceptance.

A final link among the works of the marginalist trio, which is related to the above link, is their shared methodological vision. Their common Newtonian vision of scientific activity was explored thoroughly in Chapter 4.

Our next question is: Was there a marginalist revolution? Hutchison takes an extreme position on this question. He states: "Not only has nothing genuinely describable as 'a Newtonian revolution' taken place in economics, it is reasonable to suggest that it is not probable that anything of the sort is going to occur in the foreseeable future."[31] Discussion on such a question easily slides into a debate on semantics. For example, in reference to the Hutchison quote, one might ask: what is essential to a *Newtonian* revolution?

We shall focus our discussion by addressing some questions concerning the marginalist revolution raised by Coats, and employing the definitions of scientific revolution provided by Donald Winch and Thomas Kuhn. The rise of marginalism constituted a revolution by these criteria. A. W. Coats asks: "how far did the marginal revolution constitute a break with the past? How far were any or all of the key concepts already present in the classical literature?"[32] The marginalist revolution constituted a distinct break with the past. If we examine the six elements of the hard core of the overall marginalist programme (listed above) we find that four of the principles are not part of the central core of ideas in the classical paradigm. These four include the emphasis on the individual as a key unit of analysis, the concept of utility maximization, the marginal utility/total utility distinction, and the law of diminishing marginal utility. To say that these key concepts were already present in the classical literature would be misleading. These ideas had cropped up now and again in the literature but their employment as the foundation for a new research programme constituted a major break with the classical framework.

Donald Winch's criterion for the existence of a marginalist revolution is that there needs to have been "a decisive change in the direction, and possibly even the nature, of economics as an organized body of knowledge."[33] It is clear that the marginalist revolution marked the beginning of a new direction for the economics discipline. This is because a new direction is precisely that which defines a research programme. Given a new and different set of hard core principles, a new series of models was developed based thereupon and in the direction of the positive heuristic of the programme.

It is also possible to defend the more extended claim that the marginalist revolution marked a change in the nature of economics as an organized body of knowledge. There was a methodological notion, present in the classical tradition, that the theory of value was complete. Political Economy was considered a relatively simple fixed body of thought which could be mastered by any educated person. Craufurd Goodwin states:

At the beginning of the 1870s the discipline of political economy had not changed markedly for nearly half a century. The subject was treated as a relatively minor part of "moral science" consisting of certain immutable principles or laws which could be mastered easily by an unsophisticated layman after a minimum of study.[34]

In other words, there was no active positive heuristic within the classical framework. This is the antithesis of a research programme. With the advent of marginalism, the *incompleteness* of economics came to be emphasized. As Jevons states in his *Theory*: "It is no part of my purpose in this work to attempt to trace out, with any approach to completeness, the results of the theory given in the preceding chapters."[35] This dynamic aspect of the marginalist programme, with its emphasis on a positive heuristic, would support the conclusion that there was a revolution in economics on the methodological level as well as on the level of content.

Kuhn's criteria for a revolution are that the event be "sufficiently unprecedented to attract an enduring group of adherents away from competing modes of scientific activity"[36] and that it be "sufficiently open-ended to leave all sorts of problems for the redefined group of practitioners to solve."[37] The marginalism of the early 1870s fulfills both these criteria. The first criterion is fulfilled by the fact that marginalism became the dominant programme within less than twenty years. This is marked by the fact that by the late 1880s and the early 1890s marginalism had begun to dominate the textbooks on economics. That there was an enduring group of adherents is evidenced by such names as: Pareto, Wicksell, Pantalioni, Wicksteed, Edgeworth, Böhm-Bawerk, and von Wieser. The criterion that to be a revolution marginalism had to be "sufficiently open-ended to leave all sorts of problems" is fulfilled by the powerful positive heuristic of the new programme. The whole point of a research programme is the series of puzzles which it aligns (the positive heuristic) and the tools it gives for their solution (the hard core, core theorems, core demonstrations, etc.). We have already thoroughly explored these aspects of the marginalist programme.

These considerations lead us to our next question: Why did the professionalization of the discipline take place in the last quarter of the nineteenth century? It is evident that there had not been a strong positive heuristic within the classical framework. The typical mode of handling anomalies within the classical tradition was exception-barring. This is typified by Ricardo's "mention" of non-reproducible goods and Cairnes' listing of "non-competing groups" as exceptions to the analysis. The classical framework did not display progressive problem shifts. The possibility for progressive problem shifts within the marginalist programme appeared limitless. It is ironic that Mark Blaug states: "The fact that Jevons and Walras chose to express themselves in mathematical terms was undoubtedly responsible for further resistance to their ideas."[38] Certainly their ideas must have met a certain resistance due to their mathematical character, yet it was, ultimately, that mathematical character which, to the degree that is was associated with the articulation of the series of models of the new programme, that accounted for the rise of the discipline to professional status. It takes a trained professional to develop the positive heuristic of a scientific research programme. Conversely, the positive heuristic of a scientific research programme defines the tasks of the trained professional. It became unimaginable that the relaxed situation, in which classical economics had flourished, would continue. Craufurd Goodwin portrays, the context of classical discourse:

As a subject it was thought to be particularly appropriate for eccentric philosophers, clergymen, and lawyers. In colleges and universities lectures were seldom given by specialists and often by anyone for whom there seemed to be insufficient alternative employment, in addition to lawyers, and philosophers, the subject was taught by historians, linguists, mathematicians, scientists of all types, and even college presidents.[39].

The positive heuristic of the marginalist research programme demanded a professional's attention. In regard to the Bellagio conference on the marginalist revolution, Coats comments: "Several conference papers had suggested that the marginalist revolution marked the beginning of modern professional economics."[40] Our conjecture is that the line of causality was mainly from the rise of a marginalist research programme to the professionalization of the economics discipline.

Our next question is: Should the marginalist revolution be termed a "multiple discovery?" We may use the Lakatosian methodological framework to make a distinction between two different kinds of multiple discoveries. On the one hand, we may have multiple discoveries *within* a research programme. The independent development by two or more separate scientists of a new stage in the series of models of the programme (which incorporate particular anomalies and lead to new corroborations) may be considered as multiple discoveries within a programme. This is the type of discovery to which Merton refers when he states:

A great variety of evidence ... testifies then to the hypothesis that, once science has become institutionalized, and significant numbers of men are at work on scientific investigation, the same discoveries will be made independently more than once and that singletons can be conceived of as forestalled multiples.[41]

This is also the type of multiple discovery which Blaug argues that the marginalist revolution was not.[42] Blaug's main point in his argument that the marginalist revolution was not a multiple discovery is that the economics discipline did not have the characteristic of a mature science at that time.

It may be fruitful to distinguish a different kind of multiple discovery. The growth of science is not just marked by multiple discoveries within research programmes; it is also marked by multiple discoveries *of* research programmes. The marginalist revolution was a multiple discovery of this latter type. A possible conjecture on the timing of this multiple discovery is related to the fact that it was not until after 1850 that texts on calculus, assessable to the non-mathematician, became generally available.[43] It would have taken an act of genius as great as Newton's (or Leibniz') to have formulated the marginalist ideas into a research programme without some prior knowledge of calculus. (It is probable that Menger was well-acquainted with calculus.)

Our final question uncovered from Chapter 4 is: Given that the marginalist ideas had been available to economics at least since 1738 (and some would argue since Aristotle), why did these ideas not rise to dominance until the marginalist revolution of the 1870s? Our answer to this is, of course, that it was because the marginalist ideas had not been made available in the form of a research programme until that time.

The answers to all of the above questions are linked by their reliance upon the vision of the marginalism of the 1870s as a research programme.

NOTES

1. Joseph A. Schumpeter, *History of Economic Analysis* (New York: Oxford University Press, 1954), p. 825.

2. W. Stanley Jevons, *The Theory of Political Economy*, 2nd edn. (London: Macmillan, 1879, (1st edn., 1871), p. v.
3. *Ibid.*, p. xliv.
4. *Ibid.*, pp. 161–3.
5. *Ibid.*, p. 163.
6. *Ibid.*
7. *Ibid.*, p. 165.
8. *Ibid.*, p. 164.
9. *Ibid.*, p. vi.
10. *Ibid.*, p. 269.
11. *Ibid.*, p. 2.
12. *Ibid.*, pp. xlv–xlvi.
13. Karl Menger, *Principles of Economics*, trans. and ed. James Dingwall and Bert F. Hoselitz with an introduction by Frank H. Knight (Glencoe, Illinois: The Free Press, 1950), pp. 149–74.
14. *Ibid.*, p. 49.
15. *Ibid.*, p. 108.
16. *Ibid.*, p. 166.
17. *Ibid.*, p. 149.
18. *Ibid.*, pp. 101–2.
19. *Ibid.*, p. 169.
20. *Ibid.*, p. 173.
21. *Ibid.*
22. Schumpeter, *A History of Economic Analysis*, p. 827.
23. Leon Walras, *Elements of Pure Economics*, trans. William Jaffe (London: George Allen and Unwin, 1954).
24. *Ibid.*, p. 397.
25. *Ibid.*, pp. 399–400
26. *Ibid.*, p. 416.
27. *Ibid.*, pp. 426–7.
28. *Ibid.*, p. 47.
29. *Ibid.*, pp. 201–2.
30. Imre Lakatos, "History of Science and Its Rational Reconstruction" in R. C. Buck and R. S. Cohen (eds), *Boston Studies in the Philosophy of Science*, Vol. 8 (1971), pp. 91–136.
31. T. W. Hutchison, *Knowledge and Ignorance in Economics* (Chicago: University of Chicago Press, 1977), p. 40.
32. A. W. Coats, "Retrospect and Prospect," in R. D. Collison Black, A. W. Coats and D. W. Craufurd Goodwin, eds., *The Marginal Revolution in Economics: Interpretation and Evaluation* (Durham N.C.: Duke University Press, 1973), p. 388.
33. D. Winch, "Marginalism and the Boundaries of Economic Science," in Black *et al.*, *The Marginal Revolution in Economics*, p. 59.
34. Craufurd Goodwin, "Marginalism Moves," in Black *et al.*, *The Marginal Revolution in Economics*, pp. 286–7.
35. Jevons, *The Theory of Political Economy*, p. 266.
36. Thomas Kuhn, *The Structure of Scientific Revolutions* (Chicago: University of Chicago Press, 1970), p. 10.

37. *Ibid.*
38. Blaug, "Was There a Marginal Revolution?" in Black *et al.*, *The Marginal Revolution in Economics*, p. 13.
39. Goodwin, "Marginalism Moves," pp. 286–7.
40. Coats, "Retrospect and Prospect," p. 345.
41. R. K. Merton, "Singletons and Multiples in Scientific Discovery: A Chapter in the Sociology of Science," *Proceedings of the American Philosophical Society* 105, No. 5 (1961), p. 482 quoted in Blaug, "Was There a Marginal Revolution?" pp. 4–5.
42. Blaug, "Was There a Marginal Revolution?"
43. Jaffe, "Leon Walras's Role," in Black *et al.*, *The Marginal Revolution in Economics*, p. 134.

Bibliography

Althusser, Louis. *Essays in Self-Criticism*, trans. Grahame Lock. London: New Left Books, 1976.

Anikin, A. V. *A Science in Its Youth*: *Pre-Marxian Political Economy*. New York: International Publishers, 1975.

Bagehot, Walter. *Economic Studies*, ed. R. H. Hutton. London: Longmans, Green, 1902.

Barber, W. J. *A History of Economic Thought*. Baltimore: Penguin, 1977.

Bateson, Gregory. *Steps to an Ecology of Mind*. St. Albans, Herts, England: Granada, 1973.

Baumol, William J. *Economic Theory and Operations Analysis*. Englewood Cliffs, N.J.: Prentice-Hall, 1972.

Becker, Gary S. *The Economic Approach to Human Behaviour*. Chicago: University of Chicago Press, 1976.

Bentham, Jeremy. *An Introduction to the Principles of Morals and Legislation*, ed. J. H. Burns and H. L. A. Hart. London: Athlone, 1970.

Black, R. D. Collison, A. W. Coats and Craufurd D. W. Goodwin, eds. *The Marginal Revolution in Economics*: *Interpretation and Evaluation*. Durham, N.C.: Duke University Press, 1973.

Blaug, Mark. *The Methodology of Economics*: *Or How Economists Explain*. Cambridge: Cambridge University Press, 1980.

——*Economic Theory in Retrospect*. 2nd edn. London: Heinemann Educational Books, 1977.

——*Economic Theory in Retrospect*. 3rd edn. Cambridge: Cambridge University Press, 1983.

——"Kuhn versus Lakatos or Paradigms versus Research Programmes in the History of Economics." *History of Political Economy* Vol. 7, No. 4 (Winter 1975), p. 399–433.

——"Was There a Marginal Revolution?" *History of Political Economy* Vol. 4, No. 2 (Fall 1972), pp. 269–80.

Böhm-Bawerk, Eugen von. *Kapital und Kapitalzins*. Innsbruck: Wagner, 1909.

Boland, Lawrence. "A Critique of Friedman's Critics." *Journal of Economic Literature*. Vol 17 (1979), pp. 503–22.

Boulding, K. "After Samuelson, Who Needs Adam Smith?" *History of Political Economy* Vol. 3, No. 2 (Fall 1971), pp. 503–22.

——*Economics As a Science*. New York: McGraw-Hill, 1970.

Bronfenbrenner, M. "The 'Structure of the Revolutions' in Economic Thought." *History of Political Economy*, Vol. 3 (1971).

Brown, E. H. Phelps. "The Underdevelopment of Economics." *Economic Journal* (March 1972), pp. 1–10.

Bullock, Alan and Oliver Stallybrass. *The Fontana Dictionary of Modern Thought*. Bungay, Suffolk: Fontana 1977.

Cairnes, John Elliot. *Some Leading Principles of Political Economy Newly Expounded*. New York: Harper & Brothers, 1874.

Caldwell, Bruce. *Beyond Positivism*. London: George Allen & Unwin, 1982.

Canterbery, E. Ray. *The Making of Economics*. Belmont, California: Wadsworth 1976.

Carroll, Lewis. *Symbolic Logic*. Brighton: Harvester Press, 1977.

Coats, A. W., "Is There a 'Structure of Scientific Revolutions' in Economics?" *Kyklos*. Vol. 22, No. 2 (1969), pp. 289–94.

——"Research Priorities in the History of Economics." *History of Political Economy* Vol. 1, No. 1 (Spring 1969) pp. 9–18.

Collingwood, R. G. *The Idea of History*. Oxford: Oxford University Press, 1946.

Commins, Saxe and Robert N. Linscott, eds. *Man & the Universe: The Philosophers of Science*. New York: Washington Square Press, 1954.

Cournot, Antoine Augustin. *An Essay on the Foundations of our Knowledge*, trans. and intro. Merritt H. Moore. New York: Liberal Arts Press, 1956.

——*Exposition de la théorie des chances et des probabilités*. Paris: Hachette, 1843.

——*Principes de la théorie des riches*. Paris: Librairie de L. Hachette et Cie, 1863.

Deane, P. *The Evolution of Economic Ideas*. Cambridge: Cambridge University Press, 1978.

Debreu, Gerard. *Theory of Value*. New Haven: Yale University Press, 1959.

Descartes, Spinoza, Leibnitz. *The Rationalists* (Readings), trans. respectively by John Veitch, R. H. M. Elwes and George Montgomery with Albert R. Chandler. Garden City, New York: Doubleday, 1969.

de V. Graaf. J. *Theoretical Welfare Economics*. Cambridge: Cambridge University Press, 1957.

Dobb, Maurice. *Welfare Economics and the Economics of Socialism: Towards a Commonsense Critique*. Cambridge: Cambridge University Press, 1969.

Dolan, Edwin G., ed. *The Foundation of Modern Austrian Economics*. Kansas City: Sheed & Ward, 1976.

Duncan, Ronald and Miranda Weston-Smith, eds. *The Encyclopedia of Ignorance*. New York: Simon and Schuster, 1977.

Dupuit, Jules. *De l'utilité et de sa mesure*. Torino: La Riforma Sociale, 1934.

Eagly, Robert V., ed. *Events, Ideology and Economic Theory*. Detroit: Wayne State University Press, 1968.
——*The Structure of Classical Political Economy*. New York: Oxford University Press, 1974.
Edgeworth, F. Y. *Mathematical Physics*. London: Kegan Paul and Co., 1881.
Einstein, Albert and Leopold Infeld. *The Evolution of Physics*. New York: Simon and Schuster, 1966.
——*The Meaning of Relativity*. Princeton, N.J.: Princeton University Press, 1956.
Ekelund, R. B., Jr., E. G. Furubotn and W. P. Gramm, eds. *The Evolution of Modern Demand Theory*. Lexington, Mass.: Lexington Books, 1972.
Eves, Howard. *An Introduction to the History of Mathematics*. 4th edn. New York: Holt, Rinehart and Winston, 1979.

Fetter, F. "The Rise and Decline of Ricardian Economics." *History of political Economy* Vol 1, No 2 1:11 (Spring 1969), pp. 67–84.
Feyeraband, Paul. *Against Method*. London: Verso, 1976.
——*Science in a Free Society*. London: Verso, 1978.
Friedman, Milton. *Essays in Positive Economics*. Chicago: University of Chicago Press, 1953.

Goodwin, C. "Economic Theory and Society: A Plea for Process Analysis." *American Economic Review* (May 1972), pp. 409–15.
——"Toward a Theory of the History of Economics." *History of Political Economy* Vol. 12, No 4 (Winter 1980), pp. 610–19.
Gordon, D. F. "The Role of the History of Economic Thought in the Understanding of Modern Economic Theory." *American Economic Review*. Papers and Proceedings Vol. 55 (1965), pp. 119–27.
Gossen, Hermann Heinrich. *Entwickelung der Gesetze des menschlichen Handeln*. Berlin: R. L. Prager, 1927.

Habermas, Jurgen. *Knowledge and Human Interests*. Boston: Beacon Press, 1968.
Harcourt, G. C. *Some Cambridge Controversies in the Theory of Capital*. Cambridge: Cambridge University Press, 1972.
Harrod, R. F. *John Maynard Keynes*. Harmondsworth, Middlesex: Penguin, 1972.
Hearn, William Edward. *Plutology*. Melbourne: G. Robertson, 1963.
Hegel, G. W. F. *The Phenomenology of Mind*, trans. J. B. Baillie. New York: Harper & Row, 1967.
Heilbroner, R. L. "Modern Economics as a Chapter in HET." *History of Political Economy* Vol. 11, No 2 (Summer 1979), pp. 192–8.
——*The Worldly Philosophers*. New York: Time Inc. 1953.
Heisenberg, Werner. *Physics and Philosophy: The Revolution in Modern Science*. New York: Harper & Row, 1958.

Hempel, Carl G. *Aspects of Scientific Explanation*. New York: The Free Press, 1956.

Henderson, James and Richard E. Quandt. *Microeconomic Theory*: *A Mathematical Approach*. Tokyo: McGraw-Hill Kogakusha, 1958.

Hicks, J. R. *Value and Capital*. Oxford: Oxford University Press, 1939.

Hofstadter, Douglas R. *Gödel, Escher, Bach*: *An Eternal Golden Braid*. Brighton: Harvester Press, 1979.

Hollis, Martin and Edward Nell. *Rational Economic Man*: *A Philosophical Critique of Neo-Clasical Economics*. Cambridge: Cambridge University Press, 1975.

Hunt, E. K. *History of Economic Thought*: *A Critical perspective*. Belmont, California: Wadsworth Publishing Co. 1979.

Husserl, Edmund. *Ideas*: *General Introduction to Pure Phenomenology*. London: Collier Macmillan, 1931.

Hutchison, T. W. *A Review of Economic Doctrines 1870–1929*. Oxford. Clarendon Press, 1953.

——*Knowledge and Ignorance in Economics*. Chicago: University of Chicago Press, 1977.

——*On Revolutions and Progress in Economic Knowledge*. Cambridge: Cambridge University Press, 1978.

Intriligator, Michael D. *Mathematical Optimization and Economic Theory*. Englewood Cliffs, N.J.: Prentice-Hall, 1971.

Jenkin, Fleeming. *Papers*, *Literary*, Scientific, *Etc.*, ed. Sidney Colvin and J. A. Eging. London: Longmans, Green, 1887.

Jevons, W. Stanley. *The Coal Question*. London: Macmillan, 1865.

——*Elementary Lessons in Logic*: *Deductive and Inductive*. London: Macmillan, 1902.

——*The Principles of Science*. London: Macmillan, 1874.

——*The Theory of Political Economy*. 2nd edn. London: Macmillan, 1879. 1st edn. 1871.

Kauder, Emil. *A History of Marginal Utility Theory*. Princeton, N.J.: Princeton University Press, 1965.

Keynes, J. M. *Essays and Sketches in Biography*. New York: Meridian Books, 1956.

——*The General Theory of Employment, Interest, and Money*. New York: Harcourt, Brace & World, 1936.

Klamer, Arjo. *Conversations with Economists*. Roman & Allanhead, 1983.

Knight, Frank H. *On the History and Method of Economics*. Chicago: University of Chicago Press, 1956.

——*Risk, Uncertainty and Profit*. Chicago: University of Chicago Press, 1971.

Koopmans, Tjalling C. *Three Essays on the State of Economic Science*. New York: McGraw-Hill, 1957.

Kuhn, Thomas S. *The Copernican Revolution.* New York: Vintage Books, 1957.
——*The Essential Tension: Selected Studies in Scientific Tradition and Change.* Chicago: University of Chicago Press, 1977.
——*The Structure of Scientific Revolutions.* Chicago: University of Chicago Press, 1970.

Lakatos, Imre and Alan Musgrave, eds. *Criticism and the Growth of Knowledge.* Cambridge: Cambridge University Press, 1970.
——"History of Science and it Rational Reconstructions." In Buck and Cohen, *Boston Studies in the Philosophy of Science,* Vol. 8 (1971), pp. 91–170.
——*Proofs and Refutations.* Cambridge: Cambridge University Press, 1976.
Lange, Oscar, *Political Economy.* Vol. 1, trans. A. H. Walker. New York: Macmillan 1963.
Latsis, Spiro J, ed. *Method and Appraisal in Economics.* Cambridge: Cambridge University Press, 1976.
——"Situational Determinism in Economics." *British Journal of the Philosophy of Science* (1972), pp. 207–45.
Leijonhufvud, A. "Life Among the ECON." *Western Economic Journal.* Vol. 11, No. 3 (September 1973), pp. 327–37.
Lekachman, Robert. *A History of Economic Ideas.* New York: McGraw-Hill, 1959.
Leslie, T. E. Cliffe. *Essays in Political and Moral Philosophy.* London, 1888.
Little, I. M. D. *A Critique of Welfare Economics.* Oxford: Oxford University Press, 1950.
Lloyd, W. F. "The Notion of Value." *Economic History, Economic Journal Supplement* (May 1927), pp. 170–83.
Longe, Francis D. *Francis D. Longe on the Wage-Fund Theory, 1866.* Baltimore: The Lord Baltimore Press, 1904.
Longfield, Montifort. *The Economic Writings of Montifort Longfield,* intro. R. D. Collison Black. New York: A. M. Kelley, 1971.

Maddock, Rodney Russell. *Rational Expectations, Political Business Cycles, and the Course of Macroeconomic Theory.* Duke University: Ph.D. Thesis, 1979.
Magee, Bryan. *Karl Popper.* New York: Viking Press, 1973.
Marshall, Alfred. *Principles of Economics.* London: Macmillan, 1920. 1st edn., 1890.
Marx, Karl. *Capital: A Critique of Political Economy.* Moscow: Progress Publishers, 1977. 1st edn., 1867.
——*The Poverty of Philosophy.* Moscow: Progress Publishers, 1975. 1st edn., 1847.
——*Theories of Surplus-Value.* Moscow: Progress Publishers, 1963. 1st edn., 1905.

Mason, Stephen F. *A History of the Sciences*. New York: Oxford University Press, 1972.

Mates, Benson. *Elementary Logic*. New York: Oxford University Press, 1972.

McCloskey, Donald N. "The Rhetoric of Economics." *Journal of Economic Literature*. Vol. 21 (June 1983), pp. 481–517.

Meek, R. L. "Marginalism and Marx." *History of Political Economy* Vol. 4, No. 2 (Fall 1972), pp. 499–511.

——*Studies in the Labor Theory of Value*. New York: Monthly Review Press, 1956.

Menger, Karl. *Principles of Economics*, trans. and ed. James Dingwall and Bert F. Hoselitz with an introduction by Frank H. Knight. Glencoe, Illinois: The Free Press, 1950.

——*Problems of Economics and Sociology*, ed. and intro. Louis Schneider. Trans. Francis J. Nock. Urbana: University of Illinois Press, 1963.

Mermelstein, David, ed. *Economics: Mainstream Readings and Radical Critiques*. New York: Random House, 1970.

Merton, R. K. "Singletons and Multiples in Scientific Discovery: A Chapter in the Sociology of Science." *Proceedings of the American Philosophical Society*. Vol. 105, No. 5 (1961).

Mill, James. *Elements of Political Economy*. London: Baldwin, Cradock and Joy, 1821.

Mill, John Stuart. *Auguste Comte and Positivism*. Philadelphia: J. B. Lippincott, 1866.

——"Notice of Mr. Thornton's Book *On Labour*." *Fortnightly Review* (March 1869).

——*Philosophy of Scientific Method*, ed. and intro. Ernest Nagel. New York: Hafner, 1950.

——*Principles of Political Economy*. London: J. W. Parker, 1848.

——*A System of Logic, Ratiocination and Inductive, being a Connected View of the Principles of Evidence, and the Methods of Scientific Investigation*. London: John W. Parker, 1843.

Montmort, P. R. de. *Essai d'analyse sur les jeux de hazard*. 2nd edn. Paris. Quillan, 1713.

Moss, Laurence S. 'Montifort Longfield's Supply and Demand Theory of Price and Its Place in the Development of British Economic Theory." *History of Political Economy* Vol. 6, No. 4 (1974).

Newman, James R., ed. *The World of Mathematics*. 4 Vols. New York: Simon and Schuster, 1956.

Newman, Peter, ed. *Readings in Mathematical Economics Vol. 2 Capital and Growth*. Baltimore: Johns Hopkins University Press, 1968.

O'Brien, D. P. *The Classical Economists*. Oxford: Clarendon Press, 1975.

Pantaleoni, Maffeo. *Pure Economics*, trans. T. Boston Bruce. London: Macmillan, 1898.

Pareto, Vilfredo. *Manuel d'économie politique*. Paris: V. Giard & E. Briere, 1909.

Petrella, Frank. "Individual, Group, or Government? Smith, Mill, and Sidgwick." *History of Political Economy*. Vol. 2 (1970), pp. 152–76.

Piaget, Jean. *Structuralism*. New York: Harper & Row, 1970.

Polanyi, Michael and Harry Prosch. *Meaning*. Chicago: University of Chicago Press, 1975.

——*The Tacit Dimension*. Garden City, N. Y.: Doubleday, 1966.

Popper, Karl. *Conjectures and Refutations*. London: Routledge and Kegan Paul, 1972.

——*The Logic of Scientific Discovery*. London: Hutchison, 1977.

——*Objective Knowledge*. Oxford: Oxford University Press, 1979.

——*The Open Society and Its Enemies*. Princeton, N.J.: Princeton University Press, 1962.

——*The Poverty of Historicism*. Boston: Beacon Press, 1957.

——and John Eccles. *The Self and Its Brain*. New York: Springer International, 1977.

Quetelet, Lambert Adolphe Jacques. *Théorie des probabilités* Bruxelles: Societé pour l'emancipation intellectuelle, A. Janar, Pref., 1853.

Quirk, James and Rubin Saposnik. *Introduction to General Equilibrium Theory and Welfare Economics*. New York: McGraw-Hill, 1968.

Rader, Trout. *Theory of Microeconomics*. New York: Academic Press, 1972.

Remenyi, Joseph. *Core-Demi-Core Interaction*. Duke University: Ph.D. Thesis, 1976.

Ricardo, David. *On the Principles of Political Economy and Taxation*. Vol. 1 of *The Works and Correspondence of David Ricardo*, ed. Pierro Sraffa with the collaboration of M. H. Dobb. Cambridge: Cambridge University Press, 1951.

Rima, I. H. *Development of Economic Analysis*. Georgetown, Ontario: Irwin-Dorsey, 1972.

Robbins, Lionel. *An Essay on the Nature and Significance of Economic Science*. 2nd edn. London: Macmillan, 1935.

Robinson, Joan. *Contributions to Modern Economics*. Oxford: Basil Blackwell, 1979.

——*Economic Heresies*. London: Macmillan, 1971.

——*Further Contributions to Modern Economics*. Oxford: Basil Blackwell, 1980.

Roll, Eric. *A History of Economic Thought*. Englewood Cliffs, N.J.: Prentice-Hall, 1956.

Routh, Guy, *The Origin of Economic Ideas*. New York: Vintage Books, 1975.

Russell, Bertrand. *A History of Western Philosophy*. New York: Simon and Schuster, 1945.

Ryle, Gilbert. *Dilemmas*. Cambridge: Cambridge University Press, 1966.

Samuels, Warren J. "The History of Economic Thought as Intellectual History." *History of Political Economy* Vol. 6, No. 3 (1974), pp. 303–23.

Samuelson, Paul. "Problems of Methodology: Discussion." *American Economic Review, Papers and Proceedings*. Vol. 53 (1963), pp. 231–6.

Sartre, Jean-Paul. *Being and Nothingness*, trans. Hazel E. Barnes. Secaucus, N.J.: The Citadel Press, 1956.

——*Between Existentialism and Marxism*, trans. John Mathews. New York: William Morrow, 1974.

Say, Jean Baptiste. *Catecismo de economia politica*. Madrid: Imprenta de Alban, 1822.

Schumpeter, Joseph A. *History of Economic Analysis*. New York: Oxford University Press, 1954.

Sen, Amartya K. *Collective Choice and Social Welfare*. San Francisco: Holden-Day, 1970.

Senior, Nassau William. *Letters on the Factory Act*. London: B. Fellowes, 1837.

——*Political Economy*. London: C. Griffen, 1863.

Shackle, G. L. S. *The Years of High Theory: Invention and Tradition in Economic Thought 1926–39.*. Cambridge: Cambridge University Press, 1967.

Shaw, George Bernard. "The Jevonian Criticism of Marx." *Bernard Shaw and Karl Marx: A Symposium*, 1884–1889. New York: Random House, for R. W. Ellis: Georgian Press, 1930.

Sidgwick, H. *Principles of Political Economy*. London: Macmillan, 1883.

Skemp, Richard R. *The Psychology of Learning Mathematics*. Harmondsworth, Middlesex: Penguin, 1971.

Skinner, B. F. *Science and Human Behavior*. New York: Hafner, 1948.

Smith, Adam. *Adam Smith's Moral and Political Philosophy*, ed. and intro. Herbert W. Schneider. New York: Hafner, 1948.

——*An Inquiry into the Nature and Causes of the Wealth of Nations*. London: J. M. Dent, 1776.

Spiegel, H. W., ed. *The Development of Economic Thought*. New York: Wiley, 1964.

——*The Growth of Economic Thought*. Englewood Cliffs, N.J.: Prentice-Hall, 1971.

Sraffa, Piero. *Production of Commodities by Means of Commodities*. Cambridge: Cambridge University Press, 1960.

Stigler, George J. *Essays in the History of Economics*. Chicago: University of Chicago Press, 1965.

——*Production and Distribution Theories*. New York: Macmillan, 1941.

Tabibian, Mohammad. *An Empirical Investigation in the Theory of Consumer Behavior*. Duke University: Ph.D. Thesis, 1980.

Tarascio, Vincent J. "Some Recent Developments in the History of Economic Thought in the United States." *History of Political Economy* Vol. 3, No. 2 (1971), pp. 419–31.

Thornton, W. T. *On Labour.* 2nd edn. London: Macmillan, 1870.

Todhunter, I. *A History of the Mathematical Theory of Probability.* London: Macmillan, 1865.

Toulmin, Stephen. *The Philosophy of Science.* New York: Harper & Row, 1953.

van Doorn, J. *Disequilibrium Economics.* London: Macmillan, 1975.

von Mises, Ludwig. *The Ultimate Foundation of Economic Science.* Princeton, N.J.: D. Van Nostrand, 1962.

Vonnegut, Kurt, Jr. *Cat's Cradle.* New York: Dell Publishing Co., 1963.

Walras, Auguste. *De la nature de la richesse et de l'origine de la valeur.* Paris: Felix Alean, 1938.

Walras, Leon. *Elements of Pure Economics*, trans. William Jaffe. London: Allen and Unwin, 1954.

——*Etudes d'économie politique appliqué.* Lausanne: Rouge, 1898.

——*Etudes d'économie sociale.* Paris: R. Pichon et R. Durand Auzias, 1936.

Walsh, Vivian Charles. *Introduction to Contemporary Microeconomics.* New York: McGraw-Hill, 1970.

Weber, Max. *The Protestant Ethic and the Spirit of Capitalism*, trans. Talcott Parsons with a foreword by R. H. Tawney. New York: Scribners, 1930.

Weintraub, E. Roy. *General Equilibrium Theory.* London: Macmillan, 1974.

Whitehead, Alfred North. *Essays in Science and Philosophy.* New York: Philosophical Library, 1947.

Wicksell, Knut. *Lectures on Political Economy*, trans. E. Classen. ed. and intro. Lionel Robbins. London: G. Routledge, 1935.

Wicksteed, Philip Henry. *An Essay on the Co-ordination of the Laws of Distribution.* London: Macmillan, 1894.

Wieser, Friedrick von, *Natural Value*, Trans. Christian A. Mallock. Ed. and with a preface and analysis by William Smart. London: Macmillan, 1893.

Winch, D. "The Emergence of Economics as a Science: 1750–1870." In C. M. Cipolla, ed. *The Fontana Economic History of Europe.* London: Collins, 1971, pp. 5–64.

——"Marginalism and the Boundaries of Economic Science." *History of Political Economy* 4:2 (Fall 1972), pp. 325–7.

Wittgenstein, Ludwig. *Philosophical Investigations.* 3rd edn., trans. G. E. M. Anscombe. New York: Macmillan, 1958.

Index

223